Commonsense Methods f
Students with Special Ne
and Disabilities

This fully revised ninth edition continues to offer teachers practical advice on new evidence-based approaches for teaching and managing students with a wide range of abilities, disabilities, and difficulties.

Based on topical international research from the field, this new edition provides practical advice for teachers and tutors to enable them to adapt evidence-based methods when working in inclusive settings with students with special needs, including gifted and talented students. Throughout the text, approaches to teaching and classroom management have been clearly described. New methods, programmes, and interventions are reviewed, and there is increased coverage of digital technology and e-learning. Teachers will also find support and guidance for working with students with learning difficulties in literacy and numeracy, teaching students with physical, sensory, and intellectual disability, fostering students' autonomy, social skills interventions, approaches to autism spectrum disorders, and much more. All new information in every chapter is fully supported with reference to the most recent writing and research.

This continues to be an invaluable resource for practising and trainee teachers, tutors, teaching assistants, and other education professionals responsible for supporting students in inclusive schools.

Peter Westwood has taught in primary, secondary, and special schools and for many years has been involved in teacher education in England, Australia, and Hong Kong. He has published 14 books with Routledge.

Commonsense Methods for Students with Special Needs and Disabilities

Ninth Edition

Peter Westwood

Routledge
Taylor & Francis Group

LONDON AND NEW YORK

Ninth edition published 2025
by Routledge
4 Park Square, Milton Park, Abingdon, Oxon OX14 4RN

and by Routledge
605 Third Avenue, New York, NY 10158

Routledge is an imprint of the Taylor & Francis Group, an informa business

© 2025 Peter Westwood

The right of Peter Westwood to be identified as author of this work has been asserted in accordance with sections 77 and 78 of the Copyright, Designs and Patents Act 1988.

First edition published by by Routledge 1989
Eighth edition published by Routledge 2020

British Library Cataloguing-in-Publication Data
A catalogue record for this book is available from the British Library

ISBN: 978-1-032-98441-4 (hbk)
ISBN: 978-1-032-98438-4 (pbk)
ISBN: 978-1-003-59867-1 (ebk)

DOI: 10.4324/9781003598671

Typeset in Galliard
by SPi Technologies India Pvt Ltd (Straive)

Contents

Introduction

This new edition has been revised to keep pace with current issues in the field of inclusive education and students with special needs. The text represents the most recent research, policies, and practices as reported in the professional literature. This edition continues to provide practical advice for teachers and tutors to enable them to apply evidence-based methods when working with students with special needs and disabilities in inclusive settings. A chapter is also devoted to the needs of gifted and talented students. Throughout the book, approaches to teaching and classroom management have been described, with an increased coverage of the contribution of digital technology and e-learning.

While inclusion is undoubtedly a very worthy ideal, no attempt is made here to make inclusive education sound easy to achieve. Many challenges have been encountered over the years since first implementation, and these are discussed with particular reference to their effects on students with special needs. Strong links are made to the various multi-tiered systems of support that can provide different levels and intensities of teaching assistance to students.

Without exception, all new information in every chapter is fully supported by the most recent writing and research up to and including 2024. I have continued to take an international perspective on all topics addressed in the book, drawing heavily on research, policies, and practices in Britain, Australia, the United States, and parts of Asia.

I hope that all readers will find something of value in the material here.

My sincere thanks to Jayati Tripathi, Suba Ramya, and my copyeditor Stephen Poole for their very efficient management of the production process for this new edition. Sincere gratitude also to Alison Foyle of Routledge for her support over many years.

Peter Westwood

DOI: 10.4324/9781003598671-1

Chapter 1

Meeting 'special needs' in the era of inclusion

Exploring 'special needs'

The special needs of students with disabilities and learning difficulties tend arise from two main sources—those associated with *cognitive factors* that affect learning and those that stem from *psycho-social and emotional problems* affecting a student's personal development, mental and emotional well-being, behaviour, and social adjustment. The two categories are not mutually exclusive, and many students have special needs in both areas.

Cognitive difficulties cause major problems in processing information, remembering, reasoning, and responding within the school curriculum. The difficulties can be linked to a variety of factors, including the level of a student's intelligence, reasoning ability, verbal skills, perceptual abilities, information processing efficiency, attention, and memory. These factors will be discussed in later chapters in the context of particular disabilities and also as they relate to learning within particular areas of the curriculum.

Psycho-social and emotional difficulties are related to personal characteristics such as poor self-esteem, lack of confidence, anxiety, poor self-regulation, negative attitude, low aspirations, poor social skills, and limited resilience when faced with difficulties (Schwab, 2019). Many students with special needs display at least some (often several) of these characteristics, which teachers and school counsellors must seek to change for the better. Schools that have the services of a student counsellor are fortunate because that person can help directly with addressing the psycho-social needs of students and can work closely in tandem with teachers.

Students' special needs must be identified and addressed as early as possible to ensure that their time in pre-school and school is profitable and that they maintain good motivation to learn. When a student's learning difficulty or disability results in frequent experiences of failure rather than success, the path ahead can be daunting without necessary support and encouragement. In the past, this support was provided mainly through withdrawal groups, special classes, and special schools, but now it is expected to be implemented as far as possible within the inclusive class. The challenges that the inclusion policy creates for teachers are discussed later.

DOI: 10.4324/9781003598671-2

Who are the students?

In most countries, students with special needs who are included in relevant policies are usually those with intellectual impairment, autism spectrum disorder, a physical or sensory disability (vision or hearing), reading and writing problems, or behavioural and social or emotional difficulties. In some countries, students with health problems or attention deficits are also included. It is reported that approximately 15–17 per cent of the overall school population in most developed countries has special needs spread across these categories. Some schools may have more than 17 per cent, as discussed later.

Educators in the USA prefer the term 'exceptional children' rather than 'students with special needs.' Exceptional children are described as having differences that occur to such an extent that they require additional services and modification to school practices. Some 14 categories of disability or special need are specified in the reauthorized Individuals with Disabilities Education Act (IDEA) (US Department of Education, 2004). These categories are autism, developmental delay, intellectual disability, orthopaedic impairment (physical disabilities), specific learning disability, speech or language impairment, traumatic brain injury, hearing impairment, deafness, deaf-blindness, visual impairment (low vision) or blindness, multiple disabilities, emotional disturbance, and health impairment. Under IDEA, individuals with special needs, as identified by appropriate professionals, are entitled to support from the ages of 3 to 21 years. Data from 2021–2022 indicate that some 15 per cent of the US public school population was being served under IDEA (NCES, 2023), a slight increase in recent years.

There are other students in every country who fall outside any official classification of 'disabled' or 'exceptional' but who experience learning difficulties, particularly in acquiring functional literacy and numeracy skills. In the past, these students have been referred to by many different labels—'slow learners', 'the-hard-to-teach', 'under-achievers', and 'students who struggle.' When these students are also taken into account together with those formally identified as above, it is estimated that in most countries about 20 per cent of school-age children have some form of special need, either long-term or short-term. The actual proportion in any one school varies greatly according to influences such as the level of socio-economic disadvantage in the catchment area served by the school, the economic status of parents, parental support for education, the quality of teaching, and the absence rate of students.

In an attempt to simplify identification of the population of students with special needs in various countries, the Organization for Economic Cooperation and Development (OECD) (2007) created three convenient categories. These categories of special need and exceptionality are addressed in the later chapters of this book where the nature of the support and teaching they require is considered. The categories are useful in that they neatly summarize the diverse group of students with learning problems and special needs found in inclusive classrooms today:

- students with identifiable disabilities and impairments
- students with specific difficulties in learning or with behavioural and/or emotional disorders
- students with difficulties arising from socio-economic, cultural, or linguistic disadvantage (including those struggling to learn English as a second or additional language).

Other students not specifically named in most special education policies may also require additional support in schools. These students include those who are academically gifted or with a specific talent that needs to be developed. In the USA and Canada, gifted students are regarded as part of the population requiring special provision, but in the UK and Australia, they are recognized instead in separate policies and curriculum guidelines, particularly in reference to providing early identification, acceleration, extension, and enrichment programmes.

Disabilities and impairments

Some students have special educational needs because they have an identified disability. These disabilities could include *intellectual disability* (previously referred to in some countries as 'mental retardation' or 'mental handicap'), *hearing impairment, vision impairment, physical disability, autism,* and *a speech and language disorder.* Associated with any of these disabilities one may also find some degree of emotional disturbance, behaviour problems, social relationship failures, and communication difficulties. Significant emotional and behavioural difficulties are reported in approximately 9 per cent, and double that number of children are judged to be at risk for developing such problems. The number of children with social, emotional, and behavioural problems has increased very significantly in recent years.

Intellectual disability is discussed fully in Chapter 2, covering all degrees of cognitive impairment from mild to profound. Intellectual disability is sometimes also referred to as a *developmental delay* or *intellectual developmental disorder* (American Psychiatric Association [APA], 2013). Over the past decades, the prevalence of intellectual disability among children has remained fairly stable at 2 to 3 per cent. Some children with intellectual disability may have additional sensory, physical, or communication impairments and are described as having *complex multiple disabilities.* These students usually require intensive support throughout school life and beyond.

Chapter 3 provides information on autism spectrum disorders that may or may not be accompanied by intellectual disability. Autism is sometimes classified as a *pervasive developmental disorder* (PDD). In recent years, there has been a marked increase in the number of students identified with autism. In the US, this group now represents almost 9 per cent of students served under the IDEA (NCES, 2023).

Physical disability (Chapter 4) is regarded as a fairly low-incidence category, accounting for no more than 1 to 2 per cent of the school population. The most common physical disabilities include cerebral palsy, spina bifida, acquired brain injury, epilepsy, and chronic health problems such as asthma, cystic fibrosis, type 1 diabetes, and allergic reactions. Many of these students have normal cognitive ability but may have problems attending school regularly and accessing resources and therapy. In the case of students with a significant physical disability, there are often mobility problems causing difficulties accessing some school buildings and in participating in off-campus activities.

Vision impairment and hearing impairment (Chapter 5) are also regarded as fairly low-incidence disabilities—together accounting for no more than 2 to 3 per cent of the school population. Hearing impairment includes students who are profoundly deaf and others with varying degrees of hearing loss. Vision-impaired students are those who are blind and others with low vision (partial sight). A very few individuals may have both significant hearing loss and blindness (deaf-blind students).

Students with general *learning difficulties* comprise much the largest group requiring support and intervention, and they are described in more detail below. The vast majority of these students are enrolled in inclusive mainstream classes.

Learning difficulties: General and specific

Learning difficulties are found across all ages, socio-economic levels, and ethnic groups. The major difficulty for these students tends to be an ongoing problem in gaining proficiency in reading and writing. This weakness then prevents them from keeping up with their peers in academic performance across the curriculum.

Students with learning difficulties come from one of two possible subgroups: (i) those with *general* learning difficulties but with no disability or impairment and (ii) those with a *specific learning disability* (SpLD), sometimes referred to as a *learning disorder* (LD). As explained later, learning disabilities are further categorized into two subtypes: *language-based* and *non-verbal*.

Almost all students with learning difficulties or a specific learning disability begin to exhibit their problems very early in their school life, so the sooner they receive targeted support, the better for their long-term prospects. All students with learning problems, regardless of underlying cause, need systematic and direct teaching, as described and advocated strongly throughout later chapters.

General learning difficulties

The term *general learning difficulties* is used throughout this book when discussing students of average or a little below average intelligence who are not in any way intellectually disabled and do not have a sensory or physical impairment. Students with general learning difficulties comprise the largest group of those needing support, representing an estimated 15 per cent of the overall school population. In the past, these students have often been labelled 'slower learners', with IQs typically reported to be below 100. In the case of students from disadvantaged backgrounds, their *potential* IQ can sometimes be well above 100.

The cause of general learning difficulty cannot be attributed to a single factor, and many learning problems arise from a complex interaction among variables such as the learners' cognitive ability, effectiveness of the teaching received, relevance of curriculum content, emotional and financial support from home, absences from school, the student's confidence and motivation, and availability of individual support when necessary. Some schools in disadvantaged areas may have more than 20 per cent of students with poor achievement, due to such factors. Poverty, disadvantage, absenteeism, and struggling with English as a second language are all known to be major contributory factors in students' general learning difficulties in school.

Additional factors contribute to a failure to learn, such as a student's health, attention span, and motivation; the interpersonal relationship between teacher and learner; and social relationships within the peer group. Until recently, teaching methods and instructional materials were rarely investigated as possible causes of a learning difficulty, but now it is readily acknowledged that poor-quality teaching and inappropriate curriculum materials can present major barriers to learning.

While cognitive, psycho-social, and environmental problems do exist for students with learning difficulties, these problems should not be viewed as obstacles that are too difficult for teachers to overcome. Rather they should be recognized as clear indications of areas of need that must be targeted through high-quality instruction. The evidence clearly shows that teaching for these students should involve explicit instruction in basic skills, active engagement by the students, guided practice with constructive feedback, followed by independent practice and application. These students also benefit from more frequent revision and review of previous learning. Digital technology is increasingly proving useful for motivating students with general learning difficulties, providing extra practice, and improving basic academic skills (e.g., Cranmer, 2020; Drushlyak et al., 2023; Mutflu & Akgün, 2019).

Specific learning disability

The APA (2024) describes a specific learning disability as a condition that interferes with an individual's ability to read, write, speak, spell, and compute in mathematics. The disability is evident even in a few intellectually gifted individuals. The APA also points out that their difficulties in learning are not due to conditions such as intellectual disability, vision or hearing problems, economic or environmental disadvantage, or lack of instruction. A specific learning disability is reported to be present in some 4 per cent of students of average or above average intelligence. Unless provided with effective teaching, some of these students may go on to develop serious social and emotional problems associated with constant failure in school, and some exhibit major behaviour problems (Horbach et al., 2020).

In recent years, rather than relying solely on the traditional criterion of a significant discrepancy between measured intelligence (IQ) and a student's scores on academic tests, clinicians now identify a specific learning disorder through a comprehensive clinical review of the student's developmental, medical, educational, and family history; test scores; teachers' observations; and the student's previous response to any remedial intervention. Early identification and effective intervention remain high priorities in improving the educational opportunities for these students.

Beyond compulsory school years, universities and colleges are beginning to realize the need to provide specific support for students with a learning disability who are intellectually very capable but have problems with basic literacy and study skills. Such support may include accommodations made in the time allowed for assignments and assessments, note-taking assistance, and additional guidance on locating online resources for researching assignments.

Students with a *language-based learning disorder* are those whose literacy difficulties are usually associated with general expressive and receptive language weakness and sometimes a speech problem. Language-based difficulties tend to affect acquisition of phonic decoding skills, expressive vocabulary, reading comprehension, and writing and spelling (HASA, 2019; Snowling et al., 2019). Dyslexic students typically have great difficulty developing awareness of the phonological aspects of oral language—understanding that spoken words are composed of sequences of separate sounds. As a result, they fail to develop fluency in decoding words, and their oral reading performance tends to be very slow and laboured. They tire easily and avoid reading whenever possible. Lack of practice then exacerbates their problem. Literacy intervention for children with a language-based disability must include a focus on improving oral language skills as well as explicit teaching and practice of effective decoding strategies. Direct help is also needed for strengthening reading comprehension. Much more is said about intervention methods for literacy in Chapter 10.

Students with a *non-verbal learning disorder* (NLD) form the smallest subgroup. The measured verbal IQ of these students is usually very much higher that their non-verbal score, and their oral verbal skills are usually within the normal range. Their difficulties are not associated with speech or language deficiencies but are due mainly to problems with fine motor coordination, spatial awareness, directional sense, and pattern recognition (Forber-Pratt et al., 2024).

Non-verbal learning difficulties are associated most obviously with problems in fine motor control and spatial awareness (Debenham, 2018). To some extent, non-verbal learning disability shares some characteristics with a condition known as *dyspraxia*, although the two conditions are not the same. The student may appear to be clumsy and poorly balanced and does not enjoy physical education and sport. Fine motor skills such as handwriting, setting down columns of figures, or drawing diagrams are often problematic. Students with NLD can be helped significantly once their problem is identified, because speaking and listening are their best channels for learning. Often students with NLD will leave assignments unfinished. To overcome this tendency, they can be taught self-regulation strategies to enable them to approach classroom tasks systematically and to see them through to completion (see Chapter 7). More than a usual amount of guidance may be needed to help these students set out their bookwork appropriately.

'Mainstreaming for some' becomes 'inclusion for all'

Before the 1970s, students with special educational needs and disabilities were routinely placed in special schools or in full-time or part-time special classes within mainstream schools. It was firmly believed that in these settings the students would receive an adapted curriculum and teaching methods designed to meet their needs. It was also assumed that it would be almost impossible for most teachers in mainstream classes of 25+ students to provide enough daily individualized support for a student with special needs.

In the late 1960s, a few studies had suggested that some students with only a mild degree of learning difficulty or disability could actually succeed quite well in the regular classroom if provided with additional support from the teacher or classroom assistant (Carlberg & Kavale, 1980; Dunn, 1968). Following these reports, and strongly influenced by the prevailing advocacy for the rights of persons with disabilities, the 1970s saw the advent of an era of 'integration' or 'mainstreaming.' Many more students with mild disabilities and learning problems began to be placed in regular classes in their local school instead of a special school or unit. In many regular primary and secondary schools, these students often (but not always) received additional tutoring in part-time withdrawal groups. This mainstreaming trend continued into the 1990s, alongside ongoing use of separate special schools, special classes, and units for students with the most complex special needs.

In 1994, policies and practices in most developed countries began to change again, following dissemination of the *Salamanca Statement and Framework for Action on Special Needs Education* (UNESCO, 1994, 2020). This statement called for schools everywhere to accept and educate the full range of students from their neighbourhood, regardless of a student's level of ability or disability. In 2006, the UN Convention on the Rights of Persons with Disabilities also confirmed the need to develop a more inclusive education system. It was believed that this was the route to creating a society that is more accepting and tolerant of individual differences. It was anticipated that eventually separate special schools and classes would no longer be required.

Challenges faced by implementing inclusive education

The *Salamanca Statement* has been a very worthy and influential international policy—but it has not proven easy to implement in practice (Kohout-Diaz, 2023; Taylor & Sailor, 2024; Tiernan, 2022). In particular, the notion of *full* inclusion, with students with severe intellectual and developmental disability placed in mainstream classrooms, has proven to be unrealistic and not in the students' best interests. Many educators are beginning to argue that rather than focusing entirely on placement in the mainstream, provision for students with special needs should ensure they have access to an *appropriate* curriculum and teaching methods, regardless of place of delivery (Leijen et al., 2021; Stanczak et al., 2024; Tiernan, 2022). According to Hornby and Kauffman (2023), there is really no hard evidence proving that full inclusion in mainstream for students with disabilities is more effective for learning and well-being than special education placement.

Although it was anticipated that the inclusion movement would result in closure of special schools and classes, few countries have achieved this change. In many countries, the number of students enrolled in special schools and special units has actually increased in recent years (Department for Education, 2023; Hingstman et al., 2023; Thomas et al., 2023). Students most likely to be refused full-time admission to their local school are those with autism spectrum disorder, significant cognitive impairment, or emotional and behavioural problems (Soares et al., 2022). It is also reported that students with special needs who are admitted are often not included fully in the core curriculum or in extra-curricular activities (Adams, 2019; Australian Alliance for Inclusive Education, 2020; CYDA, 2019; Ofsted, 2021).

In most countries, there are definite obstacles that are slowing progress towards inclusion. In 2020, data from 31 countries across Europe indicate that all countries still use some form of segregated settings for students with special needs (Ramberg & Watkins, 2020). Referring to the UK, Shaw (2017) was almost certainly correct in predicting that special schools were likely to remain a feature of the education system.

One of the main obstacles to implementing inclusive practices in all schools is classroom teachers' very understandable lack of confidence in their own ability to teach students with disabilities and special needs. Experienced teachers and pre-service teachers both express the view that while they support the concept of inclusion, they feel they have not received the necessary training to actually teach diverse groups of students (Lindner et al., 2023; McCracken et al., 2023). They also point to large class size in many mainstream schools, restricting the feasibility of giving adequate special support to just a few students in a class (Bondebjerg et al., 2023; Westwood, 2021).

It should also be noted that not all parents are in favour of mainstream placement for their child with a disability (Cologon, 2022; Satherley & Norwich, 2022). Many parents believe that the small class size in special schools will enable their child to receive much more personalized care and attention (Thomas et al., 2023). Parents of children with intellectual disability, emotional disorders, or autism tend to have the greatest doubts about inclusion (Paseka & Schwab, 2020).

Reasons for slow evolution of inclusive schooling are actually complex, and they go well beyond teachers' attitudes, insufficient professional preparation, and parents' doubts. Other influences include inadequate funding given to mainstream schools to enable them to establish and maintain an effective internal support system and the lack of ongoing professional support for teachers of inclusive classes. There is also a dilemma created by the current 'standards agenda' that has created tension between the notion of increasing student diversity in the classroom while insisting that schools focus on teaching to raise the standard of academic achievement for all students.

But the main reason for the slow progress of inclusive practice is that *it is definitely not easy to implement.* Some of the commonsense teaching interventions described in this book are most easily applied when students with special needs are taught for at least part of the time in small groups (or even individually for short periods) rather than within the whole-class setting. This separate assistance is achievable if a school can implement a form of tiered support, as described later.

Support for learning in inclusive schools

Inclusive schools are expected to make reasonable provision so that students with special needs are afforded the support necessary for them to have the same opportunities to learn as all other students (Gov.UK, 2022). These opportunities will be made available through such measures as the use of evidence-based instruction, modified curriculum when necessary, and differentiation in teaching approach. In recent years, support has also been provided through assistive technology, flexible grouping of students, additional tutoring, peer assistance, and (where available) the use of classroom assistants and volunteers. These issues are discussed later in Chapters 14 and 15.

The principle that students with special needs should be educated in the mainstream as far as possible continues to present many challenges for schools and teachers. Inclusive schools must devise systems that use all available human and material resources to provide the best additional supports and adapted teaching. The actual system adopted in a school will depend on the number of students needing support, the material and professional resources available, flexibility of timetables, and the aims of the support policy in that school.

Multi-tiered systems of support

Currently, primary and secondary schools are tending to adopt variations of the three-tier Response to Intervention Model (RTI) (Zhang et al., 2023). Tier 1 in this model provides effective evidence-based teaching for the whole class to facilitate learning and to minimize failures. This style of teaching is discussed fully in Chapter 14. Tier 2 provides extra tutoring in small groups for any students already known from the previous year to have ongoing difficulties or who are found to be struggling now in Tier 1 (Sonnemann et al., 2023). Most Tier 2 intervention has a focus on literacy skills. Tier 3 provides individual tutoring for any student who has a history of serious learning difficulty or has a disability that needs ongoing intensive support. This will include students with prescribed individual education plans (IEPs) (Morse, 2023). Finally, Tier 3 will also service any student not benefitting currently from the Tier 2 intervention. It is important to stress here that Tier 2 and Tier 3 interventions are intended to *supplement but not replace* a student's engagement in the general curriculum with other students (Inder et al., 2023). It must be noted that Tier 2 and Tier 3 not only must address basic literacy and numeracy learning within the curriculum but must include any necessary personal counselling a student may require for emotional well-being, strengthening resilience, and restoring motivation (Clement, 2023; Westwood, 2024).

Some schools like to use the term Multi-tiered System of Support (MTSS), implying that it may sometimes be necessary to have more than three tiers to address not only tutoring within the curriculum but also counselling, behaviour modification, speech therapy, physiotherapy, and English-as-a-second-language sessions (Bahr et al., 2023; Fleming et al., 2024; Miesner et al., 2023; Sonnemann et al., 2023).

MTSS is somewhat easier to implement in primary schools, where timetabling is flexible and class teachers teach their students for most subjects. Secondary schools tend to have a more rigid timetable with more subject specialization, creating difficulties for implementing Tier 2 and Tier 3 teaching (Grant-Skiba, 2023).

The following four chapters deal in more detail with disabilities and the effect they can have on learning and development. Later chapters describe effective methods of teaching and assessment that can be used at the various tiers in a response-to-intervention model.

Resources

Online

- Children with special educational needs and disabilities. https://www.gov.uk/children-with-special-educational-needs

- Special educational needs and disabilities code of practice: 0 to 25 years [UK].https://www.gov.uk/government/publications/send-code-of-practice-0-to-25
- Special education and inclusion: Best practices to support inclusion. https://www.thoughtco.com/special-education-and-inclusion-3111343
- Inclusive solutions. https://inclusive-solutions.com/blog/what-are-the-opportunities-and-challenges-of-inclusive-education/
- UNESCO. What you need to know about inclusion in education. https://www.unesco.org/en/inclusion-education/need-know

Print

Ainscow, M. (2024). *Developing inclusive schools*. London: Routledge.

Causton, J., MacLeod, K., Pretti-Frontczak, K., Rufo, J.M., & Gordon, P. (2023). *The way to inclusion: How leaders create schools where every student belongs*. Alexandria, VA: ASCD.

Graham, L. (Ed.) (2023). *Inclusive education for the 21st century: Theory, policy and practice* (2nd ed.). London: Routledge.

Hallahan, D., Kauffman, J., & Pullen, P. (2022). *Exceptional learners* (15th ed.). Upper Saddle River, NJ: Pearson.

Lush, V. (2023). *Building your inclusive classroom*. London: Speechmark Publishing (Routledge).

Obiakor, F., Banks, T., Graves, J, & Rotatori, A.F. (2019). *Educating young children with and without exceptionalities: Contemporary perspectives in special education*. Charlotte, NC: Information Age Publishing.

Chapter 2

Students with intellectual disability

The most obvious characteristic of students with intellectual disability is that they tend to experience significant difficulty learning and remembering almost everything that most other students can learn with relative ease. In some cases, there may also be problems with attention to task, language development, social interaction, acquiring everyday living skills, and emotional control. In general terms, students with a significant degree of intellectual disability usually appear much less mature than their age peers. Their behaviour, reasoning, and self-control are more closely related to their stage of mental development rather than to their chronological age. They have great difficulty in what is termed *executive functioning*, which includes the use of mental processes that help an individual plan, monitor, and successfully work towards their learning goals (Gravråkmo et al., 2023). These key processes include attention control, working memory, interpreting information, and solving everyday problems.

The current view of educators is that all students with intellectual disability can learn and make progress if provided with teaching methods and materials oriented to their needs and abilities and if given all necessary support (Lequia et al., 2023). It is vital that we do not sell these students short by expecting too little from them. In an endeavour to facilitate the provision of essential support, several countries now provide schools with an individual education plan (IEP) for any student identified as having special needs. In the UK, the Education, Health and Care Plan (EHCP) serves a similar purpose. These plans contain the goals to be achieved and are then clear to teachers and parents.

DOI: 10.4324/9781003598671-3

Intellectual disability

Intellectual disability was previously referred to for many generations as mental handicap or mental retardation, and the term intellectual disability was not officially introduced until the fifth edition of the *Diagnostic and Statistical Manual of Mental Disorders* (DSM-5) (APA, 2013). The term 'intellectual development disorder' has also entered into use, particularly among medical professions.

It is generally accepted that individuals with intellectual disability comprise some 2 per cent of the general population. Diagnosis is based on an evaluation of the individual's developmental history and the current repertoire of knowledge, skills, and behaviours that person has acquired (Lee et al., 2024a). The degree of difficulty that each person encounters in learning (mild, moderate, severe, or profound) is directly related to their level of cognitive impairment (Gluck, 2024). Students with mild intellectual disability form the majority of this group (80+ per cent), whose IQ is usually in the range of 50–70. They are only a little slower than average students in learning new information and skills and so can usually be educated in mainstream schools if provided with regular additional support. If provided this support at Tier 2 or Tier 3 intervention (see Chapter 1), many of these students can acquire basic literacy between grade 3 to grade 5 standard by the end of adolescence.

Students with moderate intellectual disability constitute approximately 10 per cent of the those with intellectual disability, whose IQ is usually between 35 and 50. Their education can still be provided in a mainstream school if the school has an effective multi-tiered support system and access to suitably qualified special education teachers and aides. Approximately 4 per cent of students with severe intellectual disability have IQs below 35 and are still mainly placed in special schools or centres, although some preschools, kindergartens, and a few mainstream primary schools have made efforts to accommodate them. Students with profound intellectual disability (1–2 per cent) are low-functioning in most areas and have very high and ongoing support needs. Their need for constant care and full-time management means that mainstream school placement is clearly inappropriate.

Intellectual disability impairs cognition in several key areas—language, reasoning, memory, reading, writing, and number skills. However, children with this disability may have problems not only with schoolwork but also in developing self-management and acquiring everyday living skills. Functioning is affected in the domains of interpersonal communication, social judgment, and the ability to make and retain friends (Schwab, 2019). Teenagers and adults with intellectual disability may be very naïve in their approach to and interaction with others in the community, leaving them vulnerable to exploitation or possibility of sexual abuse. Many individuals with moderate to severe intellectual disability may also have physical or sensory impairments, and some students may also have attention-deficit/hyperactivity disorder (ADHD) (Arias et al., 2019), a condition discussed fully in Chapter 8.

Priorities in teaching students with intellectual disability

In an increasing number of countries, almost all students with mild disabilities will attend mainstream schools and are helped to access the mainstream curriculum. Where necessary, adjustments and adaptations are made to classroom programmes and teaching methods to accommodate their learning needs. Only those with severe disabilities and high support needs will receive their education in a special school or centre. This could be regarded as the extreme form of Tier 3 intervention.

Mild intellectual disability

When students with mild intellectual disability are in inclusive mainstream classrooms, the intention is undoubtedly that they will follow the normal curriculum as far as possible. This arrangement is preferable to providing an alternative programme because it includes the students more effectively in the total classroom experience. However, these students may need to produce work at a slower pace and possibly use different learning materials (e.g., simpler text with more illustrations; structured notes; less-challenging worksheets; different ways of producing written work). The use of a word processor has been found to assist these students to type their work and check spelling, and a calculator can help with mathematics (Sherawat & Punia, 2022). Any necessary adaptations to methods or materials are usually specified in the student's IEP or similar document, along with personalized goals for learning. Students with mild intellectual disability will also need more frequent direct guidance, emotional support, and encouragement from the teacher, classroom assistant, and peers. Chapter 15 describes a number of strategies for adapting teaching methods and curricula.

Moderate to severe disability

In the case of students with moderate to severe intellectual disability, additional adaptations are required. This degree of disability often results in significant limitations of development in the following areas, and these must represent priorities for intervention and teaching:

- language and communication
- self-care and daily living skills
- social development
- self-regulation, self-direction, and autonomy
- basic academic skills (literacy and numeracy)
- transition to employment or sheltered work
- independent functioning in the community.

The great dilemma facing those who wish to educate children with moderate to severe disabilities in the mainstream is how to meet their needs for effective training in self-care and everyday living skills within an environment where a subject-based academic curriculum prevails. Some experts have queried whether the potential benefits of normalization in the mainstream can outweigh all the problems involved in supporting these children in a curriculum that is not necessarily very relevant to them. Some years ago, Dymond and Orelove (2001, p. 111) warned that 'Functional skills, which were once widely accepted as the basis for curriculum development, have received limited attention as the field has moved to a more inclusive service delivery model.' In recent years, little has changed, and the same observation could be made today. There is growing concern in some quarters that 'full inclusion' is unrealistic for the most disabled students and may even result in some learners receiving an education that is clearly not appropriate to meet their needs.

For some students with moderate to severe intellectual disability, a special education setting still offers the best environment to meet their needs. The purpose of having special schools and special classes was—and still is—to create an environment in which objectives for learning, curriculum content, resources, and methods of instruction can be geared appropriately to the students' abilities. A priority in designing such a curriculum is to use content and teaching approaches that will best prepare intellectually disabled students for an independent adult life.

Learning characteristics of students with intellectual disability

It is generally accepted that children with intellectual disability pass through the same stages in cognitive development as all other children but at a much slower rate. In most aspects of conceptual development, school-age children with mild to moderate intellectual disability tend to be functioning at what Piaget (1963) referred to as the 'concrete operational level'—they understand and remember best the things that they can directly experience. Teaching for them must always be reality-based and must involve 'learning by doing'. Students with severe to profound disability may be at an even earlier cognitive stage, tied closely to sensory awareness. Programmes for these most disabled students are described later.

Attention

Attention is a fundamental prerequisite for the process of taking in information and adding it to working memory, retaining that information, and retrieving the information as required (Shaw, 2023). Individuals with intellectual disability appear often to have problems maintaining attention or focusing attention on the relevant aspects of a learning situation. For example, when a teacher is showing the student how to form the numeral 5 with a pencil or how to use scissors to cut a shape from paper, the student is attracted to the ring on the teacher's finger rather than the task itself. This tendency to focus on irrelevant detail or to be distracted easily from a learning task is a major problem for a student with intellectual disability when placed in an inclusive classroom without close supervision. Without adequate control of attention, any student will fail to learn or remember what the teacher is trying to teach. Attention and memory can both be improved when a learning task is interesting and motivating, involves action on the part of the student, and is paired with encouraging feedback.

Memory

Many students with intellectual disability have difficulty storing information in long-term memory. This problem is linked, in part, with failure to attend closely to the learning task, as discussed above; but failure to remember is also due to a lack of effective strategies for facilitating memorization. To minimize this memory problem, students with intellectual disability require much greater amounts of repetition and practice to ensure that important information and skills are eventually stored and can be recalled when needed. Many opportunities must be provided for guided and independent practice, revision, and overlearning in every area of the curriculum. Often, it takes longer than expected for these students to reach the desired state of automaticity in even the most basic skills.

Generalization and transfer of learning

For any learner, the final and most difficult stage of mastering new learning is that of *generalization*. The stage must be reached when a student can automatically apply new learning in other situations not directly linked with the context in which it was first taught. It is typical of most students with intellectual disability that they do not easily transfer what they learn in new contexts. They may learn a particular skill or strategy in the classroom or workshop but fail to transfer it to a different situation. It is recommended that teachers consider ways of facilitating generalization and transfer when planning lessons for students with special needs—for example, by re-teaching the same skills or strategies in different settings. Gradually increase the range of contexts where practice is carried out, challenge students to decide whether a skill or strategy could be used in a new situation, and praise (reinforce) any evidence of students' spontaneous generalization of previous learning.

Language development and language delay

Language is important for cognitive and social development for the following reasons:

- language enables an individual to make his or her needs, opinions, and ideas known to others
- language is important for cognitive development; without language, one lacks much of the raw material with which to think and reason
- concepts are more effectively stored in memory if they have a representation in words as well as in sensations and perceptions
- language is the main medium through which school learning is mediated
- positive social interactions with other persons are heavily dependent upon effective language and communication skills
- inner language (self-talk) is important for regulating one's behaviour and responses.

A characteristic of many children with moderate and severe intellectual disability is the very slow rate at which they acquire speech and language. Some have a definite speech disorder that makes it extremely difficult for them to communicate. These children often require ongoing speech therapy. The frustration of failing to communicate can give rise to emotional reactions and the onset of challenging behaviour. A few individuals with severe and complex disabilities never develop speech, so for them alternative methods of communication, such as sign language or picture communication systems, may need to be developed.

Early intervention programmes in the preschool years place heavy emphasis on developing children's language skills. These interventions should also be family-focused as much as possible, and parents can be trained to engage more proactively in stimulating the speech development of their child with language delay (Knoche et al., 2023).

The development of communication skills is given very high priority in special school curricula and will be no less important for intellectually disabled students included in mainstream settings. Two obvious benefits of placing a child with mild to moderate intellectual disability in a mainstream class are immersion in a naturally enriched language environment and the increased need for the student to communicate with others.

Language is best acquired naturally, through using it to express needs, obtain information, and interact socially. Where possible, naturally occurring opportunities within the school day are used to teach and reinforce new vocabulary and language patterns. This *milieu approach* is found to be more productive in terms of generalization and transfer of learning to everyday use than are the more clinical approaches to 'teaching language'. However, teachers do not always find it easy to integrate specific language development objectives for an individual student into their content-based mainstream class lessons.

Many students with intellectual disability require the services of a speech therapist, but while some individuals make great strides with this, others make only very slow improvement. This is because the individual receiving help may not understand the need for it and therefore may have no motivation to practice and use what is taught. There is also the usual problem of lack of generalization – what is taught in a clinical therapy setting does not necessarily transfer to the student's everyday speech.

Social development

For many individuals with intellectual disability, the development of social competence and skills presents many ongoing difficulties. The presence or absence of social skills in these students tends to be related to the extent to which they have had an opportunity to socialize in environments other than the home. Within the family, the social interactions between the child and others are likely to be mainly positive, but the same assumption cannot be made for contacts within the community and at school or work. Although community attitudes towards people with disabilities have become more positive and accepting, there is still likelihood that some children with intellectual disability will experience difficulty gaining acceptance and making friends – particularly if they display some challenging behaviours. Some students with intellectual disability are rejected and marginalized by their peers more often on the basis of their irritating behaviour than because they are disabled. For example, the presence of inappropriate aggression and temper tantrums makes it difficult for some of these children to be socially accepted. Intervention is needed to eliminate negative behaviours and replace them with pro-social behaviours (see Chapter 8). If the student with a disability is to make friends and be accepted in the peer group, social skills training may be needed (Hallahan et al., 2023).

Strategies for developing social skills are described in Chapter 9, but helping students with intellectual disability form lasting friendships with other children in the mainstream is actually quite difficult. Often students in the peer group who start out with good intentions to associate with a disabled peer lose interest and fade away. In post-school years, socialization remains difficult for many individuals with intellectual disability, and often they require regular and ongoing support from a social worker.

Social interaction with others does indeed need to increase, but students with intellectual disability (male and female) also need to be taught *protective behaviours* to reduce the possibility that they become victims of financial or other forms of exploitation. The lack of social judgment of some teenagers and young adults with intellectual disability causes them to be rather naïve and trusting. Because they may not really comprehend right from wrong in matters of physical contact, there is also a risk of sexual abuse from peers or adults. For their own protection, they need to be taught the danger of going anywhere with a stranger, accepting rides in a car, engaging in online chat with a stranger, or taking gifts for favours. They need to know that some forms of touching are wrong, and they also need to know that they can tell some trusted adult if they feel they are at risk from some other person. These matters must be dealt with openly in schools and also reinforced by parents. Sex education is an important priority for these students.

Self-regulation and self-determination

In recent years, much emphasis has been placed on using cognitive methods to increase executive functioning (self-regulation and self-monitoring) in students with intellectual disability (see Chapter 7). While this approach is proving useful for students with mild disabilities, it is very difficult indeed to employ cognitive training with low-functioning students, for reasons that will be discussed later in connection with autism.

Self-determination and autonomy are topics that currently attract more attention in the education of individuals with intellectual disability (Carey et al., 2023; Friedman et al., 2019; Meral et al., 2023). It is recognized now that too much of the life of a person with moderate or severe disability is typically determined by others. These students need adequate autonomy if they are to have reasonable independence in adult life. In recent years, educators and caregivers have been encouraged to find many more ways of ensuring that persons with disabilities have many opportunities to exercise choice and make decisions. To facilitate this process, goals must be included in the IEP and in the curriculum for increasing the individual's independence and self-management. Parents, paraprofessionals, and carers may need to be reminded to allow children with disabilities in their care to *do more for themselves.*

Physical fitness

It is reported widely that students with intellectual disability often fail to take regular exercise and have a tendency to become overweight and unfit (Pierce & Maher, 2020). The issue of childhood obesity is considered in more detail in Chapter 4. A poor level of fitness exerts a negative influence that can affect their overall well-being. As far as possible, schools must endeavour to include these students fully in physical education (PE) and games activities and should also encourage out-of-school participation in sports. Interventions that include fitness training have been shown to have positive effects (Bibro & Zarów, 2023; Hassan et al., 2019). Parents also need to be reminded of the need for their child to engage more in physical activities.

Teaching approaches for students with intellectual disability

Taking into account the stage of cognitive development of most students with mild to moderate intellectual disability, the priority for teaching is to make the curriculum *reality-based* and *relevant*. For example, for students at the concrete operational stage in cognition, the principle of 'learning by doing' certainly applies. If they are to learn important number skills, for example, they should learn them not only from computer games, instructional materials, and practice sheets but also from real situations such as shopping trips, stocktaking, measuring, estimating, counting, grouping, recording data, and comparing quantities. A mathematics programme for students with mild intellectual disability should link the regular practising of functional number skills directly to real-life situations, so that basic mathematical thinking, rather than rote learning, is encouraged. Where firsthand experience of such quantitative situations is not immediately available, using videos of situations involving measuring, weighing, and giving change can be beneficial for improving students' mathematical understanding. Videos therefore offer an innovative solution for bringing more of the school curriculum to life for these students.

Similarly, reading skills should be developed and practiced by using recipes, brochures, comic books, and information on the computer screen, in addition to vocabulary-controlled reading books, games, and flashcards. Writing for authentic purposes should be taught directly, with a focus on 'planning-before-you-write', self-monitoring, and practice, in addition to any exercises in sentence construction and sentence combining (Güler Bülbül & Özmen, 2021; Rodgers & Loveall, 2023).

In addition to reality-based learning, children with moderate intellectual disability need to have the academic curriculum content broken down into simple steps and to be taught with high-quality explicit instruction to ensure high success rates (Macquarie University, 2023). Explicit instruction is among the most extensively researched teaching methods and has consistently proven more effective than unguided learning for most purposes. Lessons that employ explicit instruction present information and skills clearly, teach students effective ways of learning, and obtain many successful responses from students during the time available. There is heavy emphasis on practice and reinforcement with feedback from the teacher. Frequent prompting by the teacher or instructor during learning plays an important role in helping students process information, respond correctly, and acquire new skills. It has been found that this type of teacher-led instruction is extremely effective for all students in the initial stages of new learning and is of particular help to students with disabilities. The method is discussed fully in Chapter 14.

Preparation for work

Transition from school to adult life and work requires extremely careful planning for intellectually disabled students in the adolescent age range. In the past, senior special schools usually rose to the challenge of developing students' readiness for employment by providing a strong emphasis on practical skills, work routines, reliability, punctuality, and work experience. It is proving to be much more difficult to provide these opportunities for senior students in inclusive mainstream schools. This problem is yet to be resolved—which may explain why many intellectually disabled students of secondary school age have remained in senior special schools in the UK rather than entering the mainstream (Black, 2019). A study of young adults who had successfully made the transition from special school to work identified key factors that had helped them succeed; these factors included encouraging them to develop self-determination, support from family, school–workplace collaboration, and individual accommodations in an inclusive work environment (Sigstad & Garrels, 2023).

Specific approaches for students with severe intellectual disability

Several unique approaches have been developed to meet the special needs of students with severe and complex intellectual disabilities in special schools. Many of these students have no speech, and some have restricted mobility. The approaches described below also have some application with students with severe autism.

Applied behaviour analysis

Applied behaviour analysis (ABA) is a broad term that encompasses several different approaches that can be used within special education (e.g., behaviour modification, discrete trial training, pivotal response training, and task analysis). The underlying principle is *operant conditioning*, and the underpinning belief is that new skills and behaviours can be taught, shaped, and reinforced by rewards or eliminated by negative consequences. As a teaching technique, ABA involves setting clear behavioural objectives for a student and devising a schedule for rewarding him or her at every incremental step when moving successfully toward that objective (Alberto et al., 2021). The approach has been extensively researched and found to be effective in teaching new behaviours to children with intellectual disability or autism and students with behaviour disorders. The topic is discussed in much more detail in Chapter 8.

It should be noted that while the traditional form of ABA involves setting extremely detailed and specific behavioural objectives that could be used to measure accurately the effectiveness of an intervention, more recent applications (as used with severely disabled students) have found that general objectives are more functional because they are easier for support persons and parents to understand and observe.

Discrete trial training

Discrete trial training (DTT) is an ABA method for teaching a skill or behaviour using simple and structured steps, with practice and reinforcement provided for all correct responses at each and every step (Zauderer, 2023). It is an approach to building a more complex skill by practising each small step on the way. DTT is used in domains such as speech and language training, self-help skills, discriminating among colours or shapes, and recognizing letters and numbers. Task analysis has usually been conducted first to identify the best sequence of steps necessary to master any given skill or process.

Many therapists suggest that DTT is a particularly effective strategy for teaching skills to children with intellectual disability and autism, but it is difficult to implement in anything other than one-to-one teaching situations (Rabideau et al., 2018). It is an approach that can be taught to parents of children with intellectual disability or autism.

Constant time delay

Often, in one-to-one teaching situations, a teacher or tutor tends to step in too quickly after asking a question or giving an instruction. It has been found more effective if the tutor waits for a response for around 5 seconds before praising the student for a correct response or before providing a correction or prompt. A meta-analysis of this approach has indicated that it is simple to apply and more efficient than many other commonly used instructional practices (Horn et al., 2020). Constant time delay also has a part to play in remedial reading tuition at Tier 3 intervention, with the teacher waiting for a few moments longer before prompting to assist word recognition.

Intensive interaction

A method known as *intensive interaction* has been developed for use with individuals who have severe and complex disabilities, lack verbal communication, and have limited social interaction with others (Berridge & Hutchinson, 2021). The interactive approach tries to ensure that much of the informal teaching that takes place is based directly on the individual's *self-initiated* actions and reactions (no matter how small) rather than on any preplanned curriculum.

The approach was developed in England in the 1980s by teachers working in long-stay residential institutions for children and adults with severe and complex disabilities. It evolved from a technique known at that time as 'augmented mothering'—a term that sums up the essence of the interactions involved. In many ways, the method is similar to the natural approach used instinctively by parents when responding to a baby's actions. Something the child does spontaneously leads the adult to react, rather than the adult imposing communication on the child. For example, responding to the child by smiling, reaching out, touching, stroking, and vocalizing—and, by doing so, reinforcing the child's behaviour. There is a vital ingredient of natural warm social interaction and communication involved. Often playing very simple touching or laughing games or using sensory or tactile equipment will create a context for this to happen.

Since 2021 in the UK, an assessment approach known as the Engagement Model has been in use with individuals who are severely or profoundly disabled and who cannot be assessed within the usual framework of National Curriculum subjects, even at the most basic level (Gov.UK, 2020). The Engagement Model employs the basic principles of intensive interaction and has replaced what was previously referred to as 'Level P' assessment in the National Curriculum. The model involves a person who knows the individual well using natural interaction and observation to gain information on current alertness and responses. The observations are made regularly and are used to reveal any progress that is being made over time and to identify what the next goals must be. This approach fits very comfortably alongside the intensive interaction method.

Intensive Interaction has been adopted by several other countries, including Australia, for use with severely intellectually disabled and autistic individuals. Research findings suggest that intensive interaction has most positive effect with individuals who do not display very high levels of emotional disturbance and challenging behaviour (Tee & Reed, 2017).

Preference-based teaching

This approach has similar theoretical underpinnings to intensive interaction, and the two can be used in a mutually supportive manner. Preference-based teaching (PBT) is based on the belief that students enjoy engaging in learning activities much more, and attention is more effectively gained and maintained, if the mode of teaching and the materials used are compatible with their personal preferences. For example, a child may enjoy engaging in sand play rather than water play or singing with a caregiver rather than listening to a story (Watkins et al., 2019). When a child is engaged in this way, there are fewer behaviour problems. This is a very important consideration when working with children with severe disabilities and challenging behaviour. Cerveny (2016) conducted a study to determine if PBT embedded as part of DTT led to more learning than DTT alone. It was found that learning occurred in both conditions, and there was no clear difference between PBT alone and the combined version.

Snoezelen Multi-Sensory Environments

For many years, it has been believed that severely disabled children can be helped most by methods that incorporate sensory awareness and sensory stimulation. The Snoezelen approach developed in Holland uses structured multi-sensory environments containing lights, textures, aromas, sounds, and movement for therapeutic and educational purposes (Carter, 2023b). The Snoezelen approach provides both sensory stimulation and relaxation for severely or profoundly disabled individuals (including adults) and has been adopted in a number of special schools in Europe and Australasia.

Snoezelen is reported to have particular benefits for calming intellectually disabled or autistic individuals who also have emotional and behavioural problems. In some cases, Snoezelen has proven useful for reducing self-injurious behaviour. It is suggested that, in work with the most severely disabled individuals, an assessment should be made of that person's preference for certain stimuli rather than others in order to tailor a Snoezelen sensory environment to that person's preferences (see PBT above). It is also useful to identify what types of stimuli (colour, lights, music, tastes) can be used most effectively as reinforcers in other learning situations (Fava & Strauss, 2010; Grattan & Demchak, 2014). Researchers have found that giving autistic individuals some control of what happens in the Snoezelen room increases their attention and reduces anxiety and repetitive behaviour (Unwin et al., 2021).

More about Snoezelen can be found at https://www.montessori-theory.com/snoezelen-a-multi-sensory-therapeutic-approach/.

Some individuals with intellectual disability also have some degree of autism, but autism can also be present in individuals whose intelligence is within the normal range or even above. The next chapter provides an introduction to children with autism spectrum disorder. They comprise a very diverse group, with a range of mild to severe difficulties that span learning, communication, socialization, self-regulation, and independent functioning. Those students with moderate to severe autism and disruptive behaviour are often regarded as the most difficult to place successfully in inclusive classrooms.

Resources

Online

- Information on intellectual disability at American Psychiatric Association (2024). *What is intellectual disability?* https://www.psychiatry.org/patients-families/intellectual-disability/what-is-intellectual-disability
- ADCET (Australian Disability Clearing House on Education and Training). (2024). *Intellectual disability.* https://www.adcet.edu.au/inclusive-teaching/specific-disabilities/intellectual-disability

- mentalhelp.net (2024). *Effective teaching methods for people with intellectual disabilities.* https://www.mentalhelp.net/intellectual-disabilities/effective-teaching-methods/2024.
- Classful website. (2024). *Students with an intellectual disability (5 methods to help).* https://classful.com/students-with-an-intellectual-disability/
- Information on *Intensive Interaction Approach* can be found at https://integratedtreatmentservices.co.uk/wp-content/uploads/_mediavault/2015/01/intensive-interation.pdf
- Discrete Trial Training is described clearly at https://www.educateautism.com/applied-behaviour-analysis/discrete-trial-training.html

Print

Beckett, A.E., & Callus, A.M. (2024). *The lives of children and adolescents with disabilities.* Abingdon, UK: Routledge.

Glidden, L.M., Abbeduto, L., McIntyre, L.L., & Tassé, M.J. (Eds.). (2021). *APA handbook of intellectual and developmental disabilities: Clinical and educational implications: Prevention, intervention, and treatment.* American Psychological Association.

Orsolini, M. & Ruggerini, C. (Eds). (2022). *Understanding intellectual disability: A guide for professionals and parents (understanding atypical development).* New York: Routledge.

Richards, S.B., Brady, M.P., & Taylor, R.L. (2024). *Understanding intellectual disabilities* (3rd ed.). Abingdon, UK: Routledge.

Storey, K., & Haymes, L. (2023). *Case studies in applied behavior analysis for individuals with disabilities* (2nd ed.). Springfield, IL: Charles Thomas.

Chapter 3

Students with autism spectrum disorder

Autism spectrum disorder

Autism (as it was first termed) was originally identified in the 1940s and was regarded at first as a single disability that affects communication, emotional development, and social competence. The condition is now referred to as *autism spectrum disorder* (ASD) to reflect the fact that it is not a single condition with clear-cut characteristics but actually manifests itself along a continuum with varying degrees of severity and marked differences in behaviour patterns (APA, 2013; Otero & Naglieri, 2023).

ASD is regarded as a neurodevelopmental disability, and some children with autism may also have an intellectual disability that impacts their ability to learn. The fifth edition of the *Diagnostic and Statistical Manual of Mental Disorders* (DSM5) (APA, 2013) contains a very detailed description and definition of ASD, but it is not necessary to reproduce that description in full here. The main characteristics can be summarized as

- *persistent deficits in social communication and social interaction*. This may include deficits in social-emotional reciprocity; deficits in non-verbal communicative behaviours; abnormalities in eye contact and body language; deficits in understanding and use of gestures; lack of facial expressions; and deficits in developing, maintaining, and understanding relationships.
- *restricted, repetitive patterns of behaviour, interests, or activities*. This may include stereotyped repetitive movements or speech; insistence on maintaining sameness and adherence to routines; fixated interests that are abnormal in intensity; and hyper- or hypo-reactivity to sensory input such as sounds or lights.

Of course, any individual with ASD may show some but not all of these difficulties and deficits and will display them at different levels of severity from mild to severe. When an individual with ASD is officially diagnosed by a suitably qualified professional, the diagnosis must specify whether there is also an accompanying intellectual impairment and whether the individual has any

DOI: 10.4324/9781003598671-4

language impairment. The severity of the disorder is reflected in the level of support that the individual requires, ranging from 'very substantial support' to 'requiring some support'.

There are some individuals with mild autistic traits who are referred to as 'high-functioning'. Most high-functioning students receive their education in the mainstream, where their often-unusual behaviour patterns can cause them to be regarded as strange (quirky) by peers and teachers. These students may have difficulty making friends, and whereas some students with ASD may not be bothered by lack of friends, others appear to experience deep loneliness (Adams et al., 2024; Mazurek, 2014). Some high-functioning autistic students benefit from personal counselling and social training that focuses on helping them understand the feelings of others, how to initiate and maintain social interactions, dealing with their own problems or frustrations, and how to avoid trouble with other students and with teachers.

Among the group of high-functioning individuals with autism are those previously referred to as having Asperger syndrome. The *Diagnostic and Statistical Manual of Mental Disorders* no longer classifies Asperger syndrome as a distinct category (APA, 2013). These individuals are now regarded as simply located somewhere on the upper end of the autism spectrum (high-functioning). They have some of the behavioural and social difficulties associated with other degrees of autism, but they tend to have language and cognitive skills in the average or even above average range. A few may even exhibit a talent or deep knowledge in areas such as music, art, or mental calculation or can recall factual information with amazing accuracy.

Most students with mild autistic tendencies can usually be accommodated in the mainstream, but some students report that they are often bullied and can experience constant anxiety (Barna et al., 2024). Those with severe degrees of autism tend to function at a level that is too low to cope with the demands of even an adapted mainstream curriculum. In the most severe cases, the individual may not use speech and may be virtually unresponsive to social contact. It is common to find that the individual displays ritualistic habits (*stereotypic behaviours*) such as constant body rocking or self-stimulation and may be highly sensitive to any change in their routine or immediate environment. The evidence suggests that many teachers in the mainstream lack awareness of the characteristics and needs of students with ASD and are not confident or consistent in their management methods (Holmes, 2024).

Early detection remains the top priority for providing appropriate intervention for ASD. To be diagnosed as autistic, a child must show symptoms of abnormal social and interpersonal development during early childhood and must meet criteria listed in the *Diagnostic and Statistical Manual of Mental Disorders* (APA, 2013) (see *online resources*). In DSM5, a new category, *social communication disorder* (SCD), was added in order to identify individuals who have no speech disorder but display significant difficulties using spoken language to communicate with and respond to others in socially appropriate ways. They may also have difficulty interpreting non-verbal communication cues used by others (smiles, frowns, gestures). This difficulty can make it harder for a student to make and keep friends. These students do not, however, display the same repetitive and stereotypic behaviours or obsessions evident in some individuals with more severe forms of ASD.

Prevalence

ASD has been identified in all parts of the world, so the disorder does not appear to be in any way culturally determined. For many years, autism was regarded as a low-incidence disability with approximately 4 to 10 cases per 10,000 in the population. The lower figure represents the most severe cases, and the upper figure includes children with only mild autistic traits. The ratio of males to females is 4 or 5 to 1. However, in recent years, there has been a reported increase in the number of identified cases of ASD—but this may be due to greater awareness in the community and improved assessment procedures rather than any actual increase in prevalence (Izuno-Garcia et al., 2023; Nielsen et al., 2024).

Causes

The underlying cause of ASD is unknown, and current opinion is that there may be several contributory factors. Studies have tended to suggest a possible genetic influence, perhaps affecting brain processes necessary for normal social and communicative development. It is unclear whether genetic susceptibility is interacting with environmental influences and, if so, what those environmental factors may be (National Autistic Society, 2018). Several theories have been put forward—such as the possible negative effects of vaccinations in childhood—but these theories have all been refuted. The National Health Service in the UK has declared that autism is not caused by bad parenting, vaccines, diet, or infection.

Intervention for autism

Many approaches have been used to help children with autism become more responsive to teaching and management by increasing their communication skills and reducing negative behaviours (McCollow & Hoffman, 2019). Definite gains are reported from intervention programmes, but there is considerable variability in response across individuals, and some students (usually those with mild autistic traits) make much more progress than others. A few children with the most severe forms of autism and with accompanying emotional disturbance often appear to make minimal gains despite many hours of careful stimulation and teaching.

Interventions have included pharmacological (drug) treatments, diet control, psychotherapy, music therapy, play therapy, preference-based play activities, facilitated communication, behaviour modification, and cognitive self-management training. It is generally considered that behaviour modification (applied behaviour analysis) (see Chapter 2) has produced the best results to date and tends to be the most widely used approach. In some studies, after one year of consistent implementation of ABA strategies (setting of clear behaviour goals; clear modelling; practice; consistent reinforcement of required responses), many children with ASD demonstrate gains in communication skills, social interaction, and self-control (Pitts et al., 2019).

Teaching, training, and management: general principles

Teaching, training, and managing children and older students with moderate to severe autism is almost always complex and has to be ongoing and multidisciplinary. It has been said that effective intervention is characterized by structure, intensity of treatment, low adult-to-child ratio, and individualized programming (Hampshire & Hourcade, 2014). To create the optimum situation for teaching, the environment and routines must always be consistent, and teaching sessions for the student need to be implemented according to a predictable schedule. New information, skills, or behaviours need to be taught in small increments. Each student's programme must be based on a very detailed appraisal of his or her current developmental level and existing skills, so that goals can be set that help build on any existing strengths, capabilities, and preferences.

There is general agreement that the focus of any intervention programme should attempt to

- increase the individual's attention and engagement
- stimulate cognitive development
- facilitate language acquisition
- promote social interactions
- use visual cues such as pictures or hand signs as supplements to all verbal instructions and requests.

All teachers, parents, and caregivers must know the precise goals of the programme and must collaborate closely on the methods to be used with the student. The most effective interventions involve the child's family as well as teachers and therapists. It is essential that parents and caregivers also be trained in the teaching and reinforcement strategies to be used in any intervention programme in school, because the child spends more time at home than at school (Mazurek et al., 2019; Park et al., 2023). Home-based intervention programmes (or home programmes combined with clinic-based intervention) produce better results than purely clinic-based programmes.

For non-verbal autistic children, intensive use of alternative communication methods and visual cues (hand signing, pointing, gesture, pictures, and symbol cards) is usually necessary in most teaching situations. One approach to helping a student improve in self-regulation is the use of visual activity schedules, with pictures or symbols depicting what he or she must do at particular times during the school day (e.g., wash hands and dress for physical education [PE]) (Hugh et al., 2018). Such systems can also operate at home. For higher-functioning students, an electronic handheld planner can be useful for storing the daily schedule and for sending appropriate prompts at given times. Some forms of assistive technology (see Chapter 4) have also proven valuable for engaging the attention of a student with ASD and for facilitating communication.

Specific programmes and methods

Some approaches and 'treatments' advertised online are regarded as highly controversial and of doubtful value. Often these programmes are recommended on websites that provide information for parents of autistic children but give no evidence at all of the *proven* efficacy of the programme or treatment.

Pointing Therapy

Pointing Therapy addresses autistic children's tendency not to use natural gesture and pointing to focus and facilitate oral communication (Barbera, 2023; Ramos-Carbo et al., 2021). The approach teaches the child how to attract the attention of others to an object or event by finger-pointing. For example, a parent might point and say, 'Look at that big bird on the roof' or 'Where is that big bird? Show me.' The claim is that teaching the child to use pointing assists interaction and communication and may assist development of better attending behaviour.

Rapid Prompting

Rapid Prompting involves the parent or teacher using constant, fast-paced questioning and prompting to keep the child fully engaged in a communication situation. A picture book, game, or alphabet board might be a focus of attention in this interaction (Rudy, 2023). Rapid Prompting as a therapy still requires much more research to determine its effectiveness.

Snoezelen environments

The use of multisensory Snoezelen environments (see Chapter 2) has produced positive benefits for some children with autism, particularly when colours and sounds are tailored to a particular child's preferences. Spending time in the sensory environment can calm and relax an anxious or aggressive child (Unwin et al., 2021).

TEACCH

One approach that has developed in recent years is TEACCH (*Treatment and Education of Autistic and Communication-handicapped Children*) (Coleman et al., 2022; Mesibov et al., 2005). This approach is based on the need for a high degree of structure in the day for children with ASD. It uses a combination of cognitive and behavioural-change strategies, coupled with direct teaching of specific skills. Importance is placed on training parents to work with their own children and to make effective use of support services. A meta-analysis of studies involving TEACCH has suggested that it is effective for increasing social behaviour (Virues-Ortaga et al., 2013). A study by Park and Kim (2018) has also demonstrated that the structured nature of TEACCH is effective in enhancing a child's active engagement and reducing disruptive behaviour.

An important feature of this approach is that it capitalizes on some autistic children's preference for a visual system of communication rather than auditory-verbal mode. Several studies support using visual cues, prompts, and schedules to hold a child's attention and to represent information in a form that is easily interpreted (Hugh et al., 2018).

Lovaas: Young Autism Programme

One very intensive programme for autistic children devised by Lovaas (Lovaas & Smith, 2003) is also referred to as *Early Intensive Behavioral Therapy* (EIBT). The programme begins with the child at age two years and involves language development, social behaviours, and the stimulation of play activity. The programme contains elements of applied behaviour analysis and discrete-trial training, with skills broken down into their most basic components, and consistent rewarding of every positive performance with praise and other reinforcement. Excessive ritualistic behaviour, temper tantrums, and aggression are gradually eliminated. The second year of treatment focuses on higher levels of language stimulation and on cooperative play and interaction with peers.

Lovaas claimed high success rates for the programme, with almost half of treated children reaching normal functioning levels. However, the fact that this programme takes up to 40 hours per week using one-to-one teaching over two years makes it very labour-intensive and expensive. While the general principles are undoubtedly sound, it is difficult if not impossible to replicate the approach in the typical special preschool or kindergarten.

Pivotal response training

This approach, developed by Robert Koegel and Lynn Koegel and associates (2006), is based on the principle that intervention in autism should focus heavily on strengthening particular behaviours that have wide and beneficial effects on learning. Examples of pivotal behaviours are focusing and maintaining attention, responding to multiple cues, self-regulation, and the initiation of social interaction. It is hoped that, when these key areas are targeted, improvements will generalize across areas of sociability, communication, behaviour, and academic skills. Pivotal response training employs applied behaviour analysis techniques and has been used effectively in improving attention, eye contact, following instructions, play, and social behaviours (Brock et al., 2018; Ebrahim, 2019; Stockall & Dennis, 2014).

An important example of a specific pivotal behaviour is *selective attention*. If a child with ASD has major difficulty coping with distractions in the environment, training will seek to increase selective attention and reduce distractibility. Many benefits, such as improved ability to engage fully in a learning task, use of working memory, and processing information more effectively, then occur.

SCERTS model

Detailed information on SCERTS can be found in the two-volume manual by Prizant et al. (2006). The acronym SCERTS is derived from *Social Communication, Emotional Regulation, Transactional Support*, which are the areas of development prioritized within this approach. The designers of this trans-disciplinary and family-centred model stress that SCERTS is not intended to be exclusionary of other treatments or methods. It attempts to capitalize on naturally occurring opportunities for teaching that occur throughout a child's daily activities and across social partners, such as siblings, parents, caregivers, and other children.

The overriding goal of SCERTS is to help a child with autism become a more competent participant in social activities, by enhancing his or her capacity for attention, communication, reciprocity, expression of emotion, and understanding of others' emotions. There is some evidence that SCERTS can indeed improve social communication and emotional regulation in children with ASD (Yu & Zhu, 2018); however, there is a need for more research before final conclusions can be reached (Yi et al., 2022).

The Son-Rise Programme®

This training programme for parents and caregivers of children with autism is offered in face-to-face version and online by the Autism Treatment Centre of America. In some respects, this home-based intervention uses some principles of the Intensive Interaction Approach for severely intellectually disabled individuals as described in the previous chapter—for example, by building upon a child's existing abilities (no matter how small), personal preferences, and self-initiated responses as starting points for intervention and change. A basic aspect of Son-Rise is that the facilitator (adult) joins the child in his or her world, and the activities and pace of any session are directed by the child rather than by the adult. Importance is placed on having a distraction-free environment in which to interact with the child, so that attention can be maintained. Further research is needed to evaluate the outcomes from this approach (Williams, 2006).

Social stories and social thinking

Interventions for children with ASD frequently focus on improving their social awareness and social skills. These interventions aim to teach autistic individuals why they and others react socially in the ways that they do, how their own behaviours affect the way others perceive and respond to them, and how this affects their own emotions and relationships with others in different social contexts.

One approach used mainly by school counsellors that appears helpful in developing autistic children's awareness of normal codes of behaviour is the use of *social stories* (Goodman-Scott et al., 2017; Williams, 2021). These are simple age-appropriate narratives supplemented by simple illustrations and personalized to suit the child's behavioural needs. The theme and context of the story help an autistic child interpret and respond more appropriately to typical social situations—for example, sharing a toy, taking turns, or standing in line. It has also been found that simple comic strips with stick figures can be used to create situations where a child with ASD is led to think about the actions, reactions, and feelings of others (Gray, 2020).

Children's Friendship Training

Another promising approach is *Children's Friendship Training*, a 12-week parent-assisted social intervention that targets the knowledge and skills required for forming relationships (Child Mind Institute, 2023; Frankel & Myatt, 2002). The training is applicable for a wide range of children in primary schools who may have poor social skills and peer relationship difficulties.

Picture Exchange Communication System

Picture Exchange Communication System (PECS) was developed in 1984 and used in the Delaware Autistic Program. Since then, PECS has been implemented with learners of all ages who have significant cognitive and communication challenges (Vicker, 2002). The approach has been found particularly useful when working with individuals who have severe intellectual disability or autism and lack speech.

The protocol used to guide teaching with PECS includes prompting and reinforcement strategies and systematic error correction. The effectiveness of this intervention depends heavily on the adequate professional training of teachers or other adults involved (Chua & Poon, 2018). The goal of PECS is to teach a person with autism and very limited communication skills a self-initiating communication system. Children using PECS are taught to communicate their wishes, needs, requests, opinions, or ideas to another person by giving them a picture that represents the topic (e.g., a picture of a cup if a drink is being requested or a picture of playground equipment if the child wishes to go outside to play). PECS works well in the home or in the classroom; and it is reported that some learners using PECS also develop speech.

The next chapter provides coverage of students with physical disabilities and health conditions that may affect their learning and development. Chapter 5 extends the coverage to explore the needs of students with impairments of vision or hearing.

Resources

Online

- Information on autism: https://www.nhs.uk/conditions/autism/what-is-autism/
- The DSM5 criteria for diagnosis of autism spectrum disorder: https://www.autismspeaks.org/autism-diagnostic-criteria-dsm-5
- Assessment and care of children with autism spectrum disorder: https://www.who.int/news-room/fact-sheets/detail/autism-spectrum-disorders
- Teaching students with autism spectrum disorder: https://www.autismspeaks.org/tool-kit-excerpt/autism-classroom-strategies.

Print

Bass, R. (2024). *A teacher's guide to managing autism in the classroom: Teaching success from kindergarten to high school*. London: RBG Publishing.

Boucher, J.M. (2022). *Autism spectrum disorder* (3rd ed.). London: SAGE.

Grandin, T. (2024). *Autism and adolescence: The way I see it*. Arlington, TX: Future Horizons.

Meller, J. (2023). *Early intervention strategies for autism: A comprehensive approach*. Independently published.

Prizant, B.M. (2022). *Uniquely human: A different way of seeing autism*. London: Profile Books.

Chapter 4

Physical disabilities and health issues

Physical disability is a relatively low-incidence category of special educational need, but these students comprise a very diverse group. Approximately 3 students in every 100 are found to have a physical disability and receive some form of additional support. A higher figure will certainly pertain in countries with poor standards of health care and pre-natal services and in countries engaged in ongoing wars and conflict.

The education for children with physical disabilities must focus on providing them as far as possible with the same range of learning experiences and social interactions as those available to other students (ADCET, 2024). For all students with a physical disability, their greatest need is help in accessing resources and facilities, in moving around easily within the learning environment, and in forming friendships. In order to function successfully and maintain a good quality of life, some may also need support from outside services that can provide treatment, therapy, or counselling.

Learning and development

Many students with a physical disability are of average or much-higher-than-average intelligence and can cope well with the mainstream curriculum in inclusive classrooms if accommodations are made and if any necessary assistive technology is provided. Typical accommodations that may need to be provided include seating arrangements, space for a wheelchair, extra time on assignments and during examinations, and provision of peer assistance for some students in areas such as note-taking or collecting materials for a lesson. It is essential for teachers to recognize that a physical disability does not automatically impair a student's ability to learn. Assumptions should never be made about an individual's capacity to learn on the basis of a physical condition. While it is true that a disability or acquired injury that involves neurological damage can affect cognition, there are many other disabilities that do not affect intellect or learning aptitude. Teachers' expectations must always be optimistic concerning how much these students can accomplish when given appropriate access, support, and opportunity.

DOI: 10.4324/9781003598671-5

Many students with a physical disability have no problem developing friendships and interacting socially. This is particularly the case if the individual has a pleasant personality and can communicate well. However, students who lack mobility, have communication difficulties, or who have high support needs may experience much greater difficulty with socialization. Some of the strategies described in Chapter 9 will be applicable to assist with the social development and acceptance of these students.

Assistive technology

Assistive technology (AT) plays a major role in the effective education of students with physical and other disabilities by enhancing movement, participation, and communication and facilitating access to the curriculum (Baser & Arsian-Ari, 2023; Redford, 2019; Satsangi et al., 2019). The benefits of using AT are not limited to students in school but also apply to older students undertaking university or vocational training courses (Moriña et al., 2024).

The complexity of modified equipment and technology ranges from 'very low tech' such as adjustable slant-top desks, pencil grips, modified scissor grips, specially designed seating, wedges to help position a child for optimum functioning, walking frames, standing frames, and head-pointers through to 'high-tech' adaptations such as electric wheelchairs operated by head movements or by breath control, modified computer keyboards, touch screens, voice output communication aids (VOCA), and switching devices. Common devices such as smart phones and iPads have also usefully supplemented the more complex equipment needed by these students. Neese (2023) provides a useful list and description of a range of AT options (see "Resources" section below).

Augmentative and alternative communication

Many students with severe and multiple disabilities, whether congenital or acquired, may lack an oral–verbal method of communication. This can lead others to judge them, wrongly, as functioning at a low cognitive level. The priority in intervention for severely disabled persons without speech or whose speech is not intelligible is to develop an alternative method of communicating (Lillehaug et al., 2023). The ultimate aim of any augmentative or alternative communication system is to enable the individual to express his or her needs. Equally important, these aids to communication allow the person with pervasive support needs to converse about the same range of things that others of that age would discuss.

Alternative communication modes include (1) sign language, finger-spelling, cued-speech, and gesture; (2) picture and symbol systems that a person can use by pointing or by eye glance on a communication board, screen, or book; and (3) computer-aided communication.

The simplest form of alternative communication is a communication board comprising a small set of pictures or symbols that are personally relevant to the child's life and current context. For example, the board may have pictures of a television set, a glass, a knife and fork, a toilet, a toy, and an X for 'no' and a green tick for 'yes'. The child can communicate his or her wishes or basic needs by pointing to or looking at the appropriate picture. Other pictures and symbols are added as the child's range of experiences increases.

One picture communication system known as *Talking Mats* has been found to be very useful for working one-to-one with individuals who lack speech (Samuelsson et al., 2024). The system uses a 'mat' to which pictures or symbols can be attached and moved as the focus for communication (see "Resources"). *Talking Mats* have been used effectively with intellectually disabled persons and non-vocal children and adults. This picture system also exists now in a digital version that can be used on a range of mobile devices. The *Talking Mats* website has pictures of the system in use in various situations (https://www.talkingmats.com/).

Augmentative and alternative communication has been transformed in recent years by the social media revolution and the emergence of mobile technology. The immediate need now is to encourage developers of this technology to devise systems that are very easy to operate and do not require high levels of cognition and aptitude.

Cerebral palsy

Cerebral palsy (CP) is one of the more frequently occurring physical disabilities: the prevalence rate is approximately 2 cases per 1000 live births. There has been no significant decline in the prevalence rate of this disorder over recent years, even though there have been major advances in prenatal care. CP is a disorder of posture, muscle tone, and movement, resulting from damage to the motor areas of the brain occurring before, during, or soon after birth. The disability may affect one side or both sides of the body. CP is known to have a significant adverse effect on an individual's motor skills, coordination, speech production, and learning ability (Mousavi et al., 2023). CP exists in several forms (*spasticity, athetosis, ataxia,* and *mixed forms*) and at different levels of severity from mild to severe. Type and severity of the condition are related to the particular area or areas of the brain that have been damaged and the extent of that damage (Erickson & Maricle, 2021). CP is not curable, but its negative impact on the individual's physical coordination, mobility, learning capacity, and communication skills can be reduced through appropriate intensive therapy, training, and education (Golubovic et al., 2022).

Students with CP often have additional disabilities, and at least 15 per cent of cases have impaired hearing or vision defects. Epilepsy is present in up to 30 per cent of cases of CP, and a significant number of these children are on regular medication to control seizures. This medication can often have the side effect of reducing the individual's level of alertness and span of attention, thus adding to potential problems in learning. Epilepsy is discussed in more detail later.

Approximately 60 per cent of individuals with moderate to severe CP also have some degree of intellectual impairment and additional complications. It must be noted, however, that a few persons with quite severe CP are highly intelligent, and their understanding of spoken and written language is well within the normal range. There is a danger that the potential learning and development capacity of these non-verbal CP students is not recognized because of their inability to communicate. One of the main priorities for these individuals is to be provided with an alternative method of communication.

There have been many suggested treatments and therapies for CP, but few of these have been subjected to really rigorous evaluation. Even *conductive education*, a once popular and comprehensive approach originating in Hungary (Pawelski, 2007), often produces very unreliable results. It appears that only the children who have normal intelligence and mild forms of CP are likely to benefit greatly.

Instructional needs of students with cerebral palsy

Academic instruction for students with CP will depend upon their cognitive ability, their range of functional movements, and their attention span. Students with mild CP but of normal intelligence may simply be slower at completing assignments and only need more time and encouragement. Allowance may need to be made for poorly coordinated handwriting or inaccurate keyboarding. For some students, devices such as adapted pencil grips, modified keyboards, and page-turners may be required, and papers may need to be taped firmly to the desktop while working. A few students may use computers with modifications such as touch panels or voice activation rather than a keyboard or mouse.

In addition to having problems with movement and speech, many students with severe CP tend to

- tire easily and have difficulty attending to tasks for more than brief periods of time
- take a very long time to perform physical actions (e.g., picking up an object and eating a meal)
- require the teacher or an aide to move them and place them in a particular position for work, using pads and wedges that enable them to maintain their range of movements to best advantage
- need to be placed and supported in a 'standing frame' with desk-top attached
- need to be fed and toileted by an aide.

Some useful commonsense tips for including students with CP in an inclusive class can be found at https://www.cerebralpalsyguidance.com/cerebral-palsy/living/teacher-tips-inclusive-classrooms/.

Epilepsy

Epilepsy is a fairly frequent additional problem that may accompany physical disabilities that stem from neurological damage or dysfunction (McMahan & Maricle, 2020). Epilepsy is due to abnormal electrical discharges within specific areas of the brain. Severity can vary from very mild loss of awareness (mental absences lasting a few seconds) through to severe seizures in which the individual falls to the ground, convulses, and may lose consciousness (*tonic-clonic seizures*). Some instances of epilepsy that are evident in preschool or primary school years may disappear spontaneously by adolescence or adulthood; but for some individuals, the condition remains and requires a lifetime regimen of medication and management. Medication with anti-epileptic drugs is usually successful in controlling seizures in at least 80 per cent of cases.

Teachers with students who have epilepsy need to know details of each student's condition and how to manage it in the event of seizures. All seizure events should be recorded in writing and reported to parents.

Spina bifida

Spina bifida (SB) is a congenital disorder, possibly of genetic origin, and occurs when certain bones in the spine fail to seal over correctly before birth to protect the spinal cord (Silva & Maricle, 2021). SB presents with different degrees of severity and affects approximately 1 in every 1000 live births. The milder forms of SB have no significant influence on learning and mobility, and it is estimated that approximately 80 per cent of individuals with SB have intelligence within the normal range. There is no reason why the majority of students with mild SB cannot be placed in inclusive classrooms and follow the common curriculum.

Greater difficulties in learning occur with increasing severity of the disability, and learning problems are common in the remaining 20 per cent, with major deficits in sustained attention, visual perception, memory, and number skills. A study by Gaintza et al. (2018) found that successful inclusion of children with moderate to severe SB depended heavily upon schools, teachers, and families working very closely with medical and psychological professionals to provide all necessary support.

The most serious form of SB, with the greatest impact on the individual's life and development, is *myelomeningocele*. In this condition, a small part of the spinal cord protrudes unprotected from a gap in the spine. The cord is usually damaged, and bodily functions below this point, including use of lower limbs and control of bladder and bowel, may be seriously disrupted. Whereas some students with SB can walk, others may need to use a wheelchair or leg braces and must observe a careful diet and a strict toileting routine. The management of incontinence presents perhaps the greatest personal and social problem for students most severely affected by SB.

Approximately 60–70 per cent of children with myelomeningocele may also have *hydrocephalus*. In this condition, normal circulation and drainage of cerebrospinal fluid within the skull are impaired, resulting in increased intracranial pressure (Del Bigio, 2010). Treatment for hydrocephalus involves surgical implanting of a permanent catheter into a ventricle in the brain to drain the excess fluid continually to the abdominal cavity. A valve is implanted below the skin behind the child's ear to prevent any back-flow of fluid. Teachers need to be aware that shunts and valves can become blocked and that the site can become infected. If the child with treated hydrocephalus complains of headache or earache or if he or she appears feverish and irritable, medical advice should be obtained immediately.

Children with SB and hydrocephalus tend to be hospitalized at regular intervals during their school lives for such events as replacing shunts and valves, urinary tract infections, or controlling respiratory problems. This frequent hospitalization can significantly interrupt a child's schooling and can seriously fragment the coverage of curriculum content. Subjects that depend most upon carefully building sequential knowledge and skills (such as mathematics) are most affected by lost instructional time. Students in this situation require intensive 'catch up' assistance with their schoolwork in order not to fall far behind others.

Traumatic brain injury

The term *traumatic brain injury* (TBI) is used to describe any acquired damage to the brain resulting from events such as vehicle accidents, unsuccessful suicide attempts, serious falls, blows to the head, sports injury, the 'shaken infant syndrome,' and recovery after near-death drowning. The actual incidence of TBI in the population is uncertain, but many school-age students with this acquired disability are regularly recorded among those receiving special education either short term or long term (Blankenship & Canto, 2018). An increasing number of school-age individuals acquire brain injury from falls, car accidents, and partial drowning.

The detrimental effects of TBI can include

- memory problems
- attention difficulties
- slow information processing
- inability to solve everyday problems and plan ahead
- speech and language functions disrupted temporarily or permanently
- impairment of motor coordination

- onset of epilepsy
- vision problems
- severe headaches
- unpredictable and irrational mood swings or behaviour (aggressive, restless, apathetic, depressed)
- difficulty sleeping.

Students with TBI often improve dramatically in the first year following injury, but after that progress is usually much slower. There can be ongoing problems with learning, behaviour, and self-management (Kelly et al., 2023). For some individuals with TBI, there is a slight to moderate decline in functional intelligence, and skills such as reading comprehension and mathematical problem-solving present as areas of particular difficulty. Some individuals begin to have difficulty remembering a word or name (*anomia*), and this can slow down their communications and also cause great frustration. Many children with TBI express great irritation in knowing an answer to a question in class but being unable to retrieve the necessary words at the right time.

Given the complexity of the problems that can occur with TBI, it is common to find that individuals affected usually require ongoing personal counselling as well as an adapted learning programme. The main challenges for a teacher are

- finding ways of maximizing the individual's engagement and attention in a learning task by reducing distractions, providing prompts and cues, limiting the amount of information presented, and giving frequent positive feedback
- keeping instructions clear and simple and not overloading the student with information or tasks
- breaking down lesson content into manageable units of work with goals that are achievable within the individual's attention span
- helping to compensate for memory loss by presenting visual cues and graphic organizers
- rehearsing information more than would be necessary with other learners
- teaching self-help strategies such as keeping reminder notes in your pocket and regularly checking the daily schedule on a handheld electronic planner
- helping the individual plan ahead by setting personal goals and then working towards them
- accepting the student's poor ability to concentrate and to complete the work that is set.

Foetal Alcohol Spectrum Disorder

Over the past decades, there has been a marked increase in the number of children diagnosed with *foetal alcohol spectrum disorder* (Gill & Thompson-Hodgetts, 2018). It is likely that children with this syndrome had been present in classrooms long before the disorder was identified and that the children were simply regarded as slow learners.

FASD is caused by a mother having consumed significant amounts of alcohol during pregnancy, causing impairment to the child's developing brain. FASDs range in severity from mild to moderate and manifest themselves in attention deficits, lowered intelligence, poor attainment in school, hyperactivity, behaviour problems, and poor self-regulation. It is not possible to reverse the damage done to the brain, but carefully planned and implemented intervention—particularly focused on strengthening self-management and behaviour control—can help these children develop their abilities as far as possible (Griffin et al., 2023). An appropriate approach will employ the same basic principles as described in Chapter 1 for students with learning problems but could include some strategies listed above for students with TBI.

Childhood obesity

Certain students with disabilities, including those with a disability that restricts their mobility and those with an intellectual disability who spend a great deal of passive time at home, are particularly prone to weight problems (McConkey et al., 2019). While childhood obesity is not classified as a physical disability, its effects can be disabling. A report from the Organisation for Economic Co-operation and Development (OECD) (2019a) has observed that children who are overweight do less well at school, have a higher absence rate, and are more likely to be bullied. Children who are significantly overweight risk a number of health problems as they get older (e.g., asthma, type 2 diabetes, and hypertension). Obese children are more likely than others to have poor social life and low self-esteem.

The growing number of overweight children is an issue of concern in schools (and in society generally) (Gov.UK, 2023a; Olivieri, 2020). The increase in obesity within the general population is mainly associated with a contemporary lifestyle of sedentary occupations, such as sitting at a computer for hours at a time, easy access to fattening foods, and advertising that actively promotes such activities and foods. Children seem now to engage less in 'running about' and playing in vigorous games at recess time in the school yard, so it is essential that schools do all they can to increase children's awareness of the benefits of exercise, a good diet, and a healthy lifestyle. Where possible, a school curriculum or extra-curricular activities should increase the amount of time devoted to physical education and fitness. Children with physical and intellectual disabilities should be included fully in all such activities, as indicated in Chapter 2.

A study by Rouse et al. (2019) found that children's obesity rates increase from kindergarten through to grade 8, and they recommended that children's body mass index (BMI) should be routinely recorded in schools to help identify those at risk. This form of routine assessment has now been adopted in schools in several countries.

Asthma and allergies

Asthma has become a very common condition affecting school-age children, and it can result in frequent periods of absence from school. It is necessary to provide remedial teaching and 'catch up' homework for these children when they return to school. Asthma is due to inflammation of the bronchial airways, resulting in severe breathing problems. Parents must always notify the teacher if their child has asthma, and they must discuss the response that needs to be made if the child has an asthma attack while at school.

Allergies are causing problems for an ever-increasing number of students, and teachers need to be alert to any child who may have an extreme reaction to particular food, pollutants, chemicals, medicines, insect bites, or other agents. The most extreme reaction is referred to as *anaphylactic shock*, which can be life-threatening. Schools need to have a list of all students with allergies, together with emergency telephone contact numbers, and a response plan that is known to all teachers. Schools need to have an adequate supply of the medication epinephrine to use for treating urgent allergic or anaphylactic reactions.

A recent problem in the UK, the US, and Australia is the alarming number of young people who are taking up 'vaping'—the use of 'vapes' or e-cigarettes that were originally designed as substitute cigarettes to help adults stop smoking. These 'vapes' contain nicotine, a substance known to be highly addictive and with adverse impact on lungs, heart, and brain. At the time of writing, these countries are preparing to ban the sale of vapes to individuals under age 18.

Mental health and well-being

It is now recognized that, in addition to having health conditions that affect physical well-being, some students may have problems with their mental health (DfE, 2024). Schools are becoming more aware of the need to identify such students and attempt to help them overcome whatever is troubling them. This is never easy and usually involves gaining the confidence of the student and liaising with the parents. The 2024 publication *Promoting and supporting mental health and wellbeing in schools and colleges* from the Department of Education (UK) has much useful advice for schools.

General points for teachers in inclusive classrooms

It is not surprising that many teachers lack experience in working with physically disabled students. The following list provides some of the basic information they need to know.

• It may be necessary to rearrange the classroom desks and chairs to give easier access and a wider corridor for movement for students in wheelchairs or walking with sticks.

- Some students with physical disabilities will need to use modified equipment and assistive devices, so it is the teacher's responsibility to ensure that the student does use these items.
- Secondary school students with physical disabilities may have great difficulty taking notes. To overcome this, the teacher could establish a peer support network and allow the student to photocopy notes of other students or use a scribe.
- Assignments could be submitted as an audiotape rather than an essay.
- Some students with physical disabilities have a high absence rate due to therapy or treatment appointments during school hours or due to frequent health problems. The teacher will need to provide short-term catch-up work (e.g., textbook reading or a video to watch) for the student to do at home.
- Some students with epilepsy are likely to be on medication that tends to lower their level of responsiveness in class. If seizures appear to increase in severity or frequency, check that the student is actually taking the medication. Report all cases of seizure to parents.
- While applying all commonsense safety procedures, teachers should try not to overprotect students with physical disabilities. Whenever possible, these students should be encouraged to take part in the same activities enjoyed by other students. Teachers of PE and sport need to get practical advice on ways in which physical activities can be adapted to include students with physical disabilities.

The following chapter extends the coverage of disabilities by presenting information on students with impairments of vision or hearing.

Resources

Online

- ADCET (Australian Disability Clearinghouse on Education and Training). (2024). Physical Disability. https://www.adcet.edu.au/inclusive-teaching/specific-disabilities/physical-disability
- AITSL (Australian Institute for Teaching and School Leadership). (2020). Inclusive education: Teaching students with a disability. Melbourne: AITSL https://www.aitsl.edu.au/research/spotlights/inclusive-edu.ation-teaching-students-with-disability
- Neese, B. (2023). 15 assistive technology tools & resources for students with disabilities. https://www.teachthought.com/technology/assistive-technology/
- Picture communication system Talking Mats. https://www.talkingmats.com/talking-mats-in-action/for-health-and-social-care/
- Children with disabilities (2024). https://www.unicef.org/disabilities

Print

Foster, R., & Barber, L. (Eds.). (2021). *Physical education for young people with disabilities*. London: Routledge.

Giannoni, P., & Zerbino, L. (2022), *Cerebral palsy: A practical guide for rehabilitation professionals*. New York: Springer.

McMahan, A., & Maricle, D.E. (2020b). Epilepsy: What school psychologists should know. *Communique*, 49(2), 10–13.

National Academies of Sciences, Engineering, and Medicine (2023). *Advances in the diagnosis and evaluation of disabling physical health conditions*. Washington, DC: The National Academies Press.

Tiedmann, C.W. (2021). *College success for students with physical disabilities*. London: Routledge.

Wicks, B. & Walker, S. (2018). *Educating children and young people with acquired brain injury*. Abingdon, UK: Routledge Taylor & Francis.

Chapter 5

Students with sensory impairments

Students with sensory impairments comprise a varied group within the population of those with special needs, covering a broad range of cognitive ability, aptitude, and behaviour. It is reported that 1 in every 6 children may suffer from a sensory disability that negatively affects their learning ability and personal development (Khalid, 2021). These students often require adaptations to be made to teaching approaches, resource materials, and methods of communication in order to learn effectively. Given that the majority of students with sensory impairments are now placed in inclusive classes and taught by mainstream teachers, it is essential that all teachers have a knowledge of how best to accommodate them within the curriculum, how to use effective teaching strategies and assistive technology, and how to assess their learning (Rosenblum et al., 2018).

Vision impairment

In some countries, the term *vision impairment* is replacing the older term *visual impairment*. When a child is described as vision-impaired, it does not necessarily mean that he or she is blind; it means that the child has a serious defect of vision that cannot be corrected by wearing spectacles. In the population of children with impaired vision, there are those who are totally blind, those who are 'legally' blind, and those with low vision (partial sight). Taken together, these categories represent between 2 per cent and 3 per cent of individuals below the age of 18 (Ruderman, 2016), but the actual prevalence in any particular country or region depends greatly on factors such as quality of health care and availability of early assessment and intervention.

During early childhood, children with significant vision impairment tend to experience delay in cognitive development and language acquisition and later, when they are of school age, frequently experience lower levels of educational achievement (WHO, 2023). Impaired vision occurs quite frequently as an additional condition in many cases of severe and multiple disability. For example, many students with cerebral palsy also have serious problems with vision, as do some individuals with traumatic brain injury. There is also a very small

DOI: 10.4324/9781003598671-6

population of students who are both deaf and blind and who therefore require extremely skilled teaching.

Impaired vision has many causes, including structural defects or damage to the retina, lens, or optic nerve; inability of the retina to transmit images to the brain; or inefficiency in the way the brain processes visual information. Prematurity and very low birth weight are often associated with vision problems in childhood, and *retinopathy of prematurity* (ROP) is reported as one of the most common causes of impaired vision in newborn children. Some vision problems, including those associated with *albinism*, congenital cataracts, and degeneration of the retina, are inherited; others may be due to disease or to medical conditions such as diabetes.

Special educational needs of students with impaired vision

Early years

Blind children and those with very low vision may often be delayed in acquiring basic motor skills such as crawling, walking, and feeding, because vision is important for observing and imitating the actions of others. Young children with impaired vision benefit from physical activities that help them develop body awareness, movement, and coordination. From an early age, these children need to be encouraged, within the realms of safety, to explore and interact with their immediate environment.

Absence of sight can also lead to delays in cognitive development and concept formation. Early sensory stimulation is vital for young blind children, and they should be given different objects to explore through touch in order to build relevant concepts such as shape, texture, weight, and moving parts. These experiences need to be accompanied by constant verbal input from the parent or caregiver—for example, supplying concept words like 'soft', 'hard edges' 'bigger than', 'next to', 'inside', and 'heavier than.' This approach is often referred to as 'touch-listen-learn'. Children with impaired vision are obviously much less able to acquire knowledge and skills through observation, so the environment and events happening within it must be described by others to increase the child's awareness of things he or she cannot see. Auditory skills need to be strengthened through activities that involve careful and focused listening and responding.

Social and emotional development

Impaired vision can affect an individual's confidence to move about and interact with the wider environment, and this in turn can reduce willingness to initiate social contacts. This is partly due to lack of opportunity to mix and interact with other children from an early age—and thus observe and acquire social behaviours. It is also due to the fact that blind children can't see important non-verbal aspects of social interaction and communication such as nodding in agreement, looking surprised, smiling, and respecting personal space when engaging in conversation. Lack of social interaction with peers can negatively affect a blind student's self-esteem and emotional well-being. Teachers can be proactive in helping blind and partially sighted students become more involved in the social groups within the classroom. Fostering prosocial skills should also be an essential component in any special interventions delivered to students with impaired vision (Caron et al., 2023).

For vision-impaired students who are able to learn in the mainstream, inclusion can be extremely beneficial for social development. However, for some students, socialization in the classroom and in the playground can be problematic. Social development is further restricted if members of the peer group lack confidence to interact with a fellow student who is blind or partially sighted. It is sometimes helpful to foster better understanding in the peer group by discussing openly with the class the problems that a person with impaired vision may have in dealing with schoolwork and with the physical environment. Obviously, if such discussion is attempted, it must be done with due sensitivity and should be done only with the student's agreement.

Accessing curriculum and environment

There are several areas in which blind children and those with seriously impaired vision need to be taught additional skills. These areas include mobility, orientation, the use of Braille, and assistive technology. Mastery of mobility and orientation are two of the main goals in helping a blind student move towards increased independence. Studies have indicated that individuals who successfully achieve independent orientation and mobility manifest a higher level of well-being and increased social interaction (Idawati et al., 2020; Malik et al., 2018).

Mobility

Increased mobility adds significantly to the quality of life for persons with impaired vision and can aid social development (Idawati et al., 2020). Blind students and those with very low vision need to be taught mobility skills to enable them to move safely and purposefully in their environment, including such abilities as crossing the road, catching buses or trains, and locating shops. In special schools for blind students, a mobility-training specialist usually carries out the detailed planning and implementation of the programme, but classroom teachers and parents can certainly assist with development of mobility skills, including

- *self-protection techniques*: for example, holding the hand and forearm loosely in front of the face for protection while trailing the other hand along the wall or rail in unfamiliar environments; checking for doorways, steps, stairs, and obstacles; finding one's position in a room by using auditory information (e.g., air-conditioner, pot boiling on a stove, and an open doorway with traffic noise)
- *long-cane skills*: moving about the environment with the aid of a long cane swept lightly across the ground ahead to locate hazards and to check surface textures
- *using electronic travel aids*: for example, 'sonic spectacles' with a built-in device that emits a sound warning to indicate proximity to objects
- *using public transport*: teaching the individual how to use and negotiate buses and trains.

Orientation

Orientation is the term used to explain the awareness a person with impaired vision has of his or her own exact position in relation to a particular environment. They need to know where they are and where things like steps, furniture, and open doors are located in that environment. For the safety and convenience of students with vision impairment, the physical classroom should remain reasonably constant and predictable. If furniture has to be moved or some new static object is introduced into the room (e.g., a fish tank on a stand, a large television), the blind student needs to be informed of that fact and given the opportunity to locate it in relation to other objects. In classrooms, it is necessary to make sure that equipment such as boxes, books, and gym apparatus are not left on the floor and that doors are not left half open with the edge projecting into the room.

Braille

Braille, the tactile method of communication that replaces print, is of tremendous value as a medium for those students who are blind or whose remaining vision does not enable them to perceive enlarged print. A Braille supplement known as Nemeth Braille Code for Mathematics and Science Notation has been developed to provide students and transcribers with a system of tactile notation to represent signs, symbols, and usages employed in technical texts (BANA, 2022). A simplified system similar in principle to Braille is called Moon. It is reported to be easier to learn, particularly for children who have additional disabilities. Moon uses only 26 raised shapes, based on lines and curves, to represent the standard alphabet, plus ten other symbols.

In recent years, there has been debate around whether communication technology such as screen-to-speech and text-to-speech applications for computers has made Braille obsolete. Persons in the blind community have expressed varied opinions, but most believe that Braille is still very important because it provides an independent means of accessing, recording, storing, and revisiting information at any time. It is deemed more effective for deep study than relying on audio recordings.

Braille is a complex code, so its use with students who are below average in intelligence can present difficulties. Obviously, if an individual's cognitive level is such that he or she would experience difficulty learning to read and write with conventional print, Braille is not going to be an easier code to master. However, if a child's intelligence is adequate, the younger he or she begins to develop some Braille skills, the better, as this will prepare the child to benefit from later schooling and university study. There is some evidence that employing an enlarged size of Braille can result in faster learning in the youngest children (Barlow-Brown et al., 2019).

Assistive technology

In the same way that students with physical disabilities can be helped to access the curriculum and participate more effectively in daily life through the use of assistive technology, children who are blind or with low vision can also be greatly assisted (Satsangi et al., 2019). Many devices have been designed to enable partially sighted students to cope with the medium of print. *Low vision aids* are magnification devices or instruments that help the individual with some residual sight to work with maximum visual efficiency. The devices include a variety of handheld devices or desktop magnifiers and closed-circuit television or microfiche readers (both can be used to enlarge an image).

Despite the value of this technology, many students try to avoid using these devices in mainstream class because they feel that it draws unwanted attention to their disability. This emotional sensitivity to assistive technology as a marker of disability can begin in the primary school years but occurs most frequently among vision-impaired students in secondary schools. Teachers in mainstream classes may need to actively encourage a student to overcome this avoidance behaviour, because the assistive device is of very great benefit to them.

Other forms of technology

The use of 'talking books' technology has been found to benefit blind students and has application in most areas of the curriculum (Argyropoulos et al., 2019). Calculators and clocks with audio output, dictionaries with speech output, compressed speech recordings, and thermoform duplicators used to reproduce Braille pages or embossed diagrams and maps are all of great value (Mukamal, 2021). Despite the potential value of using information and communication technology (ICT) and other technology with vision-impaired learners, evidence to date suggests that schools in some countries are not yet employing the medium to its maximum potential (Ramos & de Andrade, 2016).

In subjects such as science, teachers have devised methods for helping blind students understand physical changes that can occur that sighted students can observe by eye—for example, what happens when you switch on an electric current and produce light or filling a flask to a certain level—by supplementing the visual event with an accompanying sound (a buzzer or bell) or tactile effect (Kizilaslan, 2019; Okcu & Sozbilir, 2019).

It is increasingly evident that digital technology in the form of handheld devices, though not specifically designed as assistive in a narrow sense, is being welcomed and used by individuals who are vision-impaired. Students with low vision benefit from the use of electronic tablets that allow them to adjust font size, style, colour, and contrast. It has been observed that students using an iPad app in mathematics lessons are more motivated and tend to answer more problems correctly than during a traditional approach (Beal & Rosenblum, 2018). One important new area of technology with great potential for learners who are blind is 3D printing (Dominquez-Reyes et al., 2023; Karbowski, 2020). This technology can be used for making tactile and 3D instructional materials (e.g., relief maps, models, figures, and embossed diagrams) to accompany lessons in science, history, geography, and the arts. The *Tactile Images Reader Mobile App* is also showing promise. For more information on this, see the "Online" list in the "Resources" section at the end of the chapter.

Adults with impaired vision

Many older students with impaired vision but adequate intelligence now move from school to undertake higher education courses at university. These students report that the greatest obstacles they encounter are navigating the campus buildings, finding technology to access information, lack of staff awareness of their needs, and problems with social interactions within the peer group (Shafiullah & Akay, 2023). These problems could be reduced if university staff knew more about impaired vision and how to make necessary accommodations. There also needs to be an efficient support service available on campus to provide such assistance as counselling, loan of mobile apps for voice reading of text, and volunteer helpers to assist with orientation or note-taking (Yildirim & Roveshenov, 2022).

Teaching students with impaired vision

Teachers in the mainstream with no experience of vision impairment in children may wrongly tend to hold fairly low expectations of what these children can accomplish. Having a problem with vision should not exclude any students from access to normal classroom experiences, although significant modifications to materials and methods often need to be made. The following general advice may help teachers in inclusive classes to provide vision-impaired students with the best opportunities to learn.

- Always remember to apply the principle of 'touch-listen-learn'. Use very clear verbal descriptions and explanations because words must compensate for what the student cannot see.
- Read written instructions aloud to students with impaired vision (a) to reduce the amount of time required to begin a task and (b) to ensure that the work is understood.
- Almost all students with impaired vision in mainstream classes will have *low vision* (partial sight) rather than total or legal blindness, and it is essential to encourage them to use their residual vision.
- Seat the student in the most advantageous position to be able to see the whiteboard, computer, or large screen.
- Ensure that your material written on the whiteboard, PowerPoint, or computer screen is neat and clear, using larger script than usual. Always keep the whiteboard surface clean to ensure clarity of text.
- Enlarge the font used in all notes, on-screen material, and handouts to one of the following point sizes: **24 36**
- Use a photocopier when necessary to make enlarged versions of notes, diagrams, and other handouts.
- Avoid overloading worksheets with too much information.
- Allow partially sighted students to use a thicker black-tip pen that will produce clear, bold writing.
- When necessary, prepare exercise paper with darker ruled lines.
- Allow much more time for students with impaired vision to complete their work.
- Use concrete materials for early number work (counters, abacus, and models) to facilitate manipulation and touch.
- Train other students and the classroom aide to support the student with impaired vision when necessary—for example, by taking notes during the lesson, repeating the teacher's explanations, and clarifying points.
- Call on blind students frequently by name during lessons to engage them fully in the group-learning processes. Verbally acknowledge and value their contributions.
- Call upon other students clearly by name so that the blind student knows who is responding.
- Make sure that any specialized equipment is always at hand and in good order. If the student with impaired vision uses magnification or illumination aids or other devices, make sure that you know when and how the equipment needs to be used and that the student does not avoid using it.

- Some forms of vision impairment respond well to brighter illumination, but in some other conditions, bright light is undesirable. Obtain advice on illumination from specialist support service personnel who are aware of the student's vision characteristics.
- If the student has extremely limited vision, make sure that any change to the physical arrangement of the room is explained and experienced by the student to avoid accidents. The student needs to develop fresh orientation each time an environment is changed.
- Try to help the student establish a network of friends within the class because social interaction is often not easily achieved without assistance.

Transition to work or further study

Helping vision-impaired students prepare for post-secondary school transition to work or further study requires that careers teachers and counsellors familiarize themselves with possible barriers that may exist. The following strategies are regarded as important when preparing vision-impaired students for transition.

- Discuss with the student his or her strengths, interests, and aspirations and provide appropriate career counselling and informed advice.
- Encourage and facilitate a student's increasing independence, self-confidence, resilience, and assertiveness.
- Assist the student directly by arranging suitable job placements and trial internships.
- Give adequate time to teaching 'interview skills', so that they can present themselves well during interviews for employment or university.
- For students contemplating tertiary study, help them explore the support services that will be available for them in that setting.
- Ensure that the student leaves school or college with an up-to-date knowledge of all forms of assistive technology that may continue to help him or her function.

Hearing impairment

Hearing impairment is a general term used to describe all degrees and types of hearing loss and deafness. Early identification of hearing impairment is essential in order to provide appropriate intervention for the child and to alert parents to the actions they need to take (WHO, 2024). Many students with impaired hearing have no other disability, but hearing impairment can often be present as a secondary problem in children with intellectual disability, cerebral palsy, or language disorders (Peterson et al., 2023). Having impaired hearing does not mean that an individual cannot detect any sounds—he or she may simply hear some frequencies of sound much more clearly than others.

Individuals are usually referred to as *deaf* or even *profoundly deaf* if they are unable to detect speech sounds and if their own oral language development is disordered. In some countries, those who can hear some sounds and can make reasonable use of their residual hearing are often termed *partially hearing*. In the US, the most widely used term for this is *hard of hearing*.

Hearing impairment is often accompanied by speech difficulties. Many factors—time of onset, severity, type of hearing loss, and exposure to speech models—all interact to produce large variations in deaf children's spoken language. The speech of many children with impaired hearing often has an unusual quality and can be difficult to understand. Any improvement in speech and language will allow each child to make better use of his or her intellectual potential, understand much more of the curriculum, and develop socially and emotionally.

In some situations, speech and auditory training sessions are advocated for hearing-impaired students. Speech therapists may use forms of phonological and articulation coaching that involves modelling, imitation, reinforcement, and shaping. In recent years, however, speech therapists and teachers have placed much more importance on trying to stimulate language development through the use of naturally occurring activities in the classroom (*milieu approach*). Such teaching is thought to result in the best transfer and generalization of vocabulary and language patterns to the child's everyday life. Clinical one-to-one training rarely transfers as effectively to everyday natural settings.

Many hearing-impaired children are now included in inclusive classes where accommodation and adjustments to teaching need to be made. It is argued that in these classrooms they have an opportunity to mix with other students who provide good models of natural spoken language. At the same time, students with normal hearing can develop improved understanding of and empathy for individuals who have difficulty hearing.

Types and degrees of hearing loss

Most hearing loss can be classified as either *conductive* or *sensori-neural*. The key features of each type of are summarized below.

Conductive hearing loss

Conductive hearing loss occurs when sounds do not reach the middle ear or inner ear (cochlear) because of some physical malformation, blockage, or damage. Common causes are excessive build-up of wax in the ear, abnormality of the ear canal, a ruptured eardrum, dislocation or damage to the tiny bones of the middle ear, or infection in the middle ear (*otitis media*). Hearing loss due to middle-ear infection is usually temporary and will improve when the infection is treated. If infections are allowed to continue untreated, damage may be done to the middle ear, resulting in permanent hearing loss. The use of a hearing aid may significantly help an individual with conductive hearing loss.

Sensori-neural loss

Sensori-neural hearing loss is related to the inner ear and the auditory nerve. The most serious hearing losses are often of this type. Many sounds go unheard, and even those that are heard may be distorted. The problem of distortion means that the wearing a hearing aid may not always help, because amplifying a distorted sound does not make it any clearer. Some individuals with sensori-neural loss are particularly sensitive to loud noises, perceiving them to be 'painfully' loud.

Level of hearing loss

Hearing is measured in units called decibels (dB). Zero dB is the point from which people with normal hearing can begin to detect the faintest sounds. Normal conversation is usually carried out at an overall sound level of between 40 and 50 dB. Loss of hearing is expressed in terms of the amplification required before the individual can hear each sound. The greater the degree of impairment, the less likely it is that the child will develop normal speech and language, and the more likely it is that they will need special education services. Individuals with a hearing loss above 95 dB are usually categorized as 'deaf' or 'profoundly deaf', and losses between 15 and 40 dB are classified as slight to mild. The difficulties experienced by children with slight to moderate hearing loss often remain undetected for several years, placing the child at risk of failure in school. This is particularly the case if the hearing problem is intermittent and related, for example, to head colds or middle-ear infections.

Impact of moderate to severe hearing loss

Social and emotional development

Children who have a hearing impairment are at risk of lagging behind their peers in age-appropriate social and emotional development. It is suggested that the social and emotional well-being of some deaf students can be negatively affected in inclusive classroom situations if their peers are not openly accepting of them (Partington et al., 2024). Their communication difficulty makes it awkward for them to mix effectively with their peers and be understood. Their lack of easy comprehension in a verbal environment can lead to frustration and result in inappropriate behaviour. It is also acknowledged that their problems with social-emotional development can be linked with poor academic performance. Much learning in school and in the world outside depends on having a system with which to communicate with and comprehend others; helping children improve their understanding and use of language is therefore a priority in the early years.

Helping a deaf child acquire intelligible speech can be a long and difficult process, so early intervention with active parental involvement is essential. Even before a child reaches primary school age, preschool teachers need to work closely in collaboration with outside experts such as speech therapists in order to implement the most effective support for language development (Dorn, 2019). During the school years, effective inclusion of students with impaired hearing relies heavily on the continuing availability of expert advice from visiting teachers and regional hearing-support services.

Basic academic skills

It is frequently reported that the academic attainment level of students with impaired hearing in areas such as reading, spelling, and number skills lags well behind that of their hearing peers. It is typical of these students that as they progress through the primary school years, they fall three to four years behind in reading ability. This lag has a detrimental impact on their performance in all subjects across the curriculum.

With hearing-impaired students in early primary school, careful attention must be given to the explicit teaching of reading and spelling skills. Whereas the beginning stages of reading instruction can focus on building a basic sight vocabulary by visual methods (recognizing words by sight), later teaching for students (other than those who are profoundly deaf) must embody explicit instruction in decoding skills. This advice also applies to teaching reading and spelling to students with cochlear implants (Werfel & Hendricks, 2023). Perhaps counterintuitively, phonics-based instruction is viable for these students if it is supplemented by visual materials and, in some cases, by cued speech. Without decoding skill, students' ability to read and spell unfamiliar words will remain seriously deficient. It is also essential when providing reading instruction for hearing-impaired students that due attention be given to developing vocabulary and effective comprehension strategies.

Instruction in spelling needs to be direct and systematic rather than incidental. For deaf students, it is likely that more than the usual amount of attention will need to be given to developing visual memory, to enable them to store word images and to check words 'by eye' as well as by ear. The 'look-say-cover-write-check' strategy is particularly helpful and needs to be taught thoroughly (see Chapter 12).

The written expression of deaf children is also often problematic, and syntax and vocabulary are major weaknesses (Pistav Akmese et al., 2023). Difficulties include inaccurate sentence structure, incorrect verb tenses, difficulties representing plurals correctly, and inconsistencies in using correct pronouns. The written work of older deaf students has many of the characteristics of the immature writing of younger children.

Modes of communication

Oral–aural approach (oralism)

The belief underpinning an oral–aural approach is that in a hearing world you need to be able to communicate through oral–verbal methods in order to be accepted socially and to succeed. Students relying on an oral–aural approach often require and benefit from speech training from a speech therapist. The approach stresses the use of residual hearing, supplemented by lip reading. Teachers should note, however, that the ability of many hearing-impaired students to lip read is often greatly overestimated—it is actually very difficult.

While listening and speaking remain the preferred methods of communication for students with mild and moderate degrees of impairment, for those who are severely deaf, alternative manual methods may be needed. Manual methods include natural gesture, sign language, cued speech, and fingerspelling.

Sign language

There are different forms of sign language in different countries, all having obvious characteristics in common but also having some unique features (e.g., British Sign Language, Signed English, Auslan, and American Sign Language). Deaf children from deaf families will almost certainly have been exposed to, and become fairly competent in, manual communication even before entering formal education. Experts suggest that sign language should be respected as a valid language system in its own right, having its own vocabulary and syntax that contribute to cognitive development. There is evidence suggesting that acquisition of sign language does not impede development of spoken vocabulary, and it should be valued and encouraged as an effective mode of communication (Pontecorvo et al., 2023).

Fingerspelling

Fingerspelling is usually used as a supplement to sign language, to spell out terms for which there is no clear hand sign. Fingerspelling is also incorporated into certain other signals to help convey exact meaning. Walsh-Aziz et al. (2024) have suggested that teachers of hearing-impaired children in early-elementary classes could usefully introduce fingerspelling to supplement and reinforce learning of basic word recognition.

Cued speech

A manual system known as *cued speech* was developed to help resolve the many visual ambiguities inherent in 'reading the lips.' Cued speech uses eight hand signs in four positions of the hand alongside the mouth of the speaker to differentiate between similar sounds or words. More information and illustrations can be located at the cued speech website (see "Online" list in the "Resources" section).

Total communication approach

The relative popularity of signing versus oralism ebbs and flows from decade to decade. In response, *total communication* (TC) or *simultaneous communication* (SC) deliberately combines gesture, signing, fingerspelling, and oral–aural methods to help deaf students comprehend and express ideas and opinions (Waters, 2020). A combination of oral and manual training at an early age appears to foster optimum communicative ability.

Assistive technology

Hearing aids

Hearing aids are designed to amplify sound and are of various types, including the typical 'behind the ear' or 'in the ear' aids and radio frequency (FM) aids. A hearing aid is prescribed by an audiologist to suit the individual's sound-loss profile. The aid is adjusted as far as possible to give amplification of the specific frequency of sounds needed by the student. No hearing aid fully compensates for hearing loss, even when carefully tailored to the user's characteristics. The great limitation of the conventional hearing aid is that it amplifies all sound, including background noise in the environment.

The advantage of the radio frequency (FM) aid is that it allows the teacher's voice to be received with minimum interference from environmental noise. The teacher wears a small microphone and the student's hearing aid receives the sounds in the same way that a radio receives a broadcast transmission. The student can be anywhere in the classroom and does not need to be near to or facing the teacher, as with the conventional aid. Childress (2015) describes the 'induction loop system'—a perimeter of wire that surrounds a designated area like a classroom and sends auditory information to a T-coil setting on either a hearing aid or a cochlear implant. The use of wireless remote microphones (WRMs) as secondary assistive devices for students with hearing aids or cochlear implants is reported to have very positive effects on students' sustained engagement in lessons (Gabova et al., 2024).

Many hearing-impaired students do not like to be seen wearing a hearing aid, especially in mainstream secondary schools, and students with intellectual disability often neglect to wear the aid (Nipe et al., 2018). Some students take every opportunity to hide an aid away and not use it. Some report that they feel more socially at ease, and thus able to fit in more easily with their peers, if they do not wear the aid. Teachers thus have a responsibility to make sure a hearing aid is used during lessons and is maintained in good order.

Cochlear implants

A cochlear implant is a device used to produce the sensation of sound by electrically stimulating the auditory nerve. The device has four parts: processor, transmitting coil, receiver, and electrode array. The implant is able to bypass the functions of the hair cells in the inner ear that are often damaged or defective in cases of sensori-neural loss.

Many developed countries now carry out the surgery required to implant this form of assistive device at a very young age. Cochlear implants are normally recommended only for children who are profoundly deaf and cannot benefit at all from a hearing aid. While the child can begin to perceive the electrical stimulation soon after surgery, it normally takes at least a year for gains in the child's language skills to become evident. The child's effective adaptation to the cochlear implant needs much support and encouragement from parents. Specific intervention by a speech and language therapist is also required in order to improve the clarity of spoken language (Mieres et al., 2024).

Many individuals with implants still rely on supplementary sign language or gesture to understand fully what is said, but the consensus is that having an implant is beneficial. For example, a study by Michael et al. (2019) indicated that parents of children with a cochlear implant report that their children exhibit lower levels of hyperactivity and inattention and higher levels of pro-social behaviour compared with children with a traditional hearing aid.

Other forms of technology

There is increasing evidence that integrating various forms of technology and software such as text-to-speech (TTS) and speech-to-text (STT) technology into the teaching of students with impaired hearing can bring positive results (Connelly & Doyle, 2023). Technology has also been used effectively within alternative and augmentative communication methods (Mood et al., 2022).

For information on various devices and apps that have relevance for assisting those with impaired hearing, see the "Online" list in the "Resources" section.

Teaching students with impaired hearing

The following strategies for teaching hearing-impaired students may also be helpful for teaching students with other learning difficulties in the classroom.

- The student with impaired hearing should be seated where he or she can see you easily, can see the whiteboard, and can observe the other students.
- Do not seat the student with impaired hearing near sources of noise (e.g., open window, air-conditioner, overhead fan, or generator).
- Involve the hearing-impaired student in the lesson as much as possible.
- Make sure a deaf student can see the other students who are speaking or answering questions when group discussion is taking place.
- Repeat the answer that another student has given in class if you think the hearing-impaired student may not have heard it.
- Check frequently that the student is on task and has understood what he or she is required to do.
- Make greater use of visual methods of presenting information whenever possible (whiteboard, overhead projector, computer screen).
- Do not give instructions while there is noise in the classroom.
- Write any important instructions as short statements on the whiteboard whenever possible.
- Always attract students' full attention when you are about to ask a question or give out information.
- Repeat instructions clearly while facing the class.
- Use simple language and clear enunciation when explaining new concepts.
- Do not talk while facing the whiteboard—a deaf student needs to see your mouth and facial expression.
- Do not walk to the back of the room while talking and giving out important information.
- Teach all new vocabulary by writing new words on the whiteboard, ensuring that students with hearing impairment see the word and say the word.
- Revise new vocabulary regularly and revise new language patterns (e.g., 'Twice the size of...', 'Mix the ingredients...', 'Invert and multiply...').
- When possible, provide senior students with printed session notes to ensure that key content from the lesson is available for later study.
- Encourage other students to assist the hearing-impaired student complete any work that is set—*but* without doing the work for the student.
- Make sure that you check the student's hearing aid on a daily basis.
- Modify assessment and testing procedures when necessary (e.g., more time; assistance with reading a question).
- Seek advice regularly from the regional advisory service and the visiting support teacher and integrate such advice into your programme.

Sensory processing disorder

There is continuing debate over whether sensory processing disorder (SPD) really exists separate from the many learning problems that accompany other conditions such as autism spectrum disorder or intellectual disability (Loh et al., 2023). SPD is not recognized as a separate condition in the current edition of the *Diagnostic and Statistical Manual of Mental Disorders* (DSM-5).

However, it is claimed by some educators in the field of learning difficulties that a few individuals do have a condition that causes the brain to experience difficulties processing sounds, visual stimuli, and even touch, taste, and smell in the normal way. For example, they may display oversensitivity in a room where there are bright colours or loud sounds, or they may have a very strong negative reaction to a certain sound, taste, or scent. The problem may affect only one sense or several senses. When learning to read and spell, they may have extreme difficulty matching sounds in spoken words with the appropriate letters in print and remembering certain visual sequences and patterns, or they have problems learning to associate the spoken name for a given numeral.

Regardless of whether SPD exists or not, commonsense treatment for any students who have oversensitivity to certain stimuli include avoiding the use of teaching materials or situations that create the problem. In some cases, it is worth attempting to desensitize the individual over time by gradually increasing exposure. The controversial approach known as sensory integration therapy has been suggested for use, but it lacks hard evidence of effectiveness and is regarded by some as a fake therapy (Smith et al., 2015).

For more information on SPD, see the "Online" list in the "Resources" section.

The following chapter provides an overview of the characteristics and needs of gifted and talented students. A few of these students may also have a physical disability, a sensory impairment, or a specific learning disability.

Resources

Online

- Cued Speech https://www.cuedspeech.co.uk/what-is-cued-speech/
- Other forms of technology (The *Tactile Images Reader Mobile App)* https://tactileimages.org/en/library/
- Other forms of technology (devices and apps for those with impaired hearing) https://www.osspeac.org/wp-content/uploads/2017/08/childress.connectanddiscover.100817.pdf
- Sensory processing disorder (SPD) https://eput.nhs.uk/media/b2sdvcsb/sensory-processing-disorder-information-leaflet-for-parents.pdf
- *Sensory impairment—What it is, how it affects child development and how tohelp.*https://www.teachearlyyears.com/a-unique-child/view/sen-understanding-sensory-impairment

- *Strategies for teaching students with impaired vision*: https://www.pathstoliteracy.org/strategies-teaching-students-who-are-blind-or-visually-impaired/
- American Foundation for the Blind. *Blindness and low vision.* https://www.afb.org/blindness-and-low-vision
- *A resource guide to assistive technology for students with visual impairment.* https://qiat.org/docs/resourcebank/TEBO_VI_Resource_Guide.pdf
- Examples of technology for blind persons. https://www.bbvaopenmind.com/en/technology/innovation/technology-for-blind-people-beyond-braille/
- WHO (2024). *Deafness and hearing loss.* https://www.who.int/news-room/fact-sheets/detail/deafness-and-hearing-loss
- Information on deaf and hearing-impaired students: https://www.myschoolpsychology.com/wp-content/uploads/2014/02/nichcy.org-Deafness_and_Hearing_Loss.pdf
- *Physical and sensory impairment.* https://www.eln.co.uk/blog/physical-sensory-impairment

Print

Crossland, M. (2024). *Vision impairment: Science, art and lived experience.* London: UCL Press.

Dale, N., Salt, A, Sargent, J., & Greenaway, R. (Eds). (2021). *Children with vision impairment: Assessment, development and management.* London: Mac Keith Press.

Dispenza, F., & Martines, F. (Eds.). (2019). *Sensori-neural hearing loss.* Hauppauge, NY: Nova Science.

Knoors, H., & Marschark, M. (2014). *Teaching deaf learners: Psychological and developmental foundations.* New York: Oxford University Press.

Ravenscroft, J. (Ed.). (2020). *The Routledge handbook of visual impairment.* London: Routledge.

Rotfleisch, S., & Martindale, M. (2021). Listening and *spoken language therapy for children with hearing loss: A practical auditory-based guide.* San Diego, CA: Plural Publishing.

Chapter 6

Gifted and talented students

It is now accepted that gifted and talented students do require additional consideration and support, in terms of both academic programming and their social and emotional needs (Maker et al., 2024; Montacute, 2018). In an ideal world, there would be a comprehensive approach to identifying gifted students in schools, but most countries have a laissez-faire approach. Unfortunately, as a result of this approach, many students with good potential but only average classroom performance tend to fall through the net.

Many intellectually gifted students—but by no means all—are high achievers in most academic subjects across the school curriculum. Many may display exceptional ability and creativity in a specific area such as art and design, the sciences, technology, music, drama, dance, sports, gymnastics, and interpersonal skills or leadership. These talented students also require special attention to enable them to develop their talent to the full. It is also suggested that the notion of 'giftedness' is applicable in contexts other than learning in school and university. For example, Sternberg and Rodriguez-Fernández (2024) refer to 'humanitarian giftedness' in situations when individuals deliberately use their gifts and talents in ways that benefit society.

The nature of giftedness, talent, and creativity

Over the years, experts have debated the nature of giftedness and whether it stems entirely from innate potential or arises as a result of hard work. The consensus is that giftedness, talents, and creativity do have a genetic component that represents a potential for advanced development, but such development occurs only if many factors combine in positive ways. These factors include helpful attributes in the individual such as motivation, perseverance, and resilience and a context that provides good opportunities and resources for learning. The evidence suggests that an individual's giftedness and specific talents will develop only as a result of opportunity, sustained personal effort, and long-term commitment.

DOI: 10.4324/9781003598671-7

Some authorities suggest that giftedness arises from a positive interaction among three human traits: above-average ability, a high degree of motivation and effort, and creativity. Some suggest that creativity is always a component in all forms of giftedness and talent, and others have suggested that creativity, while clearly essential in some fields, is not a necessary ingredient in *all* forms of outstanding ability or talent. Certain intellectually and academically gifted students are not necessarily highly creative in the artistic or performance sense, although they may be extremely creative in solving problems and in generating new ideas. What is generally agreed now is that creativity, when present, is a multifaceted and valued attribute that merits specific support and encouragement within the school curriculum.

Prevalence

It is generally agreed that when measured intelligence is used as the criterion for giftedness, between 3 per cent to 5 per cent of the school population can be regarded as intellectually gifted. In Britain, these students are referred to now as '*highly able students*' or students with '*high learning potential*' (Kendall, 2023; Shepherd, 2021). Within this population, there are said to be varying degrees of giftedness, ranging from 'moderate' to 'profound'. Less than one child in every 100,000 would be classed as 'profoundly gifted'. Taken together, intellectually gifted and other talented students comprise some 10 to 15 per cent of the school population.

Separation or inclusion?

One of the enduring debates in education concerns the appropriate placement for gifted and talented students within the school system (Marsili et al., 2023). The current policy of inclusive education has called into question their placement into specialist schools or full-time classes for the gifted. These options are often frowned upon now because they separate gifted students from their mixed-ability age group. Instead, it is argued that gifted students should remain in the mainstream and receive a suitably differentiated programme to match their learning rate, abilities, and talents (Kaplan, 2024; OECD, 2022). A gifted student's programme would be one of several alternative programmes operating in a mixed-ability classroom under the system known as 'tiered instruction'. It is envisioned that an ideal programme for a gifted student would involve a mix of teacher-directed instruction accompanied by learning activities with personalized goals that embody opportunities for independent study, extension, and enrichment (Altintas & Özdemir, 2015; Kaplan, 2024; VanTassel-Baska, 2015). Digital technology and online resources have opened up new options for teachers to direct gifted students into new areas of independent learning

(McKoy & Merry, 2023). The potential benefits claimed for a differentiated approach are that students of high ability remain as members of a mixed-ability class and are able to interact socially and intellectually with other students of differing abilities and interests. The high-achieving students also act indirectly as role models for other students in the class in terms of study habits, work output, and motivation.

The potential disadvantage of attempting differentiation (and it is a serious disadvantage) is that many teachers do not feel confident to identify students' individual needs and to provide for them (Porta & Todd, 2024). They find it almost impossible to sustain different levels of activities operating at the same time within the classroom (Abu et al., 2017; Papanthymou & Darra, 2022). As a result, studies have found that very little differentiation of instruction actually occurs for gifted students in many typical classrooms (e.g., McGrath, 2019; VanTassel-Baska, 2019). When these students finish assignments quickly, they tend to be given 'more of the same' or 'busywork' rather than extension and enrichment.

It must be recognized that differentiation is indeed a very complex task (see Chapter 15), and most teachers (and teacher educators in universities) have not been trained to work efficiently in this way. The larger the class size, the more difficult that multi-tasking and multi-tier programming become. These points are made here not to suggest that adopting a differentiated approach is not worthy but rather to indicate that almost all teachers require far more training and supervised practice in differentiated teaching strategies than they currently receive (Kokkinos, 2020). Rarely are trainee teachers evaluated on their ability to *demonstrate* successfully the use of differentiated teaching during their teaching practice in schools. One specific initiative that should be encouraged is the production of training videos of real classrooms where differentiation is being employed effectively. Viewing such examples of good practice will achieve much more than listening to professional training lectures about how to differentiate.

In contrast to those who advocate for full inclusion with differentiation in the mainstream as the ideal model for students of high ability, educators and researchers working specifically in gifted education believe that there must be a *continuum of placement* and delivery options, ranging from staying in a regular class to being in a special group (Gilson & Lee, 2023; Vogl & Preckel, 2014). It is argued, for example, that gifted students can be in an inclusive class for much of the time and not require differentiation but that at other times they benefit greatly from working in a special group or with a mentor. When special groups operate, it is argued that teachers can be more effective in designing a challenging curriculum and enabling a faster pace of learning. Grouping by ability at certain times also allows gifted and talented students to work closely and productively with others of similar or higher ability (Loveless, 2024). It has been found in at least one study that students in gifted classes exhibit more interest in school and report better student–teacher relationships than similar students retained in regular classes (Vogl & Preckel, 2014).

Identifying gifted learners

There is general agreement among experts in gifted education that identification should combine relevant information from parents and teachers, evaluation of work samples, and curriculum test results, together with formal psychological assessments of intelligence and aptitude. Sternberg (2024) suggests that assessment procedures and intervention design should always take full account of the family environment in which the student lives. In reality, identification of giftedness and talent usually occurs through recognizing high standards in a student's classroom work and test results, appreciating their valuable contribution to class discussions, and their higher-than-average interest in and commitment to learning.

In the US and Australia, there is no national mandate that all states must identify their gifted and talented students and make special provision for them. It is left to individual states to determine their own policy and practices—and many have done so. In the UK, the Department for Education and Employment introduced a gifted and talented education policy in 1999. At that time, the Government requested all schools to prepare a written policy on gifted and talented students, with details of how these students would be identified and what provisions would be made for them. However, it was not made mandatory that a specific support system be established in a school; and two decades later, concern continues to be expressed that many very capable students are still not being identified and fully supported by their schools. A document prepared by Loft et al. (2020) summarized the support for 'more able and talented children' provided at that time in the UK.

In an effort to improve provision in the UK, it was determined that regular school inspections should in future include a focus on how well a school is meeting the needs of highly able students. There is growing evidence that high-ability students from lower socio-income families are less likely than students from higher socio-economic families to be identified for access to enriched academic opportunities (Plucker et al., 2018). A high priority in preparing teachers for working in disadvantaged schools should be an improvement in their expertise in identifying capable students and in implementing a differentiated approach to meet their needs. In the US, the influential National Association for Gifted Children (NAGC) and the Council for Exceptional Children (CEC) have attempted to address this problem by recommending standards for the training of all teachers in gifted education (NAGC-CEC, 2013). Worldwide there have been serious attempts to increase the number of training programmes on gifted education available for teachers (World Council for Gifted and Talented Children, 2021).

Underachievement

Studies have shown that teachers in general are fairly poor at identifying gifted students who are *underachieving* (Collins et al., 2023). Gifted underachievers tend not to be recognized as such because they produce classroom work and test results that are satisfactory but not outstanding. Their high potential remains unrecognized, so nothing is done to vary their programme. Underachievement is often associated with early dropping out from school—which in turns can affect long-term life prospects for the individual. Intervention is needed, and accurate identification should be a priority where any student is achieving at a lower standard than could be expected based on their obvious potential ability (Jackson & Jung, 2022).

There are many reasons why some high-ability students may underachieve in school. Among the most common reasons are the following:

- *Boredom*: The curriculum is not sufficiently challenging to hold the student's interest and attention. The pace at which topics are covered in the mainstream programme may be much too slow for students who are able to learn at a much faster rate. There may also be too much time devoted to revising material they have already mastered. Even in early childhood education settings, there is evidence that the daily programme contains too little of intellectual challenge for young children of high ability. Inattention is a major problem for some gifted students who have attention-deficit/hyperactivity disorder (ADHD) (McCoach et al., 2020).
- *Personal or emotional problems*: The student may be experiencing difficulties at home or within the peer group, and these problems can severely undermine the ability to concentrate and devote effort to study. Some highly gifted individuals are also prone to experience stress, anxiety, and depression (Duplenne et al., 2024). A few students of high ability are obsessed with producing results that are always perfect, and they are constantly fearful of failure. This *perfectionism* can have very negative long-term effects on their school progress mental well-being and life satisfaction (Hüseyin & Nüket, 2023).
- *Peer pressure*: A few students of high ability may underachieve by concealing their talents from classmates in order not to stand out as 'different'. For example, they may be reluctant to hand in work of a high standard, or ask questions and contribute to class discussions, even though they have much to offer. Both boys and girls may deliberately underachieve so as not to be thought 'too smart'. This is especially true during adolescence.
- *Poor study habits*: Some gifted students are not naturally inclined to work hard, set themselves goals, make a commitment, and devote the necessary effort. The fact that a student has high potential does not in any way ensure that he or she is motivated to develop that potential through hard work. In addition, a few gifted students lack effective study strategies, so they do not always tackle assignments efficiently or successfully.

- *Disability*: It must be recognized that some students with physical or sensory disabilities may also be gifted and talented, but their disability often hides their potential. A few students who are very talented and of high intelligence may have a specific learning disability in areas such as reading, spelling, writing, or mathematics, or they may have ADHD (Neumeister, 2024). Dyslexic students, for example, may be intellectually gifted but have chronic problems with writing their assignments and reading comprehension. These students with a specific learning disability are often referred to as 'twice exceptional', and some may experience problems securing peer group acceptance because of their learning difficulties or behaviour. The danger is that gifted students with these basic skill difficulties may be thought by the teacher to be low-achievers and may even be placed in a low-ability group.
- *English as a second language*: Gifted students whose first language is not English can have difficulty performing to the best of their ability in schools where English is the medium of instruction. The problem relates not only to difficulties with understanding spoken and written language but also to a reluctance (sometimes related also to cultural differences) to participate actively and ask and answer teachers' questions in class or to request additional help and explanations. Many states in the US have endeavoured to cater for academically gifted English-as-a-second-language learners within their programmes for gifted and talented students (Office of English Language Acquisition, 2021).
- *Socio-economic disadvantage*: Some potentially gifted students may underachieve for a variety of reasons related to social disadvantage. For example, poverty leading to lack of resources in the home, dysfunctional family, low expectations, and lack of support for learning are all factors associated with underachievement in school (Wai & Worrell, 2021). There is also some evidence that minority students from disadvantaged families are under-represented in special programmes for gifted and talented (Pierce, 2022).

Addressing underachievement must always be an important aim within gifted education. It has been found that interventions for underachievement can be effective in increasing motivation for learning, improving self-regulation, and finding school more meaningful (Steenbergen-Hu et al., 2020). One approach that appears to be useful in this respect is the *Achievement Orientation Model* (Long & Erwin, 2020; Ritchotte et al., 2014; Siegle et al., 2017). The principle underpinning this model is that in order to do well and achieve their potential, learners need to recognize the value of an activity, put in the required effort, and build confidence in their own ability to achieve (self-efficacy). For an explanation of the model, see the "Online" list in the "Resources" section at the end of the chapter.

Meeting the needs of gifted and talented students

Effective education for gifted learners relies heavily on selecting a viable organizational model for delivery. As indicated already, the options have ranged from full-time inclusion in the mainstream and placement full-time or part-time in a special class through to enrolment in a separate school for students who have been identified as gifted. Other options include occasional withdrawal to participate in special programmes (often provided by a local university), promotion to a higher age group, modifying the curriculum so that a gifted student moves through the content more rapidly, independent study programmes, and the use of mentors. Some schools also enrol students in special after-hours or summer programmes for gifted and talented learners. Designing appropriate teaching for students of high ability, regardless of where are taught, involves three main considerations: acceleration, extension, and enrichment.

Acceleration

Acceleration refers to any method adopted to cater for a gifted student's faster pace of learning and to avoid students having to repeat material they already know. Studies have shown unequivocally that acceleration can contribute greatly to gifted students' motivation and academic achievement and in most cases has no negative effect on their social adjustment and emotional well-being (Bernstein et al., 2021; Crawford, 2018; Steenbergen-Hu et al., 2016). Acceleration can be a feature within a gifted student's differentiated programme in the regular classroom, or it can be achieved through some of the practices described below.

- *Grade skipping*: Gifted students can work with an older group or class for certain lessons, or a student may be permanently promoted to a higher age group. Some studies have found that grade skipping can be beneficial to the students, intellectually and socially. However, a review of previous studies led Miravete (2023) to conclude that, to date, evidence is inconclusive and more studies are required to assess whether grade skipping really does have a positive impact on academic achievement and is not detrimental to a student's psychosocial well-being. It should be noted that moving to a higher grade will not help a gifted student at all if the programme into which the student is promoted is of poor quality. Promotion to higher grades each year is also a difficult system to sustain over several years of schooling, particularly when a student moves to another school. Early admission to university represents another extreme example of this acceleration model. While useful for some exceptionally advanced students, the model does require a certain degree of maturity and social adaptability in the students, and it does not necessarily suit all.

- *Curriculum compacting*: In this approach to differentiation, the teacher omits certain topics or exercises in a course of study and modifies assignments so that a student of high ability can skip work already known, work on new topics, and achieve learning objectives in a shorter period of time. If the teacher is well informed of the content of online programmes, e-learning represents one way that the curriculum can be adapted for gifted learners (Calvert et al., 2023). For this compacting approach to be effective, it is essential that the teacher adapting the curriculum have deep command of subject matter, so that condensing and restructuring a course can still achieve the desired learning outcomes. It is not an easy option and seems to be seldom used in any methodical way in the typical classroom.
- *Independent learning contracts*: An individualized work plan is designed for the student of high ability, allowing him or her to work fairly independently or with a mentor for specific periods each week. The teacher and student together negotiate and agree upon the details of the contract such as what is to be the product, when it is to be completed, and what resources are need. Such contracts usually involve more challenging learning objectives and the provision of relevant learning resources (texts, computer software, Internet connection, and hyperlinks for e-learning). Independent learning contracts are a valuable option within a differentiated approach in inclusive classrooms.

Extension

Extension activities enable high achievers to go much more deeply into an area of study. This can be achieved in part by compacting the curriculum to save time and then using that time to work on more challenging and open-ended assignments. E-learning in all its forms has opened up many new possibilities for doing this in recent years. The extension approach tends to involve students in more first-hand investigation and problem-solving, with an emphasis on development of critical and creative thinking (Maker & Pease, 2021). Students may need first to receive direct teaching in the use of particular researching and data-processing skills. Extension activities often rely heavily on students' ability to learn independently and self-regulate.

Enrichment

Enrichment can be thought of as an approach that seeks to broaden a field of study to include more applications and additional examples or problems—but not necessarily more difficult concepts. The purpose is to encourage deeper knowledge through original creative or exploratory activities related to the topic or theme. Enrichment is often achieved through computer-assisted learning, project work, individual or cooperative study contracts, and the use of classroom learning centres. Enrichment is also often the main function of the extra-curricular activities organized by many schools. Often, these activities serve the purpose of encouraging growth and talent development in areas other than academic subjects. Evidence to date suggests that gifted students have very positive views on teachers' use of enrichment strategies (Desmet et al., 2023).

Mentoring systems

Both extension and enrichment goals can also be facilitated through *mentoring systems*. Mentoring can be provided for gifted students with an interest and aptitude in a particular field. Use is made of adults or older students with expertise in that particular area as tutors, guides, or critical friends. The area of study may be academic or may be related to fine arts, performing arts, recreation, sports, or technology. Often these mentoring sessions take place as extra-curricular activities. In recent years, *online mentoring* of individuals or small groups has proven to be effective as a means of providing coaching for gifted and talented learners. This was particularly the case during the Covid-19 pandemic of 2019–2022 (Kadioglu Ates & Gurdag, 2021).

General principles of teaching

No matter whether gifted and talented students are taught within the mainstream or in ability groups, their curriculum needs to be suitably comprehensive and challenging. The activities provided must engage students in knowledge acquisition, higher-level thinking, problem-solving, investigation, and creation of new ideas. It is also important to promote students' independence in learning by encouraging their curiosity, persistence, and willingness to share ideas.

Effective teaching and learning for students of high ability must include at least the following components:

- individualized goal setting
- opportunity to progress rapidly
- access to challenging topics, problems, and materials (e.g., online resources)
- direct teaching and application of age-appropriate study skills and strategies
- activities that require deep study, reasoning, critical thinking, and creativity
- opportunities to pursue personal interests and develop talents.

Specific implementation models

Many different programmes and curricula have been devised to serve the needs of gifted and talented students. It can be seen that although the programmes have different names, they all tend to have some similar features. The main aim in all cases is to provide a more challenging and motivating approach to meets the learning needs and interests of students of high ability. Some of these models are most easily implemented in situations where gifted and talented students are gathered together as a separate group rather than in mixed-ability classes.

Enrichment Triad Model and Schoolwide Enrichment

The *Enrichment Triad Model* (ETM) and the *Schoolwide Enrichment Model* (SEM) (Reis & Peters, 2021; Renzulli & Reis, 2014) are examples of well-designed approaches to foster and support gifted students and other learners through differentiation in the mainstream. Various adapted versions of ETM and SEM have emerged in different countries and for application with different age groups.

The ETM presents students with a variety of activities that enable them to explore a given topic from different perspectives and at different levels of complexity. All students first engage in a range of introductory activities (Type I enrichment) to become generally conversant with the topic and to identify interesting issues worth investigation. All students are then taught necessary investigative and data-processing skills, such as online searches, interviewing, note-taking, summarizing, tabulation, and producing graphics, required to explore and report on these issues in greater depth and breadth (Type II enrichment). Finally, students can focus on specific issues or personal interests related to the central theme and study these in much greater depth through independent or collaborative study (Type III enrichment). Type III enrichment in particular takes students of high ability beyond the regular curriculum objectives to explore new areas of interest in greater depth.

ETM is part of the *Renzulli Learning System* that assists teachers and students to meet the *Common Core State Standards* in the US. For example, the resources used in the system place a strong emphasis on problem-solving, creativity, and critical thinking. Students develop important skills that enable them to analyze informational texts, research and integrate information from multiple sources (including information and communication technology), and use mathematics and literacy skills to investigate, solve, and describe real-world problems. More information, including research findings, can be found on the *Renzulli Learning System* website (see "Online" list in the "Resources" section).

Parallel Curriculum Model

The Parallel Curriculum Model (PCM) evolved from earlier work on curriculum adaptation by Carol Tomlinson in the US. PCM is based on the premise that every learner is somewhere on a path towards gaining expertise in a particular subject (Tomlinson et al., 2008). The parallel curriculum sets out to develop further the existing abilities of all students and to extend the specific talents of students who perform at advanced levels (Hathcock, 2018; Irving et al., 2016). Four parallel components are provided: (1) a *core curriculum* of key knowledge, concepts, and skills related to the subject; (2) *connections*, helping students relate new content to prior knowledge in this and other subject areas and apply skills across disciplines; (3) *practice*, to help students function effectively in a particular discipline; and (4) *identity*, helping students identify personally with the subject more deeply by connecting it with their own lives, interests, and aspirations. These four curricular components are used by teachers as a framework when they plan units of work around a central theme. Teachers must determine each student's current ability level, and from this information develop activities that will move him or her along a continuum towards greater expertise. For an explanation of the PCM, see the "Online" list in the "Resources" section.

Autonomous Learner Model

The Autonomous Learner Model (ALM) recognizes the need for gifted students to become self-directed learners, able to take responsibility for implementing and reflecting upon their own learning processes. The model focuses on gifted and talented students across the school age range and is flexible enough to be used in the regular classroom, in small group settings (pull-out programmes) or as an individual course. Among the basic principles of the model are emphases on fostering self-understanding, and making full use of a student's personal interests and aptitudes. The approach is entirely compatible with the preference of many gifted students to be independent in their learning—but also able to call upon a mentor when necessary.

ALM has five major dimensions: (1) *Orientation*—understanding one's own abilities, aptitudes, aspirations, interests; and comprehending the scope and purpose of ALM in relation to self-development. (2) *Individual development*—acquiring powerful study and research skills needed for independent life-long learning; use of technology; career path awareness; working collaboratively with others. (3) *Enrichment*—enhanced opportunities to explore topics or problems that are not necessarily components of the core curriculum; participating in cultural activities, community service, excursions and camps. (4) *Seminars*—individual or group presentations of topics that have been studied. Small discussions, sharing advanced knowledge. (5) *In-depth study*—individual projects, group research, and mentorships.

A manual prepared by Betts et al. (2021) provides useful activities that teachers can use to implement principles of ALM. These activities are all geared to help advance the emotional, social and cognitive development of students on the road to becoming more autonomous in learning and motivation. Digital technology now has an important role to play in the design of learning activities that facilitate learner autonomy and encourage self-determination (Pratiwi & Waluyo, 2023).

For more information on the ALM, see the "Online" list in the "Resources" section.

The CLEAR Curriculum Model

This model integrates three approaches that have proven to be effective in gifted education, namely differentiation, increasing depth and complexity of the curriculum, and *Schoolwide Enrichment*. The acronym CLEAR is derived from continuous assessment, learning goals, experiences, authentic products, and rich curriculum (Azano et al., 2017). The curriculum content and activities are designed so that all students are fully engaged and appropriately challenged to facilitate higher achievement. Evaluation of the effectiveness of CLEAR Curriculum indicates that it provides a viable option to enhance students' learning and that teachers are able to implement it with moderate to high fidelity.

For a comprehensive overview of this model (with specific examples), see the "Online" list in the "Resources" section.

The following three chapters address important personal, social, emotional, and behavioural attributes of students with learning difficulties or disabilities. Topics explored include how teachers manage behaviour in the classroom, how students manage their own learning, and factors that influence students' social and emotional development.

Resources

Online

- Underachievement: *Socio-economic disadvantage.* https://thegraysonschool. org/wp-content/uploads/The-Achievement-Orientation-Model.pdf
- Renzulli Learning System (Enrichment Triad Model and Schoolwide Enrichment). https://renzullilearning.com/
- Parallel Curriculum Model. https://presentlygifted.weebly.com/parallel-curriculum-model.html
- Autonomous Learner Model (ALM). https://presentlygifted.weebly.com/autonomous-learner-model.html
- *The CLEAR Curriculum Model.* https://eric.ed.gov/?id=ED535658
- *What is giftedness?* https://www.davidsongifted.org/gifted-blog/what-is-giftedness/
- Who are the 'gifted and talented' and what do they need? https://www.npr.org/sections/ed/2015/09/28/443193523/who-are-the-gifted-and-talented-and-what-do-they-need
- In the USA the National Association for Gifted Children provides much useful information. https://www.nagc.org/

- *Support for more able and talented children in schools* (UK). https:// commonslibrary.parliament.uk/research-briefings/cbp-9065/
- A clear description of the *Enrichment Triad Model* can be found at https:// enrichmenttriadmodel.weebly.com/what-is-triad.html

Print

Eames, F.H. (2022). *The gifted learner: How to help, understand and support children and young people.* Shoreham-by-Sea, West Sussex: Pavilion Publishing and Media.

Farah, Y.N., & Johnson, S.K. (2021). *Classroom management for gifted and twice-exceptional students using functional behavior assessment.* Austin, TX: Prufrock Press.

Inman. T.F. (2023*). Educating the gifted: Wisdom and Insights for inspired teaching.* Austin, TX: Prufrock Press.

Lafferty, K. (2023). *The teacher's guide to gifted and talented education.* London: Routledge.

Skolnick, J.F. (2023). *Gifted and distractible: Understanding, supporting, and advocating for your twice-exceptional child.* London: Penguin.

Stanley, T. (2022). *A teacher's toolbox for gifted education.* New York: Routledge.

Chapter 7

Self-management and autonomy

Self-management is an essential competency that all students need to develop if they are to become confident and autonomous learners. This is particularly important now that schools are tending to use more student-centred approaches, independent studies, and e-learning, all calling for good self-direction. Studies have yielded data indicating that students who have the capability to self-regulate tend to do well in school and are more confident, diligent, and resourceful (Fu et al., 2023; Mammadov & Tozoglu, 2023; Oppong et al., 2019). Encouraging the development of this autonomy needs to begin in the preschool and early school years (Lyons, 2024).

One of the common observations concerning students with special needs or disabilities is that they are often passive learners, unable to make good decisions or regulate their own learning processes and behaviour appropriately. One of the goals of education must therefore be to help these students achieve a higher level of self-management and self-efficacy. The four components of self-management that need to be addressed are personal goal setting, self-monitoring, self-evaluation, and self-reinforcement (Howard et al., 2020). When the students acquire this capability, it is much easier for them to be engaged effectively in inclusive classrooms and to improve in their learning. Teaching of self-management must therefore be a high priority when working with students who have learning and attention problems and is essential for their successful functioning in an inclusive class.

Definition of terms

Several important terms are used in discussions on students' self-regulation, some overlapping in meaning but each used in a specific context. In the field of psychology, each has its own precise meaning.

- *Self-regulation* is the general term commonly used in relation to an individual's ability to monitor his or her own behaviour and modify responses and reactions as necessary. Self-regulation in learning usually involves the ability to 'think about one's own thinking' (*metacognition*) and control processes

DOI: 10.4324/9781003598671-8

such as selective attention, strategy application, and self-correction. Self-regulation includes the ability to manage one's emotions, to control anger or frustration, and to cope with stress. Self-regulation and metacognition in the context of classroom learning are discussed more fully later in the chapter.

- *Self-determination* refers to a person's autonomy to plan, set goals, make decisions, and take appropriate action to achieve one's goals. Too often, the life of persons with disabilities is largely controlled by others, and they are given very few opportunities to exercise self-determination.

- *Autonomy support* refers to the strategies and actions that parents and teachers employ to foster independence and self-determination in children and older students. The concept is most frequently referred to when describing behaviour improvement interventions but actually applies to all aspects of self-directed learning.

- *Self-directed learning* means that students are made responsible for monitoring and managing their own learning processes to achieve desired outcomes. The approach requires students to be intrinsically motivated and to exercise personal management over all actions taken in tackling a particular learning task. Interest has grown in recent years in promoting this self-directed learning, particularly in the final years of secondary school and in tertiary education, where it has major importance in relation to all forms of e-learning.

- *Classroom self-management* is a specific aspect of self-regulation that refers to a student's ability to function effectively in a classroom environment without the need for constant supervision or direction from others. This capability relates to such behaviours as organizing one's lesson materials, knowing what to do when work is completed, recognizing when to seek help from the teacher or a peer, understanding how to check one's work for careless errors, how to maintain attention to task, and how to observe well-established routines such as ordering lunch, having sports equipment or books ready for a specific lesson, and knowing when a change of lesson or room is to occur. All these skills are easily acquired by students without learning problems or disabilities but can be difficult for some students with special needs.

The importance of classroom self-management

Self-management by a student with a disability seems to be one of the most important factors contributing to successful inclusion. Some students—for example, those with intellectual disability or with social, emotional, or psychological disorders—frequently exhibit very weak self-management, having become overly dependent on control from others. It is essential that all students with special needs, whether placed in special settings or in the regular classroom, be helped to develop adequate levels of independence in their work habits, self-control, and readiness for learning. When students are able to manage routines in the classroom and look after their own needs during a lesson, the teacher is able to devote much more time to teaching rather than managing the group.

Teaching self-management and fostering autonomy

Evidence is accumulating to indicate that specific training in self-management and self-regulation can be effective in promoting students' autonomy (Hoff & Ervin, 2013; Lawson et al., 2021; Schulze, 2016). Intervention studies involving self-management training at various age levels have suggested that there are strong positive effects from such training (Sandjojo et al., 2019).

The specific self-management skills required by a child in school will tend to differ slightly from classroom to classroom according to a particular teacher's management style, routines, and expectations and according to the nature of the curriculum. The self-management skills required in an informal classroom setting tend to be very different from those needed in a more formal or highly structured setting. For example, in some secondary school classrooms, a premium may still be placed upon passive listening, note-taking, and sustained on-task behaviour, while in other classrooms, it is group-working skills and cooperation with others that are essential prerequisites for success. Knowing how to respond to the demands and constraints of different lessons and settings is an important aspect of a student's growth towards autonomy. To encourage students' self-management, teachers need to consider precisely which skills or behaviours are required in order to function independently in their particular environment; for example, it may be that in a certain lesson the prerequisites are staying on task without close supervision, resisting distractions, and using resource materials and technology independently. In another situation, being able to work closely with peers, sharing ideas, and showing initiative are the required behaviours.

For students with special educational needs, a five-step procedure can be used to teach self-management: (1) *Explanation*: Discuss with the student why a specific self-managing behaviour is important. Help the student identify and observe other students exhibiting that target behaviour. (2) *Demonstration*: Teacher clearly explains and models the behaviour. (3) *Role play*: The student imitates the behaviour, with feedback from the teacher or peer. (4) *Cueing*: In the natural classroom setting, the student is reminded and prompted when necessary to carry out the behaviour. (5) *Maintenance*: It is important to teach and reinforce the particular behaviour to the point where the student no longer needs to be prompted. When the student displays the behaviour spontaneously without needing a prompt, he or she is rewarded.

One approach that has received attention is the structured *Alert Program*® that uses the analogy of an 'engine' that has to be controlled in order to run on high, low, or appropriate power for the task in hand. According to the *OT Toolbox* website (2023, n.p.),

The Alert Program helps the individual to attain, maintain, and change arousal appropriately for the given situation [and] *Alert Program* goals teach students, educators, and parents the relationship between internal states and attention, learning, and behaviour ... with this support, *Alert Program* strategies help students recognize and define the self-regulation strategies in a variety of tasks and settings.

Gill et al. (2018) have supported the use of the *Alert Program*® in school settings for improving students' self-regulation, but the programme needs further well-designed research to obtain hard data on efficacy. For more information on the *Alert Program*® for self-regulation, see the "Online" list in the "Resources" section at the end of the chapter. For additional advice on fostering autonomy, again see the "Resources".

Locus of control and self-efficacy

Self-management links quite closely with two important personality constructs known to influence academic achievement, namely *locus of control* and *self-efficacy*. According to Haidari et al. (2023), self-efficacy and locus of control positively influence an individual's motivation when in a learning situation. To understand locus of control, it is necessary to recognize that individuals attribute what happens to them in any particular situation either to internal factors (e.g., their own ability, effort, decisions, or actions) or to external factors (e.g., luck, chance, or something outside their control). Students with an internal locus of control recognize that they can influence events by their own actions and believe that they do to some extent control their own destiny. At the classroom level, an example of internality might be when students recognize that if they ignore their friends' distractions and really concentrate on the task at hand, they get much better results. Appreciating the fact that outcomes are under one's personal control is a key component of one's feelings of 'self-efficacy' and a strong defense against passivity. This feeling of competence and control is as important for university students as it is for students in school (Adamecz et al., 2024).

Internalization of locus of control usually increases steadily with age if a child experiences normal success and reinforcement from his or her efforts in school and in daily life outside school. However, it has been found that many students with learning problems and others with negative school experiences remain markedly external in their locus of control in relation to school, believing that their efforts have little impact on their progress because they lack the ability to change outcomes. Young children enter school with positive views of their own capabilities, but this confidence rapidly erodes if they experience too many early failures and frustrations.

The student who remains largely external in locus of control is likely to be the student who fails to assume normal self-management in class and is prepared to be controlled by others such as the teacher, parent, classroom aide, or more assertive peers. There exists a vicious circle wherein the student feels inadequate, is not prepared to take a risk, seems to require support, gets it, and develops even more dependence upon others. This can be described as *learned helplessness* (Hwang, 2019), which can also lead quite rapidly to alienation to school. The teacher's task is one of breaking into this circle and causing the student to recognize the extent to which he or she has control over events and can influence outcomes. It is natural for a teacher, tutor, or aide to wish to help and support a student with special needs, but it should not be done to the extent that all challenge and possibility of failure are eliminated. Failure must be possible and students must be helped to see the causal relationship between their own efforts and the outcomes. Students will become more internal in their locus of control and much more involved in learning tasks when they recognize that their effort and persistence can overcome failure.

It is important that teachers and parents publicly acknowledge and praise students' positive efforts rather than emphasizing lack of effort. In general, teachers' use of *descriptive praise* has a strong positive influence on students' beliefs about their own ability and the importance of making an effort. When praise is perceived by students to be genuine and credible, it appears to enhance their motivation and feelings of control. Teachers' use of praise has been well researched, and it seems that praise is particularly important for students *provided that it is genuine and deserved* and that the praiseworthy aspects of the performance are specified. For example: 'Good work, David! You used your own words instead of simply copying from the reference book.' 'Well done, Joanne. I like the way you have used a different colour to show the higher ground.' A student should know precisely why he or she is being praised if appropriate connections are to be made in the student's mind between effort and outcome. Trivial or redundant praise is very quickly detected by students and serves no useful purpose.

Attribution retraining

A markedly external locus of control (as in learned helplessness) usually has a negative impact upon a student's willingness to persist in the face of a difficult task. It is easier for the child to develop avoidance strategies rather than persist if the expectation of failure is high. *Attribution retraining* is an approach designed to redirect students' self-blaming causal explanations for their difficulties (e.g., 'I lack academic ability' or 'I just don't understand big numbers') by encouraging them instead to attribute poor performance to controllable factors, such as the amount of effort they put in and the time they devote to the task (Chodkiewicz & Boyle, 2016; Graham & Taylor, 2022). When a task is completed successfully, students are taught to appraise carefully the results of their own efforts and encouraged to verbalize their conclusions aloud: 'I did that well because I took my time and read the question twice'; 'I listened carefully and planned my answers.' Verbalizing in this way helps students focus their attention on the real relationship between effort and the observed outcomes. In most cases, attribution retraining seems to have maximum value when it is combined with *cognitive behaviour modification*.

Cognitive behaviour modification

Cognitive behaviour modification (CBM) involves training students to gain better control over their own thoughts and actions by using inner self-talk. When used in clinical settings to modify maladaptive behaviours or emotions (e.g., phobias, anxiety disorders, stress, anger, and aggression), the approach is often referred to as *cognitive behavioural therapy* (CBT). The approach has been used successfully with a wide range of individuals who present with developmental delay, learning problems, or behaviour difficulties (Cooney et al., 2018; Garvik et al., 2014; Rutter & Atkinson, 2024).

In a school situation, a student with a behaviour or attitude problem in class is taught to memorize and use a mental 'script' that enables them to monitor and regulate their own behaviour in a particular situation. An example might be a student who has great difficulty staying on task and who often gets out of her seat to disturb others during the lesson. A small timing device with a beeper might be placed on her desk and she would be taught to monitor her own on-task behaviour every time the beeper sounds. If she is on task, she praises herself: 'Good! I am working. I am finishing the task.' At the end of each lesson, the teacher rewards the student in some way if she has achieved the set goal by remaining seated and on task. It is usual for a teacher to implement a CBM programme with advice from the school psychologist, who is able to assess the particular characteristics of the student and then recommend appropriate strategies.

Metacognition

Metacognition refers to the ability to monitor one's own thinking processes and exercise control over them. Metacognitive processes enter many aspects of cognition and the development of self-regulation and autonomy. It has been suggested that metacognition is one of the most significant predictors of academic performance, possibly even more influential than intelligence (Burns, 2024; Ohtani & Hisasaka, 2018). Metacognition helps a learner in school recognize that he or she either is doing well or is having difficulty with a particular learning task. The learner who is monitoring his or her own ongoing performance will detect the need to pause and check, perhaps begin again before moving on, weigh up possible alternatives, or seek outside help. This is clearly an important ability in almost all areas of the curriculum.

Metacognitive training focuses on assisting a learner to monitor the appropriateness of his or her thoughts when faced with a particular task or problem.

This involves self-questioning and analysis that can lead to a more considered plan of action. Teachers should provide modelling of this process by thinking aloud, to reach a decision on what action to take. Metacognitive training has to utilize authentic topics, problems, or tasks as the focus of instruction, and curriculum areas such as reading comprehension, mathematical problem-solving, and planned essay writing have been popular topics for research. The Education Endowment Foundation in the UK has stated that metacognition and self-regulation training approaches have yielded consistently high levels of impact for all learners and are particularly effective for low-achieving students (EEF, 2019).

Cognitive strategies and strategy-based instruction

A cognitive strategy can be thought of as a 'mental plan of action' that enables a student to tackle a particular task or assignment systematically. Strategy training involves a teacher providing a clear demonstration of exactly how to approach that task. The teacher who says: 'Watch and listen. This is how I do it – and this is what I say to myself as I do it', is providing the learner with a secure starting point. The teacher who simply says, 'Here is the exercise. Get on with it', is providing an invitation to failure and frustration for some students.

Although most teachers are aware of the value of implementing strategy training, too few manage to do this as a routine part of their approach. They tend to be more concerned with covering curriculum content than with helping students become more efficient at learning that content (Magnusson et al., 2019). If cognitive strategies are not taught explicitly, many students fail to discover them incidentally.

It was noted in Chapter 1 that many students with general or specific learning difficulties appear to lack appropriate strategies for tackling schoolwork. They do not seem to understand that these tasks can be completed effectively if approached with a plan of action in mind. *Strategy-based instruction* (SBI) involves teaching students to apply effective thinking procedures to guide their actions and self-monitoring when approaching a particular task or problem. Research attention has focused mainly on using SBI in teaching reading comprehension, writing skills, and mathematics (e.g., Khosravi et al., 2023; Witzel & Myers, 2023). For example, attempting to solve a routine word problem in mathematics usually requires careful reading of the problem, identification of what one is required to find out, recognition of the relevant data to use, selection of the appropriate process, completion of the calculation, and a final checking of the reasonableness of the answer. This approach to solving the mathematical problem involves metacognition, application of a cognitive strategy, and utilization of procedural knowledge (how to carry out the steps in a specific calculation).

The typical teaching procedure used in SBI usually has the basic structure described below.

- *Modelling*: teacher performs the task or carries out the new process while thinking aloud. This may involve self-questioning, giving self-directions, making overt decisions, changing one's mind, and evaluating the results.
- *Overt external guidance*: students copy the teacher's model and complete a similar task, with the teacher still providing any necessary prompting and verbal directions.
- *Overt self-guidance*: students repeat the performance with a similar task while using self-talk.
- *Covert self-instruction*: students perform several similar tasks while using inner speech to monitor their actions, guide their responses, and make decisions.

In a mathematics lesson, typical self-questions, statements, and directions a student might be taught to use when attempting to solve a problem would include

- *What exactly do I have to do? Where do I start?*
- *Don't rush.*
- *OK, I need to multiply these two numbers and then subtract the answer from 100. That's good. I know that answer is correct.*
- *I'll need to come back and check this part. Does this make sense?*
- *I think I made a mistake here, but I can come back and work it again. I can correct it.*

These self-monitoring statements cover focusing attention, goal setting, planning, checking, self-reinforcement, self-appraisal, error detection, and self-correction. These statements are applicable across a fairly wide range of academic tasks.

Students with learning difficulties tend to take very much longer than other students to adopt a new learning strategy, so abundant practice needs to be sustained until independent use is finally established. Maintenance of strategy use can be assisted by frequent discussion with students about how and when to apply the strategy and by the use of descriptive praise when a student remembers to use a strategy without prompting.

Students find most relevance in strategies they can use to complete classroom assignments and homework more successfully. Sometimes, the steps involved in tackling a specific task can be printed on a cue card to be displayed for as long as is necessary on the students' desks. The students can also be taught a mnemonic for remembering the strategy. Examples of mnemonics are provided in Chapters 10 and 13, on literacy and numeracy.

Generalization of taught strategies has always been problematic, particularly for students with learning difficulties. The students may learn how to apply the strategy successfully to one specific task but not recognize how the same approach could be used in other contexts. To help students overcome the problem of limited generalization, teachers might (1) provide training from the beginning that deliberately requires the strategy to be applied in a variety of different authentic tasks from across the curriculum and (2) review a particular strategy quite often to discuss the situations in which it could be applied.

This chapter has presented concepts and practices that relate to ways of making students more autonomous in their approach to learning and in monitoring and regulating their own responses. The next chapter looks at issues concerned with classroom behaviour more generally.

Resources

Online

- Alert Program®. https://www.alertprogram.com, https://www.theottoolbox. com/alert-program-self-regulation-program/
- *Self-regulated learning: What it is, why it is important and strategies for implementingit*.https://educationaltechnology.net/self-regulated-learning-what-it-is-why-it-is-important-and-strategies-for-implementing-it/
- Ochoa, D. (2023). *What is student autonomy and how to promote it.* https:// www.thinkific.com/blog/what-is-learner-autonomy/
- Garrido, G.L. (2023). *Locus of control theory in psychology: Definition and examples.* https://www.simplypsychology.org/locus-of-control.html
- *Strategy-based instruction.* https://www.understood.org/en/articles/ what-is-strategy-instruction
- *Teaching self-management: Practical ways to help students develop skills in this key component of social-emotional learning.* https://www.slideshare. net/TransformingEducation/teaching-self-management

Print

Allen, K.A., Furlong, M.J., Vella-Broderick, D. & Suldo, S. (Eds.). (2022). *Handbook of positive psychology in schools* (3rd ed.). New York: Routledge. [See chapter on academic self-efficacy.]

Mynard, J., & Shelton-Strong, S.J. (Eds.). (2022). *Autonomy support beyond the language learning classroom: A self-determination theory perspective.* Bristol: Channel View Publications (Multilingual Matters).

Roma, G.P. (2023). *Student success: Foundations of self-management.* State University of New York Press.

Ryan, R.M. (2023). *The Oxford handbook of self-determination theory.* New York: Oxford University Press.

Strosnider, R., & Sharpe, V.S. (2019). *The executive function guidebook: Strategies to help all students achieve success.* Thousand Oaks, CA: Corwin.

Chapter 8

Managing behaviour

Challenging behaviour is not necessarily a characteristic of students with special needs and disabilities; many students without difficulties or disabilities exhibit problem behaviour stemming from a variety of causes. However, a few students with special needs may lack self-control, and some may have social and emotional problems leading to a need for behaviour change intervention.

A well-managed classroom with a minimum of problem behaviours is conducive to positive learning opportunities for all students. Teachers in primary and secondary schools place great importance on managing students' behaviour and helping them gain control over their own conduct. Many teachers report that one of their main concerns in the classroom is the student who disrupts lessons, cannot work cooperatively with others, and seeks too much attention from teacher or peers. A teacher may know what the student needs in terms of basic instruction and support, but it proves impossible to deliver appropriate teaching because the student is unreceptive.

Unfortunately, teachers tend to be reactive to problem behaviour that arises, rather than using proactive management strategies to prevent the problems occurring (Hepburn et al., 2021). Students who are in classes containing peers with poor behaviour report that the troublesome students don't listen to the teacher and that there is almost constant noise in the classroom (OECD, 2019b). Countries reporting the highest rates of poor behaviour are France, Australia, New Zealand, and the UK. Classroom behaviour problems were less evident in China, Korea, and Japan (Earp, 2024; OECD, 2019b).

The effects of misbehaviour

There are always numerous negative outcomes from behaviour problems in school, for both the students and their teachers. Students who are creating the problems usually miss out on many important learning opportunities by spending huge amounts of time off task. They also tend to have poor quality of life in school because their social acceptance is negatively affected when they alienate members of their peer group. The general classroom climate is also

DOI: 10.4324/9781003598671-9

affected because the teacher is unable to relax and use methods which do not require tight control.

One of the main factors contributing to teachers' stress and burn-out is students' challenging behaviour (Elliott et al., 2024). Teachers need the support of the school principal and the understanding from colleagues that a particular student's challenging behaviour is not due to their own inability to exercise effective classroom control. When a school fails to adopt a collaborative and supportive approach to the management of difficult and disruptive behaviour, certain problems tend to arise: (1) individual teachers feeling that they are isolated and unsupported by their colleagues, (2) teachers feeling increasingly stressed by daily conflict with some students, and (3) the problem becoming worse over time.

Preventing behaviour problems

The fundamental requirement for preventing problem behaviour is to provide students with a safe, secure, and predictable environment in which learning can take place (Zoder-Martell et al., 2023). Positive teacher–student relationships are an essential component of proactive behaviour management (Dean & Gibbs, 2023). Lessons and the activities within them need always to employ teaching methods, activities, and resources that engage students fully in the learning process and that help them feel successful. This often requires tasks and activities to be differentiated to match the various ability levels of the students. A common cause of inappropriate behaviour or total disengagement from learning is when students are expected to undertake work that is too difficult, too easy, or boring. Teachers who are most effective in classroom management and maintaining student engagement tend to set interesting and achievable tasks for students to attempt. They also avoid 'dead spots' in lessons and check students' progress regularly to provide timely and constructive feedback and encouragement.

The underlying principle for managing students' behaviour today is to be positive rather than punitive. An example of this is the proactive approach known as *school-wide positive behaviour support* (SWPBS), which seeks to improve students' academic and behavioural outcomes by targeting the school's organizational and social culture (Reimers, 2020; Wienen et al., 2019). Under a proactive and preventive approach, teachers endeavour to 'catch students being good' and to praise them descriptively for their appropriate behaviour rather than waiting for bad behaviour to occur and having to react to it. Too often, teachers give far more attention to students who are not behaving appropriately compared with positive attention given to the other 95 per cent of well-behaved member of a class. Studies in mainstream schools have supported the efficacy of SWPBS, with reports of significantly lower truancy rates and higher reading and math proficiency (Kurth et al., 2024; Noltemeyer et al., 2019; Pas et al., 2019). In the context of students with special needs (including those with autism), this positive approach is reported to be linked to improved outcomes for the students and their teachers (Kurth et al., 2024; Walker et al., 2023; Wang & Kuo, 2019).

Behaviour management policy

At school level, it is essential to have a clear policy on behaviour management to ensure uniform and consistent implementation by all staff. This document should have been drawn up and negotiated with input from all teaching and support staff (and often also from parents) to describe ways in which matters of classroom control and discipline should be approached. Ideally, a policy will also make specific reference to the management of students with diagnosed behavioural disorders and how the school may involve outside agencies to assist. In the case of any student with chronic behaviour problems, it is essential to involve his or her parents fully in the implementation of any behaviour change programme. The parents and school staff should together agree on the goals and strategies for a behaviour management plan and then be consistent in applying the same strategies in school and at home.

It is always necessary in the classroom to establish rules for behaviour that are clearly understood by students and accepted by them as reasonable. At the core of any behaviour management policy should be the stated aim of teaching all students effective and responsible ways of managing their own behaviour. A good policy in action will help all students recognize the personal and group benefits that self-control and responsible behaviour can bring. In many ways, a school policy on student behaviour should be seen as dealing more with matters of social harmony, welfare, and safety rather than a list of procedures for enforcing discipline and punishment. This is in keeping with the belief that schools must be safe and friendly environments in which to work, play, and socialize with peers.

A three-tier model of intervention

In the same way that support for difficulties in learning is best delivered through a three-tier model (see Chapter 1), it is now accepted that managing behaviour also needs to be implemented at three levels. This tiered system can be provided as part of any school's general approach to discipline or incorporated as a feature of a SWPBS model. Tier 1 involves establishing for all students an environment in which expectations and rules for behaviour are clear to all students, and all students are helped to acquire appropriate self-management. Tier 1 involves teaching students how to use pro-social behaviours to prevent problems arising, implementing evidence-based classroom management strategies, and openly acknowledging (reinforcing) students when they display positive behaviours. Tier 2 provides additional targeted guidance for some students who at times display poor behaviour. Tier 3 involves intensive behaviour change intervention targeted at any individual student with ongoing challenging behaviour. Methods used most frequently at Tier 3 in special schools are based on principles derived from *applied behaviour analysis* (ABA) (see below), with very clear goal setting, reward systems, abundant practice, and frequent evaluation of progress (Pitts et al., 2019).

Pas et al. (2019) report that this three-tiered model is now implemented in nearly 26,000 schools in the US. Evaluations in primary and secondary settings indicate lower suspension rate (small effect size) and higher reading and math proficiency rates (small to large effect sizes) in the primary years. In secondary schools, there has been a decrease in truancy rate as well as higher reading and math proficiency.

The need for a team approach

At school level, behaviour problems are best dealt with through a team approach (Nese et al., 2023). In particular, all teachers who have contact with a student receiving Tier 3 intensive intervention need to collaborate and use a consistent approach when dealing with the problem behaviour. Occasionally, of course, it is necessary to seek outside expert advice when a student's behaviour does not respond to standard forms of effective management; but in many cases, behaviour can be modified successfully within the school setting. In some schools, *behaviour support teams* have been created to assist in this process and to ensure that all personnel who have contact with a problem student have a common goal and are consistent in their approach. These teams also have the roles of assisting with staff development, implementing behaviour policy, encouraging positive approaches to classroom management, and helping to solve specific problems related to behaviour and learning. In several countries, regional or district services have also established similar behaviour support teams or units to work with parents as well as schools.

Modifying behaviour

It should be understood that changing a student's behaviour is difficult, because a behaviour we regard as inappropriate has often proven to be quite effective for that student in attaining certain personal goals. The behaviour has been used frequently and has become a well-established characteristic of that student. In order for positive behaviour change to occur, the student must first *desire* to change, and it is then the responsibility of the teacher to help the him or her understand exactly how to bring about and maintain improvement. It is always essential for the management method employed to establish a new behaviour and eliminate an undesirable behaviour should be implemented consistently by all personnel who work with the student.

As stated above, the approach commonly used to bring about change in students with special needs (particularly those with autism, moderate intellectual disability, or behaviour disorder) is based on principles of ABA (Alberto et al., 2021). ABA makes three assumptions, namely that (1) all behaviour is learned, (2) behaviour can be changed by altering its consequences, and (3) factors in the environment (in this case, the classroom) can be engineered to reward and maintain specific behaviours.

When using ABA, a problematic behaviour is observed to identify factors that are causing and maintaining the behaviour. A programme is then designed to reshape this behaviour into something more acceptable by using a system of reinforcement. In cases of very persistent negative behaviour such as physical aggression, positive reinforcement procedures alone may not be sufficient to bring about change. In such cases, it may be necessary to introduce negative consequences and reductive procedures, such as loss of privileges, loss of points, or time out. Attention must also be given to improving the student's own self-monitoring in order to increase his or her control over the behaviour.

The behavioural approach is now regarded as an evidence-based method, its efficacy having been reported in an impressive number of research studies over a long period of time. In particular, ABA techniques are of great practical value for those working with students who have severe disabilities, autism, emotional disorders, and challenging behaviour. However, although ABA approaches have consistently proven to be effective in changing behaviour, they are sometimes criticized on the basis that control is exercised by powerful others rather than by the individual. It is suggested that manipulation of the individual's behaviour is somehow out of keeping with humanistic values and respect for personal autonomy. In reality, any behaviour change programme normally has as its ultimate goal that the individual will develop, maintain, and exhibit the new positive behaviour as part of their independent and autonomous functioning. Technology has offered new opportunities in this respect, by providing devices that enable a student to self-monitor in areas such as time on task and attentive listening. For example, there is an intervention involving CellF-Monitor, an iPad application that allows individuals to self-rate their academic engagement behaviour during independent learning activities (Schardt et al., 2019).

Increasingly, ABA approaches are being supplemented by simultaneous application of cognitive behaviour modification (CBM) (see Chapter 7). This often involves the teacher or trainer in coaching the individual to use *self-talk* to monitor and control their reactions to challenging situations. The self-talk enables the student to process aspects of the situation rationally and enables him or her to manage responses more effectively. A key ingredient in the approach is teaching the student to use statements that serve to inhibit impulsive and inappropriate responses, allowing time for substitution of more acceptable responses—for example, to approach another student in a friendly rather than confrontational manner or to ignore a teasing remark rather than respond to it with aggression. These strategies help to strengthen an individual's resilience when facing challenging situations.

Recent years in Britain have seen the introduction of 'isolation booths' in some primary and secondary schools (Weale, 2020). These are small closet-size spaces or cubicles set apart from the main classroom to which an unruly or aggressive student may be sent for time out. These isolation areas are variously referred to as exclusion units, consequence booths, time-out spaces, and calm rooms. This type of provision has come in for harsh criticism based on growing concern about the impact such punitive spaces have on a student's emotional well-being (Condliffe, 2023). There is still lack of evidence that isolation rooms are effective in modifying behaviour and may be a breach of the United Nations (UN) Charter on the Rights of the Child.

Students with learning difficulties or disabilities

There is a misguided belief that most students with special needs have some form of behaviour problem. It was this erroneous belief that caused many teachers in the beginning to have serious doubts about the feasibility of introducing inclusive education. As stated earlier, the belief is, of course, entirely untrue because many of these students are well behaved in class, cooperative, and friendly and create no problem at all for classroom management. It is true, however, that *some* students with autism and others with intellectual disability often have inappropriate ways of responding to frustration, anxiety, or stress. They may withdraw into themselves (internalizing behaviour) or instead may respond aggressively to teacher and peers (disruptive externalizing behaviour). In addition, there are a few students who are diagnosed as having an *emotional or behavioural disorder* (EBD) and who require a behaviour intervention plan (BIP) to teach them effective strategies for self-control for classroom learning (Isaak et al., 2022).

Emotional or behavioural disorders

Students with EBD comprise a diverse group, with a wide range of intellectual and academic abilities. Their social interaction with other students is often problematic, making it difficult to accommodate them in inclusive classes. They tend to do best in smaller units where they have a structured and predictable routine and where they can receive intensive Tier 3 intervention and support. This usually combines an ABA approach to reinforce positive pro-social behaviours and eliminate undesirable responses while providing individual guidance and counselling of a therapeutic nature. As stated earlier, students with an autism spectrum disorder, and others with some forms of intellectual disability, also sometimes require and benefit from a similar Tier 3 approach. In all other cases of disability or sensory impairment, the students concerned can participate in and benefit from all of the approaches described in this chapter.

Autism

One approach that has proven to be useful for children with autism, to help them understand events from the perspective of others, is *Social Stories*™ (Karal & Wolfe, 2018). These simple age-appropriate stories can focus on skills such as sharing and cooperating, how to make friends, how to cope with changes to routine, and what to do when you are angry or unhappy. They are useful also for preschool children who often need help to understand codes of behaviour, social interactions, and relationships. Social stories can be presented using pictures of children engaging in desirable and undesirable behaviour. The children are then guided to observe and reflect upon the behaviour and the reaction it gets from others. For example, a first picture might show children lining up in front of a cake stall at the school Open Day. One child is pushing another out of the line in order to take his place. The children on each side are looking very unhappy. In the next picture, two of the other children are beginning to push the naughty child away from the line and a fight starts. In the third picture, the lady in charge of the cake stall says that she will stop selling the cakes unless children line up in a neat queue. The final picture shows a neat queue of children with happy faces, each paying in turn for a cake. Simple stories of this type can also be presented in an active form, through video and virtual reality programmes (Ghanouni et al., 2019). A review of existing studies of social stories found that they can be an effective intervention for increasing appropriate behaviours and decreasing challenging behaviours (Williams, 2021).

Dealing with disruptive behaviour

Teachers can lose almost half of their teaching time in some classrooms because of students' unruly behaviour. This type of behaviour upsets the orderly conduct of teaching and prevents achievement of the objectives for a particular lesson. Frequent disruptive behaviour may also impair the quality of personal and social interaction within the group by destroying a positive classroom climate. Sometimes, simple changes such as modifying seating arrangements, restructuring working groups, clearly specifying rules for working together, reducing noise level, and monitoring more closely the work in progress will significantly reduce the occurrence of disruptive behaviour.

Analyses of various interventions used to decrease disruptive behaviour have found that the use of group rewards (group contingency interventions) can be effective (Page et al., 2023; Pokorski, 2019). Under this arrangement, all members are rewarded when behaviour in a class improves. This also has the advantages that it is easier to administer than individual reward systems, and it involves the whole class of students in monitoring and improving behaviour.

Good Behaviour Game

The Good Behaviour Game (GBG) has existed in various forms for many years but has seen an increase recently in its application. It is an approach that rewards students for displaying appropriate on-task behaviours during lessons. The class is usually divided into two teams that include any students with special needs, and points are given to a team for all appropriate behaviours displayed by its members. The team with the most points at the end of the session (or end of the week) wins a group reward. Obviously, this approach needs to be used frequently enough to have the desired impact. GBG has been found effective for reducing disruptive behaviour, increasing on-task behaviour, and increasing teachers' use of praise relative to reprimands (Fallon & Kurtz, 2019). Adapted versions of GBG have even proven useful in the preschool age range (Foley et al., 2019). Combining deliberate social skills training with the GBG approach has been found effective for bringing about improvements in the engagement and behaviour of primary school students diagnosed as having emotional and behavioural disorders (Meredith-Murphy et al., 2020). Holmdahl et al. (2023) concluded that students with special needs may especially benefit from the GBG due to its focus on clear expectations, positive reinforcement, and a more inclusive classroom climate.

ClassDojo and tootling

Technology has provided a new medium for monitoring behaviour and providing reinforcement that can improve classroom climate. One example is the use of 'tootling' in which students report positively and pro-socially on their peers' behaviour via ClassDojo technology. ClassDojo is a widely used school-based social media platform (digital app) that can provide an effective system for behaviour monitoring and control (Love, 2022; Manolev et al., 2019). Teachers can also provide on-time feedback and reinforcement to students regarding individual and group behaviour. Tootling basically encourages students to report on classmates' prosocial behaviour, and when students' tootles are displayed via a projector, appropriate behaviour can be discussed and reinforced with the group. Results from a study with primary school students indicate substantial decreases in class-wide disruptive behaviours and increases in academically engaged behaviour (Dillon et al., 2019). ClassDojo also enables teachers to share information from school to home regarding students' behaviour (Love, 2022). A study with older special education students also suggested that ClassDojo monitoring produced a reduction in problem behaviour for the classroom as a whole and for most individual students (Lipscomb et al., 2018). A similar result was obtained with high school students using tootling via handwritten notes rather than technology (Lum et al., 2019).

Behaviour contracts

Often, it is necessary to supplement any whole-class approach to behaviour management by addressing the particular problem behaviour of an individual student. A behaviour contract is a written agreement signed by all parties involved in a behaviour-change programme, including the student (Schrieber et al., 2023). After discussion and negotiation, the student agrees to behave in certain ways and carry out certain obligations. In return, the staff and parents agree to do certain things; for example, the student may agree to arrive on time for lessons and not disrupt the class. In return, the teacher will sign the student's contract sheet, indicating that he or she has met the requirement in that particular lesson, and add positive comments. The contract sheet accompanies the student to each lesson throughout the day. At the end of each day and the end of each week, progress is monitored and any necessary changes are made to the agreement. If possible, the school negotiates parental involvement in the implementation of the contract, and the parents agree to provide some specific privileges if the goals are met for two consecutive weeks, or loss of privileges if it is broken. When behaviour contracts are set up in a secondary school, it is essential that all subject teachers who have the student in their classes be informed of the details.

Aggressive behaviour

Aggression can manifest itself in many forms: physical aggression, verbal aggression, violence against persons and property, online abuse, and sexual aggression. Verbal aggression (abusive and hurtful language) is the most frequent form of aggression in American elementary and secondary schools (Poling & Smith, 2023). Teachers are very bothered by physical aggressive behaviour that is directed at them (Erskine et al., 2023). Increases in work-related stress among teachers are related in part to increases in acting-out and aggressive behaviour among their students. Teachers need to acquire some effective strategies for dealing with students' anger and potential aggression (Elliott et al., 2024).

A cognitive behavioural approach described earlier can be effective in helping students monitor and control their own anger—although the students must genuinely want to change their own behaviour if the approach is to work. Often, aggression has proven to be a useful response for a student, helping him or her establish a 'tough persona' that he or she may be reluctant to lose. It is worth noting that students with a history of physically aggressive responses are often not particularly proficient in using language to argue their point of view, and sometimes the aggression is used to compensate for their inability to win an argument or convey their feelings (Chow & Wehby, 2019). Intervention for these students may need to focus on improving their moral reasoning and empathy as well as modifying overt behaviours (Baker et al., 2023).

What really needs to be taught is how to resolve threatening situations by negotiation and compromise and not by aggression. In typical cognitive approaches, participants explore the following issues:

- the nature of anger
- when anger can be justified
- when anger becomes a problem
- things that trigger our anger
- how to take control when we are becoming angry (anger management)
- how to use self-instruction to and control to choose alternative responses.

It is reported that less aggression is found in schools where a caring and supportive environment has been nurtured and where curricular demands are realistic. Schools where there is constant frustration and discouragement seem to breed disaffection and stimulate more aggressive and anti-social behaviour in students.

Bullying

Traditional forms of face-to-face school bullying, bullying outside of school hours, and, more recently, cyberbullying are causing growing concern worldwide. A search of any research database will reveal a great increase globally of studies on this topic conducted over the past decade. Data from the US, the UK, and Australia indicate that cases of bullying are increasing every year (Unicef, 2024; Waghorn, 2024). Particularly worrying is the evidence that more girls than ever before are also engaging in online bullying and in aggressive face-to-face confrontations (Miskimon et al., 2023). An estimated 30 per cent of school students experience bullying by their classmates—but studies suggest that many more students are actually bullied but do not report it. Clearly, the increase in bullying by both boys and girls is a situation that needs to be addressed almost daily by teachers and school counsellors.

Some students are more resilient than others when experiencing face-to-face or cyberbullying, but this must not be taken as a sign that all children can cope. The lives of too many students are made miserable when they become victims of bullying. Known outcomes from becoming a victim include absenteeism, anxiety, psychosomatic illnesses, low self-esteem, a feeling of isolation, depression, and, in extreme cases, suicidal tendencies (Doremus, 2023; Miskimon et al., 2023). A large number of adults describe the severe impact that bullying at school had on them, indicating that bullying really has long-lasting effects.

Bullying may take several different forms: direct physical assault, verbal attacks, or indirect attacks such as spreading hurtful rumours verbally or online or by excluding someone from a social group. In physical bullying, bullies pick their targets very selectively, and there are often characteristics of victims that make them targets for bullies. Victims are often students who appear to be vulnerable, weaker, shy, nervous, overweight, of different ethnic background, or a 'teacher's pet.' Students in secondary schools who identify themselves as (or are thought by the peer group to be) members of the LGBTQ population are also very much at risk (Hornbeck & Duncheon, 2024). Unpopular students and those with behaviour disorders or poor personal and social skills, students with a specific learning disability, and those with an intellectual disability or autism are more likely than others to be victimized.

Many bullying incidents tend to occur in the schoolyard, the bathrooms, and cloakrooms, particularly if supervision is poor. Increased out-of-class supervision is one step that schools can take to reduce bullying. When bullying is carried out by gangs of students, factors such as the importance of status within the group come into play. Some individuals feel that they are demonstrating their power by repressing the victim. Even those who are not themselves bullies get carried along with the behaviour and do not object to it or report it. Few would ever intervene to help the victim.

School climate appears to be an influence on prevalence of bullying, and schools that have poor teacher–student relationships and a 'non-inviting' atmosphere exhibit more cases. Schools in England are required to have an anti-bullying policy; but in any country without such a policy, due attention must still be given to addressing bullying as a key topic in their behaviour management plans (Kidwai & Smith, 2024). There must be agreed procedures for handling incidents of bullying and procedures for collaborating with parents, so that all approach the problem with similar strategies. School-wide procedures also need to be in place for providing support and counselling for victims of bullying and methods for working to modify the behaviour and attitude of the bully.

Cyberbullying

Data from many countries suggest an alarming increase in cyberbullying in the form derogatory comments, malicious gossip and lies posted on social network websites, instant messaging, emails, and by mobile phone. Unfortunately, as with other forms of bullying, students often do not report such bullying to their parents. Parents therefore need to watch for any signs of cyberbullying, include the student seeming to be constantly upset or secretive after spending time on their mobile phone, and spending more time than usual in online chat rooms. The use of cyberbullying is found not only in schools but also in colleges and universities. In the case of older adolescents, the bullying can also take the form of posting online embarrassing photographs involving the victim. It is known that all forms of cyberbullying result in anxiety and depression for the victim (Hinduja & Patchin, 2019). Victims of extensive cyberbullying have been found to display poor mental well-being and are under constant emotional distress and can even contemplate suicide (Doumas & Midgett, 2023).

Teachers should discuss with their classes what cyberbullying is and its effect on the person targeted. They need, in particular, to talk about the role that other students play in passing on rumours, lies, false accusations, and fake stories to others, thus contributing to the harm that is done. Students should be encouraged to avoid joining in online attacks on a victim and to report the matter to a teacher. It is suggested that issues of bullying and cyberbullying should become the focus of attention within the school curriculum—perhaps under the general heading 'human relationships'—and should certainly be part of a safe, socially aware, and caring school environment.

For more information on cyberbullying, see '*Cyberbullying: Everything you need to know*' in the "Online" list in the "Resources" section.

Attention-deficit/hyperactivity disorder

Some students (estimated at between 5 per cent and 10 per cent) display problems maintaining attention to any learning task and are easily distracted. They may also exhibit impulsive behaviour and hyperactivity. These students are classified now as having attention-deficit/hyperactivity disorder (ADHD) and are frequently referred for psycho-educational assessment. A few of these students may also be diagnosed with *conduct disorders*—defined as a disregard for age-appropriate social norms and rules, lack of empathy and respect for others, and persistent violations of their rights (APA, 2013). ADHD can accompany certain other disabilities such as cerebral palsy, traumatic brain injury, autism, specific learning disability, and emotional disturbance. Even students who are identified as potentially gifted can exhibit distractibility and hyperactivity. Accurate diagnosis of ADHD in student is often difficult because the symptoms of inattentiveness and hyperactivity can be exhibited at times by any child.

The fifth edition of the *Diagnostic and Statistical Manual of Mental Disorders* (*DSM*) divides ADHD into two main categories: *inattention* (failure to listen or pay attention to details, distractibility, and difficulty staying on task) and *hyperactivity and impulsivity* (excessive fidgeting, random movement, an inability to remain seated, excitability, and excessive talking) (APA, 2013). In many cases, both inattention and impulsivity are present. *DSM-5* has also placed increased emphasis on the fact that ADHD is not limited to the childhood years and may be diagnosed in some adults.

Most authorities now agree that the ADHD syndrome has multiple possible causes, and no single factor has been identified. The following influences have all been put forward as possible explanations: genetic factor, central nervous system dysfunction, subtle forms of brain damage too slight to be confirmed by neurological testing, allergy to specific substances (e.g., food additives), adverse reactions to environmental stimuli (e.g., bright lights, noise), maternal alcohol consumption during pregnancy, and inappropriate management of the child at home. Some studies have found that there are gender differences in the age at which symptoms of ADHD begin and the ways in which they change across the age range (Murray et al., 2019).

Students with ADHD, while not necessarily below average in intelligence, usually exhibit poor achievement in most school subjects. Weak concentration and restlessness associated with the syndrome have usually impaired the child's learning during the important early years of schooling. Many ADHD students also have problems developing social competence and peer relationships. Some seem to lack an understanding of the emotional reactions and feelings of others, resulting in many negative confrontations and other inappropriate social interactions.

Interventions for ADHD

It is not surprising to find that many different forms of treatment and intervention are advocated. Treatments have included diet control, medication, psychotherapy, behaviour modification, and cognitive therapy. There have also been 'alternative' treatments of doubtful value. Experience seems to show that what works for one child may not work for another. The most effective treatment seems to require a behaviour management plan, parent counselling, home management programme, and (possibly) medication. In the US, almost 60 per cent of students with ADHD are taking medication such as Ritalin or Adderall to reduce their hyperactivity and to help them focus attention on schoolwork. In Britain and Australia, the use of medication as a first resort is a little less common, and the focus is more on behavioural interventions. The use of medication remains a controversial issue, and teachers often express doubts about the ethics of using drugs to control behaviour.

There is strong agreement among experts that students with ADHD need clear structure within lessons and learning materials that are comfortably within their ability range. The programme must be effective in motivating and engaging the student and holding their interest and attention. Enhancing the learning of these students may also need to involve

- providing strong visual input and hands-on activities to hold attention
- using guided computer-assisted learning
- teaching the students better self-management skills
- giving the students specific roles, responsibilities, and duties in the classroom
- monitoring them closely during lessons to find many opportunities to praise and reinforce them descriptively when they are on task and productive.

As is the case with all other areas of exceptionality and special need, there is a strong need for all teachers and other school personnel to receive adequate training in recognizing and supporting students with ADHD (Cueli et al., 2024).

The next chapter explores how students with learning difficulties or disabilities may be helped to develop more effective social skills alongside better self-management to gain greater acceptance in inclusive classrooms.

Resources

Online

- *Cyberbullying: Everything you need to know* https://www.verywellhealth. com/cyberbullying-effects-and-what-to-do-5220584
- *7 Steps to set-up an effective behavior management plan.* https://www. positiveaction.net/blog/behavior-management-plan
- Association for Positive Behaviour Support: *Positive Behavioural Support Competence Framework.* https://pbsacademy.org.uk/pbs-competence-framework/
- ClassDojo website at https://external2.classdojo.com/en-gb/
- Earp, J. (2024). [Infographic]. Classroom disciplinary climate: Global comparisons. *Teacher Magazine*, 14 March 2024. https://www.teachermagazine. com/au_en/articles/infographic-classroom-disciplinary-climate-global-comparisons
- *From chaos to calm: Effective behaviour management strategies for the classroom* (2023). https://www.routledge.com/blog/article/behaviour-management-strategies-for-the-classroom
- Gov.UK. (updated 2024). *Behaviour in schools: How school staff can develop a behaviour policy.*
- Gov.UK. *Bullying at school* [Printable version]. https://www.gov.uk/bullying-at-school/print

Print

Bates, B., Bailey, A., & Lever, D. (2019). *A quick guide to behaviour management.* London: Sage.

Bennett, T. (2020). *Running the room: The teacher's guide to behaviour.* John Catt Educational (Hodder).

Doremus, W.A. (2023b). *Prevention and intervention of bullying and cyberbullying in schools. Revised position statement.* Silver Spring, MD: National Association of School Nurses.

Singh, G. (2024). *101 ways to win in teaching in secondary school: Managing behaviour, workload and well-being.* Dunstable, Bedfordshire, UK: Brilliant Publications.

Thomsen, E., Henderson, M., Moore, A., Price, N., & McGarrah, M.W. (2024). *Student reports of bullying: Results from the 2022 School Crime Supplement to the National Crime Victimization Survey.* Jessup, MD: National Center for Education Statistics.

Walker, H.M. (2023). *Solutions to critical behavioral issues in the classroom.* New York: Guilford Press.

Weathers, M. (2024). *Executive functions for every classroom, grades 3–12: Creating safe and predictable learning environments.* Thousand Oaks, CA: Corwin.

Chapter 9

Social skills and peer group acceptance

In order to cope well in inclusive schools and be accepted into the peer group, students with learning difficulties or disabilities must possess adequate social skills for mixing and working with other students. It is for this reason that one of the most important goals for inclusive education is helping all students develop skills that enable them to engage in positive social interactions. It is evident that poor peer relationships during the school years can have a lasting detrimental impact on an individual's confidence and competence in later years.

Problems with social acceptance

Problems gaining acceptance in a social group can be just as harmful to a student's well-being in school as constant academic failure. Students who leave school with significant deficits in social skills are at risk for negative interactions in the community, delinquency, unemployment, and mental health problems. On the other hand, individuals with adequate social skills are much less likely to engage in problem behaviour, are better at making friends, are able to resolve conflicts peacefully, and develop effective ways of dealing with persons in authority.

Research has found that debilitating loneliness can occur when individuals do not make lasting relationships and often negatively affects their personality development and quality of life during adolescence and into adulthood (Kerr, 2024; Mund & Neyer, 2019). This is not to say that all persons who are not gregarious must therefore be lonely and unhappy—people differ greatly in their desire or need for constant company. This is as true of children of school age as it is of some adults who are quite happy with their own company.

Lack of social acceptance in a school peer group can be experienced by students who are in some way perceived as 'different', such as newly arrived migrants and refugees with limited English, students with disabilities, students from a different religion, students with emotional or behavioural problems, and aggressive students. Particularly at risk of social isolation are students with severe intellectual disability and developmental delay (Bradburn et al., 2024; Carter et al., 2024). Teachers in classes that contain students who are seen as

DOI: 10.4324/9781003598671-10

'different' in any way should be giving due attention to fostering acceptance. Positive social relationships can be encouraged through carefully designated cooperative groupwork, partner assignments, peer tutoring, and extra-curricular social activities (e.g., Danniels & Pyle, 2023; Diaz-Garolera et al., 2022; Hymel & Katz, 2019; Nalls & Wickerd, 2023).

Children with learning difficulties or disabilities

Inclusive education settings create the potential opportunity for children with special needs to engage in many more social interactions with their peers—but their acceptance does not occur spontaneously. Most studies of inclusion have shown that merely placing a student with a disability in the mainstream will not automatically lead to his or her social integration into the peer group. The reasons for lack of acceptance include (1) many students without disabilities do not readily initiate friendly contact with those who have a disability or choose them as a partner; (2) students with disabilities do not automatically initiate friendly contact with other students, nor do they observe and copy positive social models that are around them; and (3) some teachers do not recognize the need to intervene to help promote students' positive social interactions (Sutherland et al., 2019).

Lack of social skill is often reported, particularly in students with emotional or behavioural disorders, autism, and attention-deficit/hyperactivity disorder, and these students are often marginalized in the peer group. These students clearly need targeted support to help them acquire the social skills necessary to maintain effective communication and interactions with others. One approach that seems to be promising for building self-esteem and social confidence is to engage these students in activities that require them to take responsibility for helping others, such as in peer tutoring or acting as a leader for younger students.

Certain social skills need to be developed before children reach school age and are placed in regular classrooms, so parents must take a very active role in teaching preschool children the essential behaviours they will need later to facilitate their social acceptance in school. Among the parent-implemented strategies recommended are using social stories that depict various children interacting positively, helping others, sharing, and 'being a nice person' (see Chapter 3). When social stories are told to young children or older students with intellectual disability, the story can also involve the use of puppets to act out target behaviours. It is also important to teach and practice specific pro-social skills such as friendly greeting, active listening, making eye contact, and following an adult's directions. These behaviours all represent important pivotal responses that are effective in many situations and that facilitate further social development.

In secondary schools, there may be a need to combine pro-social skills and empathy training alongside any other behaviour change programme that may be in operation for certain individuals (Dart et al., 2024; Hopkins et al., 2023). In particular, these interventions should aim to reduce aggression and substitute a better understanding of and consideration for others. The students need to be helped to strengthen their self-monitoring and self-control. This is particularly the case in countries where youth crime and public misbehaviour have become an increasing problem.

As well as possessing appropriate social skills, a socially competent student must avoid displaying negative characteristics that impede easy acceptance by others, such as a high level of irritating behaviour, impulsive reactions, aggression, temper tantrums, ignoring rules during play, and using abusive language. In many cases, these undesirable behaviours need to be eliminated or significantly reduced by behaviour modification and cognitive self-management (see Chapters 7 and 8).

Creating opportunities

A positive and supportive school environment is fundamental for the social development of all students and provides the foundation that enables them to feel 'connected' to the school community (Zurbriggen et al., 2023). Students feel safe and connected to their school when they perceive that adults and peers in the school care about them and value them as worthy individuals. Creating classroom environments where cooperation rather than competition is a dominant element is the first step in encouraging social development.

At least three conditions must be present in the classroom for positive social interaction and development of friendships among students with and without disabilities. These conditions are opportunity, continuity, and support.

- *Opportunity*: Students need to work and play in close proximity to others frequently enough for meaningful contacts to be maintained. Inclusive classrooms provide proximity and frequency of contact, and opportunities are increased when the teacher uses cooperative learning methods and groupwork as an adjunct to teacher directed instruction. Students must be involved on a daily basis in group activities that encourage social cooperation and mutual support. These arrangements create the best chances for students with disabilities to interact positively with their peers and imitate social behaviour of others.
- *Continuity*: When students are placed together as a class unit over a reasonable period of time (school term, school year), there is continuity from day to day in getting to know and like one another.
- *Support*: Some students need more help than others to make good-quality contact with members of the class in order to work and play with them. Teachers' observation of their own classes will reveal which students need this extra support—for example, noticing any student who appears to be

without friends at recess and lunch breaks and who seems unable to relate closely with classmates during lessons.

Facilitating social interaction

The following strategies can be used to increase the chances of positive social interaction for students with disabilities.

- Use cooperative groupwork frequently as part of your teaching approach and ensure that any student with a disability is appropriately paired with a supportive classmate. Each student needs to understand clearly his or her area of responsibility—for example, 'John, you can help Craig with his writing, then he can help you with the lettering for your title board.' More is said in the next section concerning the composition of groups.
- In primary schools, sometimes make increased use of non-academic tasks because a student with special needs can more easily contribute at his or her own level of competence (e.g., painting, table games, using glove puppets, and model-making).
- Use the class activity called *Circle Time* (Koczela & Carver, 2023) as an opportunity for students to discuss age-appropriate aspects of social behaviour, such as how to make friends, helping one another, working together, preventing bullying or teasing, building self-esteem, looking for strengths in other people, and showing interest in the ideas of others.
- Encourage other students to help any classmate with special needs—if that student welcomes such assistance. Often, young students are unaware of the ways in which they can help. The support they give should not be so great that it causes the target student to become overly dependent and passive. The goal is not to do everything for the student but rather help him or her become more confident and competent. Using *Circle of Friends* as a peer-group support strategy can be beneficial. The system operates by involving a small group of classmates as a natural source of support to help a student with difficulties solve any problems that may arise during the school day.
- Establish after-school clubs and activities that students with special needs can also join. This also has the benefit of helping taught social skills to be extended beyond the classroom setting.

A difficulty that can arise with any attempt to improve social interaction is that some students actually resent obvious intervention by a teacher to 'fix them up' with a friend. This is particularly the case with adolescents who are ultra-sensitive to peer group opinion. The reality is that teachers cannot really 'force' friendships to be established between students with special needs and others; they can only establish the conditions under which this may occur spontaneously.

Groupwork

Working and playing in groups are natural ways that students of any age and ability can mix socially and acquire important social and communication skills. Careful planning is always required if groupwork is to achieve the desired educational and social outcomes. Success depends on the composition of the groups and the nature of the tasks set for the students.

When utilizing groupwork as an inclusive strategy alongside teacher-directed instruction, it is important to consider the following basic principles.

- Groupwork must be used frequently enough for the students to become familiar with the routines. Infrequent groupwork results in children taking too long to settle down and a lesson can become chaotic.
- Size of the group is important. Often, having students work in pairs (such as at the computer) is a good starting point. Select the pairs carefully to avoid incompatibilities. The teacher may need to intervene to help a particular student gain a partner or to enter into a larger group activity.
- Seating and work arrangements are important. Group members should be in close proximity but still have personal space to work on materials without getting in each other's way.
- It is not enough merely to establish groups and to set them to work. Group members may have to be taught how to work efficiently together. There is great value in discussing openly with a class the best ways of working as a team and identifying the skills necessary to cooperate productively—listening to the views of others, following instructions, sharing, praising each other, and offering help. In the early stages, many groups can be helped to function efficiently if the teacher (or classroom assistant or a parent helper) works as one group member without dominating or controlling the activity. Helping each other and sharing materials are behaviours that must be modelled and reinforced.
- Choice of tasks for group work is extremely important. It is essential that all tasks have a very clear structure and purposes that are understood by all. When tasks are poorly defined or too complex, the session can become chaotic. Tasks have to be selected that actually require students to work collaboratively. Initially, there is merit in having all groups working on the same task or activity at the same time. This makes it much easier to prepare resources and manage time effectively. When several groups are undertaking quite different tasks, it becomes a major challenge for the teacher to manage the lesson.
- Teachers should monitor closely what is going on during group activities and must intervene when necessary to provide guidance, prompts, and suggestions and to praise examples of good teamwork.
- When groups contain students with special needs, it is vital that the specific tasks to be undertaken by these students be clearly delineated. It can be

useful to establish a system whereby the results are rewarded and praised for the way in which they have *worked together* positively and supportively. Under this structure, group members have a vested interest in ensuring that all members participate and learn, because the group's success depends on the achievement of all.

It is widely claimed that too many students spend out-of-school hours alone playing video games. However, access to digital technology has also created new opportunities in school for students to work together in pairs or groups. In what has become known as *technology-enhanced learning spaces*, students can collaborate to study given topics (McKay & Sridharan, 2024; Mendini & Peter, 2019). At the moment, this form of collaborative learning has been adopted mainly in tertiary education—but it has relevance also for the senior school years, particularly for extending gifted students and involving students with disabilities. The use of digital technology for teaching at distance was instrumental in coping when many schools were closed during the Covid-19 pandemic (2019–2022). Through the media of websites, apps, emails, and online chat rooms dedicated for a particular course of instruction, students can join discussions, ask and answer questions, work on a common activity, seek and share information, make suggestions, and assist one another with understanding a topic.

Social skills training

It is evident that early social skills training can be instrumental in reducing problems in later years. Social skills training involves explicit teaching of positive pro-social behaviours and social problem-solving skills to individuals who experience difficulties with social relationships. The aim of intervention is to strengthen existing skills and teach new behaviours that can be maintained and generalized to everyday situations. These skills training approaches are usually based on cognitive behavioural principles. Social skills training needs to be intensive and long-term in nature and promote maintenance, generalization, and transfer of new skills into the individual's daily life.

Studies indicate that when well-designed social skills training is implemented, the outcomes can be very positive for individuals who lack the skills (Cuncic, 2024). This is particularly the case if parent involvement is a key feature of any programme. One example of a specific intervention for social skills is the *Programme for the Education and Enrichment of Relational Skills* (PEERS®), useful with students on the autism spectrum (Tripathi et al., 2024; Veytsman et al., 2023). This programme can be adapted to meet the needs across the age range, from preschool to adulthood (Park et al., 2023; Ridgely et al., 2023).

The teaching of social skills involves setting out to establish the following behaviours. Each behaviour should be considered relative to its appropriateness for the particular student's age and specific needs in their current social environment. Typical skills and responses at the most basic level that may need to be taught include

- making eye contact
- greeting others by name
- gaining attention in appropriate ways
- knowing when to talk, what to talk about, and when to hold back
- initiating a conversation
- talking in a tone of voice that is acceptable
- maintaining conversations
- answering questions
- listening attentively to others and showing interest
- sharing with others
- saying 'please' and 'thank you'
- helping someone
- being able to collaborate in a group activity
- taking one's turn
- smiling
- accepting praise and giving praise
- accepting correction without anger or resentment
- making apologies when necessary
- coping with frustration and managing conflict.

The most meaningful settings in which to work on a child's skills are usually the classroom and schoolyard. This is a good example of 'situated learning' in that it can result in more rapid and permanent learning and maintenance of new behaviours. To a large extent, functional social skills, once established, are likely to be maintained by natural consequences—that is, they are repeated as a result of more satisfying interactions with peers.

Many students with special needs and disabilities can make friends quite easily if they have a pleasant personality and do not have irritating and disturbing behaviours; but others may have great difficulty due to lack of basic social skills. In some cases (e.g., students with autism spectrum disorders or those with emotional and behaviour disorders), it is necessary to provide additional intensive training beyond what is possible through normal everyday activities. This type of Tier 3 social skills intervention usually uses a combination of modelling, coaching, role playing, rehearsing, feedback, and counselling.

Intensive intervention for individual students in a clinical setting typically begins by showing the student the social skill to be taught. This may be done (according to the student's age and ability) by role play, using video, pictures, or a simulation using puppets. Teacher and student together discuss how a particular skill or behaviour helps positive social interaction to occur. The teacher may say, 'Look at the two girls happily sharing the picture cards. Tell me what they might be saying to each other.' 'Here is a boy joining this class for the very first time. What would you say to him to make him feel welcome?' The student then role-plays that situation and receives informative and descriptive feedback from the teacher. 'Good try! But you've not quite got it yet. You need to look directly at him while you speak. Try it again. That's better! You looked and smiled. Well done.' Providing feedback to the student via video recording may be appropriate in some situations. It is then necessary to find authentic opportunities for the same skill to be applied in the classroom and other natural settings. Later in the week, the teacher watches for instances of the student applying the skill at other times in the day without prompting and provides praise and reinforcement.

Training in social skills is usually not a matter of simply teaching a student something that is missing from his or her repertoire of behaviours but may also involve replacing an undesirable behaviour with a new alternative behaviour. This is often difficult because a behaviour that society regards as undesirable may actually be regarded by the individual concerned as very rewarding—for example, winning an argument through aggression or by taking possession of a coveted object by stealing. The negative behaviour has already proven to work well for the individual, and it acts as a powerful force that militates against any new pro-social skills we attempt to teach. The residual influence of pre-existing behaviours is one reason why new skills taught during training are often difficult to maintain.

Finally, it seems clear that poor social acceptance is often an accompaniment to poor academic achievement in class. Unless achievement within the curriculum can also be improved, social adjustment and acceptance may remain problems for some students. With this in mind, attention in the chapters that follow are focused on evidence-based approaches for intervention in the area of literacy and numeracy.

Emerging Issues

The above basic social skills have remained relevant over the years, but the passage of time brings new and different influences that can affect social life. At different ages and stages, different issues emerge that impact upon social development and relationships. These issues during adolescence and early adulthood include consideration of how male students regard and interact with female students (Setty, 2021). In recent years, the specific topic of 'consent' has emerged in mainly Western societies as very important in the context of appropriate and acceptable intimacy (DeSipio & Pallotti, 2024; Hayes et al., 2024). Ewing et al. (2022, p. 3) have claimed that 'sexual harassment and assault are distressingly common occurrences in middle school settings.'

Other topics that merit inclusion when discussing social, moral, and behavioural codes of conduct are teenage abuse of drugs, 'vaping' (use of substitute cigarettes), communicating with strangers online, gang behaviour and other antisocial activities, and domestic violence. Esposito et al. (2021) have observed that helping adolescents think about the harm of some of these behaviours can play a key role in influencing their own decision not to engage in such conduct. If these contemporary topics are to be tackled, it must always be in age- and maturity-appropriate ways, and sensitivity is required since some students may be having direct experience within their own families.

The next chapter begins to explore commonsense methods for teaching young students to read. The coverage extends to methods for assisting struggling readers.

Resources

Online

- Useful discussions on training social skills can be found at http://www.minddisorders.com/Py-Z/Social-skills-training.html and https://www.verywellmind.com/social-skills-4157216
- A list of children's books useful for teaching social skills can be located online at https://www.pinterest.com/jillkuzma/books-i-love-for-teaching-social-skills/
- Additional information on *Circle of Friends* can be obtained from https://www.friendshipcircle.org/blog/2012/01/11/circle-of-friends-a-type-of-person-centered-planning/
- *Social skills training for kids: Top resources for teachers.* https://positivepsychology.com/social-skills-for-kids/
- *How to create a friendly classroom environment.* https://www.thoughtco.com/non-threatening-welcome-classroom-environment-3111328

Print

Baker, J. (2023). *Social skills training for children and adolescents with autism and social communication differences.* Arlington, TX: Future Horizons.

Daniels, N. (2019). *Social skills activities for kids: 50 fun exercises for making friends, talking and listening, and understanding social rules.* Emeryville, CA: Rockridge Press.

Gueldner, B., Feuerborn, L.L., & Merrell, K.W. (2020). *Social and emotional learning in the classrooms* (2nd ed.). New York: Guilford Press.

Plevin, R. (2023). *The social skills workbook for kids: Games, activities and exercises to help children make friends and understand social rules.* Eden Valley, Cumbria, UK: Life Raft Media Ltd.

Shapiro, L. (2004). *101 ways to teach children social skills: Activity* book. Bureau for at Risk Youth.

Chapter 10

Intervention for reading difficulties

Reading as an essential skill

Students who find reading difficult fall quickly behind their age peers in most areas of the curriculum; and failure to master reading then undermines their confidence, motivation, and mental health. This situation leads eventually to disengagement from learning and a growing belief that reading is simply too difficult and to be avoided. Early identification and intervention are absolutely essential for at-risk children, so that they are helped to make better progress before detrimental feelings of anxiety and helplessness set in (Fishstrom et al., 2024; Ramirez et al., 2019). For several decades in the US, Australia, and the UK, weakness in reading has remained the principal reason for the high number of referrals for additional support in schools, and poor overall standards in literacy continue to be reported in these countries.

Learning to read is a reasonably complex task, and it is not surprising that children with intellectual or sensory impairments and those with a language disorder would have difficulty coping with print. Students learning English as a second or additional language can also have difficulties with reading and spelling. However, the data from surveys of literacy find that many students who a free from any of these disabilities or problems make up the vast majority of struggling readers in primary and secondary schools. It is common to blame the time students spend playing online games or other activities with digital technology for less time in developing literacy skills, but the blame may well lie with their schools and with teacher training.

A major gap exists between what research has shown to be the essential components of beginning reading instruction and what teachers actually do in kindergartens and primary schools. Although universities and colleges do at least now mention in passing that young children need to learn skills for decoding words, their trainee teachers are rarely observed and assessed on their ability to implement lessons and activities based on phonics (Meeks & Stephenson, 2020; National Council on Teacher Quality, 2023). This seems akin to sending out surgeons who have received only a lecture or two on how to remove an appendix but have never had any supervised experience in doing

DOI: 10.4324/9781003598671-11

so. What is needed is more in line with the *Reading Apprenticeship*® model (Institute of Education Sciences, 2023), where novice teachers are coached in how to teach the beginning stages of reading by a person with proven expertise (see "Online" list in the "Resources" section). Much more needs to be done to ensure that young teachers *can actually teach* fundamental reading skills (Dennis et al., 2024; Gengler, 2023; Pilgrim, 2022). It is also essential that any teachers in the learning support role be able to demonstrate this effective teaching. Standards will not improve until all teachers are using *evidence-based methods* and all schools devote *sufficient time each day* to reading within a comprehensive literacy programme that also teaches effective strategies for comprehending, enjoying, and using text.

Tier 1 literacy teaching

Research studies over several decades have confirmed that an effective Tier 1 literacy programme for all beginners must incorporate listening for sounds in spoken words (phoneme awareness), having letter knowledge for phonic decoding, recognizing the most commonly used words by sight, building a rich vocabulary through listening to stories read aloud, and developing age-appropriate comprehension strategies (Daniel et al., 2024; Hiebert, 2023; Rice et al., 2024; Webber et al., 2024).

As students move from the beginning stages of reading, decoding and sight vocabulary building will become less a focus of attention, and higher-order processes involved in comprehending and criticizing text become very important (Sanders & Garwood, 2022). Reading programmes must also incorporate many activities to encourage aural and oral language development and vocabulary growth. Enrichment activities should encourage careful listening, establish familiarity with language patterns (particularly important for students learning English as a second language), and introduce books that foster children's interest and enjoyment in reading. In 2023, the Department for Education in England updated its *Reading Framework*, reinforcing all the above components and stressing the importance of basic phonics in the early stages (DfE, 2023).

The Tier 1 teaching method supported most by research involves instructing all beginners in letter knowledge and decoding skills, using what is known as 'systematic synthetic phonics'. This method provides beginners (and older students with learning difficulties) with a system for identifying any unfamiliar words they encounter—proving to them that learning to read does not involve trying to memorize the image of every single word. Young children cannot really become independent readers unless they master the alphabetic code and can use it to decode new words. It is absolutely essential that all teachers providing beginning-stage literacy instruction be thoroughly trained in how to use this method in order to reduce children's later failure rates in UK, the US, and Australia (Flynn et al., 2021). It is rightly claimed that '[h]igh-quality professional development can lead to increased and sustained implementation of evidence-based practices' (Dennis et al., 2024, p. 77). Evidence for the vital importance of sound teacher education is also being found in other countries (e.g., Counihan et al., 2022).

For the period from 1970 to 1999, general reading instruction at Tier 1 in most primary schools tended to be fairly unstructured and based on a belief that children will learn to read simply by engaging with print every day and with a little guidance from an adult. This 'whole-language approach' tended to rely too much on children acquiring decoding skills simply from immersion in stories. It is now recognized that most children make much better progress if phonic decoding (sounding and blending) is explicitly taught and practiced.

While decoding ability and word recognition are clearly essential for reading, children must also be able to understand the information they are decoding in a text. Any early reading programme must contain not only explicit teaching of phonic skills but also instruction in age-appropriate comprehension activities (Daniel et al., 2024). The effective teaching of reading comprehension must encourage critical thinking to evaluate ideas and propositions within a story or factual report. The explicit teaching of comprehension strategies can best be achieved through direct explanation, modelling by the teacher, and abundant guided practice. It is preferable to apply strategy training to authentic text (books, newspaper reports, magazine articles, and online documents) rather than to contrived exercises. Comprehension and study-skill strategies can also be taught through dialogue between teacher and students, working together to extract meaning from a text. Dialogue allows students and teachers to share their thoughts about the topic of the text and to learn from the successful strategies used by others. The teacher may encourage her students to challenge the accuracy of stated facts in the text, and require them to go back to re-read a passage, or seek help from others in interpreting certain details. These are strategies that need to be taught explicitly to all students at Tier 1 (Wang & Li, 2019). Dialogue between teacher and student also serves a diagnostic purpose by allowing a teacher to appraise the students' existing strategies used for comprehending and summarizing texts.

Essential comprehension strategies that need to be developed at Tier 1 include

- gaining an overview of a topic by previewing text and illustrations before reading
- generating questions about the material
- reading the text carefully and reading it again if necessary
- locating the main idea in a paragraph
- making a mental note of key points
- in narrative texts, predicting what may happen

- in expository text, looking for facts and linking them, noting any new terms, relating new terms or concepts to prior knowledge and experience, and looking for possible causes and effects
- rehearsing, summarizing, or paraphrasing the content.

Deriving meaning from different forms of text—narrative, expository, and informational—helps students acquire a broader range of cognitive strategies. Comprehension is naturally an across-the-curriculum competency, and all subject teachers in secondary schools would benefit their students if they integrate 'reading for meaning' into their own subject. Different genres of text require the teaching of specific strategies for processing the types of information and styles of language used—for example, in a science textbook vs. a history book or novel.

Reading intervention at Tier 2

Under the Response to Intervention model described in Chapter 1, students already known to have difficulties, and others who struggle with Tier 1 reading instruction during the first year of school, are very soon given additional teaching in groups of up to five students. These groups may be organized under a withdrawal system, rather than attempted within the inclusive class setting, and may be taught by a teaching assistant under the teacher's direction. Some extreme exponents of full inclusion argue that even this system causes unfortunate separation of one group of students from their peers, but it has become the default arrangement that many inclusive schools now accept.

Most effective programmes at Tier 2 for beginners usually target activities to build phonemic awareness, establish sound–letter relationships, introduce word families, and provide daily reading practice with appropriate texts to increase fluency and comprehension. The progress of students receiving Tier 2 support is closely monitored, and when any individual begins to read at the standard expected for his or her age, the additional support is phased out. It is also essential to identify any student with significant learning difficulties who must be immediately referred on for Tier 3 intensive tutoring (Jaeger, 2024).

Withdrawing students for tuition in small groups can achieve a great deal, but it is also essential that the regular classroom literacy programme be differentiated in terms of reading materials, skills instruction, and assignments to allow weaker readers a greater measure of success in that setting. Failure to differentiate the regular class programme frequently results in loss of achievement gains when students no longer receive extra assistance.

It is also essential that intervention at Tier 2 (small groups) and Tier 3 (individual) not only involve intensive re-teaching and guided practice of reading skills but also address a student's emotional reactions to failure and loss of motivation that may have developed in the past. Activities must be conducted in therapeutic ways that put students at ease and rebuild their confidence to make a new effort.

Research evidence supports the effectiveness of early intervention at Tier 2 for reducing the need for a more intensive support later for some students (Morrison et al., 2020). However, several weaknesses that are evident in many of these Tier 2 and Tier 3 systems include using untrained volunteers to do the teaching, having too few sessions of instruction each week, and lack of meaningful links with the Tier 1 class programme (McDaniel et al., 2024).

Using tutors

Skilled and experienced tutors for literacy can significantly raise students' achievement levels and confidence, and the evidence suggests that efficient tutoring yields good effects (Lindo et al., 2018; Morris, 2023). All tutors need to be trained to carry out the work (Pletcher et al., 2023a). However, often through lack of resources, some schools are tending to use unqualified parent-volunteers and classroom aides who have not been specifically trained as tutors for Tier 2 or Tier 3 interventions. Any volunteer tutor must always work under the direction of the teacher and implement activities that have been selected by the teacher to meet the student's diagnosed learning needs.

Tutors must be knowledgeable about explicit teaching of decoding skills and also how to encourage reading fluency and comprehension. Above all, tutors need to appreciate the vital contribution that active engagement, time-on-task, and *successful practice* play in facilitating students' improvement. It is also essential that tutors be aware of how to function most effectively in their role of empathic supporter. For example, they need to know how to break a reading task down into manageable steps, how to give descriptive praise and encouragement, and how to provide corrective feedback in a positive way. A tutor must always be supportive rather than critical and didactic. Often, well-meaning tutors talk too much; they need to talk less but listen more to their students.

In an ideal situation, tutors should receive constructive feedback from the teacher on their tutoring skills and their tutor–student relationship (Waltz, 2019). Gaining supervised experience as a reading tutor for individuals or small groups is one way during pre-service that trainee teachers can gain valuable skills and insights for later application (Pletcher et al., 2023b). This should perhaps become a common feature of all early childhood and primary school teachers' training (Carter, 2023a).

There are several useful strategies that can be taught to tutors, some of which can be applied at both Tier 2 and Tier 3. One such strategy is known as 'Pause, Prompt, Praise' (PPP). When a student encounters an unfamiliar word, instead of the tutor stepping in immediately and supplying the word, he or she waits for about 5 seconds to allow time for the student to recognize or decode the word. If the student is not successful, the tutor provides a prompt, perhaps suggesting that the child sound out the letters or think of the meaning of the passage. When the word is identified, the student is praised very briefly ('Good. You got it.'). If the student cannot read the word even after prompting, the tutor quickly supplies it, and the student re-reads the sentence.

It is important to point out that PPP can be used to good effect across a wide range of other situations where individuals are learning a new skill or behaviour (see *constant time delay* in Chapter 2). An example of time delay in the beginning reading stage is when a tutor displays a word and asks the student 'Please say this word', then waits for 5 seconds to allow the student to think and respond. If the response is correct, the teaching sequence moves on; if incorrect, the teacher provides the correct answer and asks the question again. The student then responds with the correct answer. Constant time delay has been used effectively with a broad range of students with learning difficulties (Borton & Herzberg, 2023; Horn et al., 2023).

Selecting text materials for Tier 2

The use of graded reading books with decodable text has been found highly appropriate in reading interventions (e.g., Summers, 2000) and also useful when working with students learning English as a second language. During the 1980s and 1990s, books for beginners that contained a high proportion of decodable words were shunned by whole-language practitioners. It was felt that the books presented unnatural language—for example, 'A dog and a frog sit on a log.' Some teachers still resist the use of such books; but times have changed and many publishers have returned to producing vocabulary-controlled books that help beginners build confidence and automaticity in applying decoding skills. With this confidence, they soon become ready to read books that are not controlled for vocabulary.

Specific interventions for students at Tier 2

Fresh Start is a Tier 2 literacy intervention for at-risk students entering secondary school with poor reading and writing skills. Students are grouped for instruction according to their level of reading ability, and they receive a very systematic and rigorous teaching of phonics, usually three times per week for 33 weeks. A large-scale evaluation of the programme concluded that *Fresh Start* shows considerable promise as an effective catch-up intervention (Gorard et al., 2016).

Rapid Phonics is a synthetic phonics intervention to improve decoding skills and reading fluency in young students in the first six years of primary school (Pearson Publishing, 2024). The focus is on mastery of basic phonics, modelled reading, independent reading, and reading at home. The programme is usually implemented for one-and-a-half hours of tuition per week for groups of four students. Use is made of graded decodable books, and digital resources are now an important component of the programme.

Specific programmes for intervention at Tier 3

Students with the most severe reading difficulties need to receive intensive individualized teaching on a daily basis, usually outside of the whole-class setting. An individualized approach, often guided by a formal individual education plan, enables the pace of instruction to be regulated carefully, and specific techniques such as multisensory and multimedia support can be used to help a student remember letter-to-sound correspondences and sight words (Seidl et al., 2024). One of the key benefits of Tier 3 teaching is that it greatly increases the opportunities for a student to actively respond during instruction and receive feedback. Research has found that more opportunity to respond successfully in individual tutoring is associated with positive improvements (Johnson et al., 2023; Martin et al., 2018; Scott, 2023).

It is, of course, possible for teachers to devise appropriate individual tutoring programmes for students with learning difficulties, after their strengths and weaknesses have been identified. However, in recent years, several structured intervention programmes have emerged. These programmes include *Reading Recovery®*, *Success for All*, *QuickSmart*, *MULTILIT*, and *Reading Rescue*.

Reading Recovery®

Reading Recovery® (RR) is an early intervention programme first developed in New Zealand in the 1970s by the late Marie Clay. It can be described as a supplemental programme to assist young primary school students' reading and writing skills through one-on-one tutoring, and the content of each lesson is based on observations of the student's strengths and weaknesses (IES, 2023). It is now used in many other parts of the world, including America, Canada, Australia, and England. RR involves intensive individual tutoring, but a few schools have adopted aspects of the model for small group teaching at Tier 2. *Every Child a Reader Project* (2005–2008) in the UK utilized RR as the main intervention. Children identified as having reading difficulties after one year in school are placed in the programme to receive individual daily tuition from a teacher specifically trained in the approach. The children receive this individual support for approximately 15 to 20 weeks.

In a RR lesson, optimum use is made of the available time and students are kept fully on task. A typical session includes seven activities:

- quick revisiting of a familiar book
- re-reading of a book introduced the previous day
- minor attention to phonics through simple spelling using plastic letters
- writing of a dictated or prepared short story

- sentence building and reconstruction from the story
- introduction of a new book
- guided reading of the new book.

The texts selected for use in RR are graded according to the child's reading ability to ensure a high success rate. Frequent re-reading of familiar stories boosts confidence and fluency. Teachers keep detailed records of children's oral reading errors and use these to target the knowledge and strategies a child still needs to learn. The intention is that the teacher or tutor operating the RR session will provide positive guidance that helps a young reader move forward in his or her zone of proximal development. RR, when correctly implemented, can be effective in raising young children's reading achievement and confidence. It is claimed that at least 80 per cent of children who undergo the full series of lessons can then read at the class average level or better. However, RR is not without its critics.

Children's individual responses to RR vary, and long-term impact on a student's reading and writing remains uncertain. Some critics claim that far too little attention is devoted to explicit instruction in phonics and decoding for children with major weaknesses in this area. In part, this is due to the fact that RR was created during the era when the whole-language approach held sway and phonics teaching was regarded as having only a very minor role in reading proficiency. It has also been noted that, in reality, only a few RR teachers actually base their teaching on carefully observed characteristics of their student (Arrow et al., 2022), and perhaps this accounts for the reports that the approach fails to meet the needs of children with the most severe reading problems (Serry et al., 2014). Other difficulties associated with RR include the need to organize regular time in the school day for some children to be taught individually and the need to provide appropriately trained personnel to give the daily tuition. The high cost of such a labour-intensive one-to-one intervention remains an unresolved issue.

For a detailed evaluation of RR by What Works Clearinghouse (2023), see the "Online" list in the "Resources" section.

Success for All

Success for All is an approach devised by Robert Slavin and his associates (Slavin et al., 2009; Slavin & Madden, 2013) with much to offer at all three tiers of the Response to Intervention model. It is a comprehensive whole-school programme intended to improve literacy teaching and prevent reading failure. Originating in the US, *Success for All* has been adopted successfully in several other countries (e.g., Hingstman et al., 2021). The reading and language lessons operate daily for 90 minutes, providing primary students with intensive instruction and practice. One unique feature of *Success for All* is that junior classes throughout the school usually group for reading at the same time, and children go to different classrooms based on their current reading ability level.

Success for All places emphasis on direct phonics instruction (segmenting words and sounding and blending phonemes). Equal importance is placed on students reading meaningful texts and self-monitor for comprehension. In an attempt to avoid the common lack of transfer of taught skills in tutoring sessions back to the student's regular classroom, *Success for All* teachers also participate in the mainstream reading programme and assist with reading lessons in the regular classroom. This helps ensure that one-to-one tutoring is closely linked to the mainstream curriculum, not divorced from it.

Success for All spans school years from kindergarten to grade 8 and also provides training and follow-up support for teachers and tutors. The programme is widely used in the US, where the *Common Core State Standards* are now incorporated into the approach (Slavin & Madden, 2013). Research evidence in general has supported *Success for All* as an effective intervention model. The *Best Evidence Encyclopedia* states, "*Success for All* has strong evidence of effectiveness for struggling readers. Across nine qualifying studies, the weighted mean effect size was +0.55" (0.55 represents a significantly positive effect).

Catch Up® Literacy

The National Literacy Trust in the UK is an independent charity that seeks to improve the opportunities for children, young people, and adults to master the literacy skills they need in life. *Catch Up® Literacy* is one approach that the Trust provides, and another is *Early Words Together*, designed to empower families to enrich the language skills of their 3- to 4-year-old children.

Catch Up® Literacy is described as a structured, 15-minute, one-to-one intervention provided at least twice a week for struggling readers. A book-based approach is used to develop and strengthen word recognition, phonic decoding, and comprehension. Sessions must be conducted by a teacher or *trained* teaching assistant.

For more details, see the "Online" list in the "Resources" section.

QuickSmart

QuickSmart is Tier 3 intervention implemented in Australia (Graham et al., 2007). It targets middle-years students (age 10 to 13 years) who exhibit ongoing difficulty acquiring functional literacy and numeracy. The reading component focuses on improving students' automaticity in common word recognition and on increasing fluency in reading connected text. Teaching focuses on mastery of sets of words, beginning with high-usage three- and four-letter words and moving later to more complex and demanding words. In addition to practicing the words in isolation, they are incorporated in two or more passages of connected text on various topics. Lesson format for *QuickSmart* is designed to ensure maximum engagement and a high success rate for students during each 30-minute session. Students are taught in pairs and the programme is normally implemented three times a week for 30 weeks. Each lesson involves brief revision of work covered in the previous session, a number of guided practice activities, independent practice, and games and worksheet activities. Strategy instruction and concept development are seen as key components of each lesson. The programme has undergone regular evaluation and revision. Results from several studies indicate that *QuickSmart* students are able to narrow the gap between their performance and that of their higher-achieving peers.

MULTILIT

The name *MULTILIT* stands for *Making up Lost Time in Literacy* (Wheldall et al., 2017). This comprehensive Tier 2 or Tier 3 approach to teaching low-progress readers (age 7 or above) addresses five key areas necessary for effective reading instruction, namely phonemic awareness, phonic decoding, fluency, vocabulary, and comprehension. It has three strands covering word attack (phonics), sight words, and reinforced reading (practice reading of meaningful text). The teaching approach within *MULTILIT* draws on evidence from research into the most powerful strategies to help readers who are significantly behind their peers.

The student is given a placement test at the beginning of intervention to ensure that he or she is placed at the correct level within the programme. It is claimed that a student undertaking *MULTILIT* can make 15 months' progress in word recognition in two terms of instruction. The programme is tutor- or teacher-led and should be delivered at least three to four times a week. Sight vocabulary is targeted, with particular reference to a list of 200 key words. Students' rapid automatic recognition of sight words helps develop their reading fluency. The other key component in the programme is termed 'reinforced reading', using books chosen carefully to be at the appropriate instructional level to enable a student to apply and generalize knowledge and skills.

The same providers have also devised *MINILIT* (Meeting Individual Needs in Literacy) (Reynolds et al., 2021; Wheldall et al., 2017). This involves a 15-week tutoring programme with groups of three to six students working daily for one hour with a tutor. Each session involves time spent on phonemic awareness, sight vocabulary, word-attack skills, text reading, and story time. The intervention paves the way for smooth entry into the classroom reading programme or into *MULTILIT* for those still needing support.

Supplementary tutoring strategies and activities

Repeated Reading

Repeated Reading is a well-known procedure used to increase fluency, accuracy, expression, and confidence in students who are already under way with reading. The procedure is equally useful in primary and secondary schools and has a place in adult literacy interventions (Kostewicz & Kubina, 2020). The approach has been found effective with students learning English as a second or additional language, secondary school students with poor reading ability, and various groups of students with learning difficulties. A particular advantage of Repeated Reading is that it can be practiced at home as well as at school (Hindin & Steiner, 2024). Most recently, Repeated Reading has been included in some digital reading apps to good effect (Alqahtani, 2023; Whitney & Ackerman, 2023).

Repeated Reading simply requires readers to practice reading a short passage aloud until their accuracy rate is above 95 per cent and the material can be read aloud fluently. The teacher first models the reading (while the student follows in the text) and then spends a few minutes making sure that the student fully understands the material. The student then practices reading the same material aloud, and corrective feedback is provided by the teacher if necessary. The student continues to practice until nearly perfect and finally records the reading on audiotape. When the recording is played back, the student hears a fluent performance, equal in standard to the reading of even the most competent student in class. This provides an important boost to the student's confidence. Greater fluency can also lead to improved comprehension because the reader is expending less mental effort on identifying each word.

Multisensory approaches

Learning through the senses, particularly touch, is basic in much of early learning and helps assimilation and retention of information (Seidl et al., 2024). The use of tactile materials for facilitating learning of sight words and letter-to-sound correspondences can have a definite role in Tier 3 interventions (Dixon, 2022; Gassid, 2023). Multisensory methods have been successful with students with intellectual disability, autism, and visual impairment who cannot easily remember letters, words, or numbers. The approach has a long history in special and remedial education, dating back to the work of Orton (1937) and later to Gillingham and Stillman (1956).

The abbreviation VAKT is often used to indicate that multisensory methods combine visual, auditory, kinaesthetic, and tactile modalities to support learning and memory. The typical VAKT approach for beginners or for those with a cognitive disability involves the learner in finger-tracing over an enlarged word, or drawing it in the air, while saying the word, hearing the word, and seeing the visual stimulus. For older learners, writing a word or using a keyboard and typing a target word several times while watching it appear on the screen are also multisensory activities.

The best-known multisensory method is the Fernald VAK Approach, which involves the following steps:

- student selects a particular word that he or she wants to learn
- teacher or tutor writes the word in blackboard-size cursive writing on a card and together they pronounce the word

- student finger-traces over the word, saying each syllable as it is traced
- this process is repeated until the learner feels capable of writing the word from memory
- when a word is mastered, it is filed away in a card index box for later revision.

It can be argued that multisensory approaches using several channels of input may help a learner integrate at a neurological level what is seen with what is heard, whether it be a letter or a word. On the other hand, VAKT approaches may succeed where other methods have failed because they *actively engage* the learner and *focus attention* more intently on the learning task. Whatever the reason for its effectiveness, this teaching approach involving vision, hearing, articulation, and movement usually does result in improved assimilation and retention.

Games and apparatus

In the early stages of any literacy support programme, it is helpful to incorporate materials that hold a student's attention most effectively and provide additional opportunities for practising important skills. Games and word-building equipment such as plastic letters, magnet boards, and flashcards can be used as adjuncts to any literacy intervention. Games provide an excellent opportunity for learners to engage in practice of material that might otherwise be perceived as boring and dull. For example, games provide an enjoyable way of discovering and reinforcing letter–sound relationships, word building, and word recognition. A game should always contribute to the objectives for the lesson—for example, by developing listening skills, strengthening phoneme awareness, reinforcing letter knowledge, and building vocabulary—rather than simply providing a distraction from 'real' learning. The use of games may also be seen as non-threatening and thus serve a therapeutic purpose within a group or individual teaching situation.

Digital technology and reading

Increasingly, digital technology has entered the literacy learning domain through motivating games and apps that help students learn and apply essential decoding, spelling, and reading skills (Ronimus et al., 2019). Handheld communication devices and e-learning apps have added considerably to the non-print media that can be incorporated into a literacy programme. The additional practice afforded by digital games is absolutely essential for children who learn at a slower rate or who are poorly motivated. In the home situation, digital materials can aid literacy development because children can work alone or with parent support on early reading and writing skills. Parents who are adequately computer literate can help their children search for, read, and interpret information from Internet for homework or personal interest.

Advances in information and communication technology have created many new and interesting ways for students with learning difficulties to engage in literacy activities for authentic purposes—for example, through sending and receiving emails, texting, surfing the Internet, using e-readers, accessing interactive reading websites, social networking, and creating blogs. Evidence supports the value of digital technology as a contemporary medium for language and literacy development and for participating in today's digital world (Scholes, 2024). A common finding is that using digital technology can be a very valuable approach for enhancing reading skills, with significant improvements in achievement, engagement rates, and attitude.

The National Literacy Trust have described children's use of digital technology as 'a polarizing topic' due to community concerns over some children's excessive use of screen time and their access to subject matter that is not age-appropriate. However, the Trust reached the conclusion that digital technology can play a useful role in supporting early communication, language, and literacy by offering new learning opportunities. The main supplementary role of technology is as a component in 'blended teaching' that combines face-to-face classes with independent (but guided) use of computer or handheld device to study the associated curriculum material.

For the various reports that the National Literacy Trust produced on this topic, see the "Online" list in the "Resources" section.

The next chapter expands the discussion of literacy by considering methods for assisting the development of writing skills.

Resources

Online

- Reading Recovery. https://eric.ed.gov/?q=Reading+Recovery+%c2% ae+&id=ED629013
- *Catch Up®Literacy.*https://literacytrust.org.uk/primary/targeted-approaches-literacy-catch-/catch-up-literacy/
- National Literacy Trust Reports. https://literacytrust.org.uk/information/ what-is-literacy/literacy-and-digital-technology/
- DfE (Department for Education: UK). (2023). *The Reading Framework.* https://assets.publishing.service.gov.uk/media/65830c10ed3c34000 d3bfcad/The_reading_framework.pdf
- Education Endowment Foundation. *Improving literacy in secondary schools.* https://educationendowmentfoundation.org.uk/education-evidence/ guidance-reports/literacy-ks3-ks4
- Gov/UK. *Literacy and numeracy catch-up strategies.* https://assets. publishing.service.gov.uk/government/uploads/system/uploads/ attachment_data/file/739722/literacy_and_numeracy_catch_up_ strategies_amended_july-2018_amended_10.09.18.pdf

- Literacy Trust. *Evidence-based interventions.* https://literacytrust.org.uk/programmes/interventions/
- Institute of Education Sciences. (2023). *Reading Apprenticeship®*. What Works Clearing House. https://files.eric.ed.gov/fulltext/ED625919.pdf

Print

Blevins, W. (2024). *Differentiating phonics instruction for maximum impact: How to scaffold whole-group instruction so all students can access grade-level content.* Thousand Oaks, CA: Corwin.

DeVries, B.A. (2023). *Literacy assessment and intervention for classroom teachers* (6th ed.). New York: Routledge.

Dymock, S., & Nicholson, T. (2024), *Teaching literacy effectively in the modern classroom for ages 5 to 8.* London & New York: Routledge.

National Council on Teacher Quality. (2023b). *Reading foundations: Technical Report.* New York: NCTQ.

Scanlon, D.M., Anderson, K.L., Barnes, E.M., & Sweeney, J.M. (2024). *Early literacy instruction and intervention: The interactive strategies approach* (3rd ed.). New York: Guilford Press.

Watkins, P. (2021). *Teaching and developing reading skills.* Cambridge, UK: Cambridge University Press.

Chapter 11

Problems with writing

The importance of writing ability

Writing is one of the most complex skills that students must learn, and it is not surprising that some individuals have difficulty achieving proficiency. They may be able to read quite well, but reading and writing are complementary but separate processes. While there is, of course, overlap between reading and writing, so that one skill set can support acquisition of the other, some aspects of reading and writing tend to draw upon different areas of knowledge and skill and are even controlled by different areas of the brain (Hand et al., 2024; Kim, 2022).

Writing can be a problem for individuals of any ability level, but those most likely to have difficulties are students with cognitive impairment, developmental language disorder, or a specific learning disability (*dysgraphia*) (Brimo et al., 2023; Kalenjuk et al., 2022; Williams & Larkin, 2023). Students who are struggling to learn English as a second or additional language can also have major problems with writing. Individuals of any age with significant difficulties associated with writing tend to display the following weaknesses:

- possessing no strategy for planning, executing and revising their written work
- difficulty generating relevant and coherent ideas
- too little time spent in thinking before beginning to write
- inability to decide upon an appropriate structure for writing on a given topic
- slowness and inefficiency in executing the mechanical aspects of writing or keyboarding
- many false starts and deletions of each attempt
- limited output in the available time
- no feeling of accomplishment.

A student who has problems writing will experience no satisfaction pursuing the task and will try to avoid writing whenever possible. Avoidance then reduces opportunities for practice, and lack of practice results in no improvement.

DOI: 10.4324/9781003598671-12

The student has lost confidence and self-esteem in relation to writing and has developed a negative attitude accompanied by learned helplessness. Difficulties in writing are evident even in some adults. The negative and harmful impact that this problem has on an individual's confidence, self-esteem, emotional well-being, and quality of life is illustrated very clearly in a TV documentary series *Lost for Words*, broadcast on the SBS channel in Australia in 2022 and 2024. For more details, see the "Online" list in the "Resources" section at the end of the chapter.

The challenge for a teacher is (a) to motivate these students to want to write and (b) to provide them with enough support to ensure increased success. It is important to give support that can restore confidence and motivation and make students feel more successful as writers. Fortunately, studies have clearly indicated that students with learning difficulties can be helped to improve in all areas of writing, and teaching approaches to achieve this improvement are discussed in this chapter.

Competencies involved in writing

The creation of written text involves two key areas of competence: (i) lower-order transcription skills such as handwriting or keyboarding and spelling and (ii) self-regulated planning for creating, sequencing, and expressing ideas through effectively composed sentences (Sumner et al., 2024). The more fluent and automatic that lower-order skills become, the greater will be the cognitive capacity available to the writer for thinking, composing, and revising. The demands of written expression include generating ideas around a set topic, organizing these ideas into a logical sequence, constructing effective sentences, using correct grammar and vocabulary, and writing in a style appropriate for a particular audience. These are extremely difficult competencies for some students to develop, because as well as needing the mechanical skills for writing or keyboarding, they draw heavily upon an individual's background experiences, general knowledge, depth of vocabulary, imagination, and sense of audience.

Teaching writing at Tier 1

Schools have always recognized the responsibility they have to guide students to become proficient writers. The traditional teacher-led approach was to implement daily highly structured activities devoted to grammar rules, sentence construction, paragraphing, punctuation, and spelling. Direct guidance was also given on how to write specific styles of text (e.g., letter to a friend, application for a job, formal essay, and report on a fieldtrip). The approach focused on providing students with the relevant knowledge, skills, and strategies needed to be a successful writer in everyday life and to ensure adequate practice to result in confidence and competence. This was the approach used in most schools until the 1980s.

Eventually, by 1980, the traditional skills-based approach was being criticized by progressive educators and some academics as being too structured and prescriptive, limiting creative expression and not really catering for student diversity (McKnight, 2023). As a result, the traditional approach was gradually replaced by a student-centred method termed *process writing* (Graves, 1983). Focus shifted from direct teaching of skills to encouraging students to experiment freely with ideas for writing. This involved producing several drafts of material, sharing these with teachers and peers, and then polishing a final draft using their feedback and encouragement (Keen, 2022). In this approach, any teaching of grammar rules and conventions occurs informally through individualized feedback. The accepted wisdom became that teachers must never teach isolated skills but instead should support students' efforts as they write freely for authentic purposes. The belief seems to be that students will become good writers if they simply engage in authentic writing every day and receive encouragement. This process writing approach, with its student-centred learning principles, became a major component within the prevailing whole-language approach to literacy.

A gradual shift back to a more skills-based approach to writing has occurred over the past two decades. The national curricula introduced in several countries all specify precisely the writing standard that students at various ages are expected to achieve. These standards have become criteria for use in any mandated testing that accompanies the curriculum. The standards have given teachers a clearer idea of what students should be achieving in writing and thus help to identify those who are having difficulties. Concern began to emerge that too many students were not reaching adequate proficiency in key literacy skills, perhaps because teachers were not directly and systematically covering the 'nuts and bolts' of writing skills needed to produce cohesive text. According to Pytash et al. (2023, p. 305), the skill of writing is 'under taught in middle and high schools.' It is now recognized that while teachers using process writing often assign stimulating and creative topics for students to talk and write about, this may not be sufficient, particularly for students who need direct guidance in the basic skills.

The stage seems to have been reached now in Britain, Australia, and the US where more priority is being given at Tier 1 to embedding skills-based teaching while still retaining students' freedom to experiment with their ideas in writing. The current view is that a balanced approach to teaching writing must include all necessary direct instruction and practice in essential composing and revising skills. In other words, teachers must teach students *how to write* rather than expecting the skills to be acquired simply by doing more writing. This situation is parallel to the view that the whole-language approach is never 'whole' unless it includes explicit instruction in phonic decoding skills.

Several overlapping Tier 1 models that have evolved from the process approach are *writers' workshop*, *shared writing*, *paired writing*, and *guided writing*. It is relatively easy to integrate more structure and direct teaching of basic skills within each of these models and to differentiate the amount of feedback and guidance given to individual students. Russell (2024) provides a good example of explicitness in teaching writing (see the "Online" list in the "Resources" section).

Writers' workshop

Writers' workshop is an inclusive approach where all students in primary or secondary school engage individually and collaboratively in a writing activity at the same time (Beschorner & Hall, 2021). Motivation during writing workshop comes mainly through the topics that students are offered (Kinberg, 2020). A topic often links with subjects being studied in the broader curriculum and may be suggested by the teacher or by the students. The underlying principle is cooperating and providing feedback to one another through group sharing and peer editing.

Students in writing workshop are assisted through all stages of the writing process (prewriting, drafting, revising, and 'publishing'), and their products can become part of the reading material available in the classroom. During the writing session, the teacher provides the necessary scaffolding, conferring with almost every student about his or her writing, providing advice, correction when necessary, and encouragement (Helsel et al., 2022). Differences in abilities among the students will determine the amount of time the teacher spends with each individual. The evidence is that teacher's daily scaffolding in writers' workshop has a positive impact on students' writing skills and over time promotes independence in writing (Brown, 2018; Nagl, 2020). Differentiated teaching, correction, and reinforcement of specific language skills during writing workshop takes place in three ways: (1) individual students receive on-the-spot guidance and feedback during the session; (2) a mini-lesson may be conducted occasionally for 5 to 10 minutes, covering, for example, a specific grammar or spelling rule or use of adverbs and adjectives; and (3) principles of grammar, style, and spelling can also be a focus in whole-class discussion and feedback at the end of any session.

Shared writing

Shared writing can be made part of any lesson that involves students writing and discussing together. By the end of primary school, most students are capable of evaluating the quality of their own writing, but they still need guidance from teacher and peers on how best to revise and improve their work. It is the responsibility of teachers to spend time modelling the critiquing process (thinking aloud and giving positive and helpful advice as well as criticism) before expecting students to do this. They need to provide examples of giving descriptive praise, highlighting good points in a piece of writing, helping to shape new ideas, and showing students how to improve what is not clear and how to polish the final product. In all approaches that involve classmates and partners giving feedback (*peer critiquing*), this needs to be done with great sensitivity, because if implemented badly it draws unnecessary public attention to certain students' weaknesses.

Paired writing

In the same way that working with a partner can improve reading skills, having a partner for writing at Tier 1 is also beneficial. A study involving fifth- and sixth-grade students who wrote with a peer found that the students were more motivated than students taught by whole-class methods (De Smedt et al., 2020). Usually, the two students work together to produce one piece of writing using ideas that both have discussed. Jointly, they polish various drafts until a final product meets their expectations.

In inclusive classrooms, the pair of students are usually good friends who work well together and do not have learning difficulties; but paired writing can also be adapted for tutoring purposes. When paired writing is used at Tier 2 or Tier 3, the pair of students working together usually comprise the student with difficulties and a very supportive helper (peer tutor). The helper's role is to stimulate ideas from the writer, to note these down, and later to offer suggestions. When sufficient ideas have been generated, the helper and writer together review the notes and discuss the best sequence for presenting the ideas. A graphic organizer or concept map format could be used to indicate visibly how the ideas will be linked. The target student then writes a first draft with input from the partner, and together they edit the draft for clarity of meaning, sequence, spelling, and punctuation. The writer produces a final copy, and together they evaluate the finished product. Word processors have provided new ways of working collaboratively with a partner on written assignments.

Guided writing

Guided writing is a variant of the process approach but involves much more direct input from the teacher, usually in the form of *strategy training*. The guided approach is thought to be more effective than unstructured use of the process method for fostering students' writing skills. Guided writing is considered a useful approach from middle primary school years into secondary school. The approach involves *demonstrating* specific writing strategies for different styles or genres, followed by *guided practice* and *independent application* by the students. Exemplary teachers of writing frequently use modelling and evidence-based strategies to improve student writers' achievements.

A teacher might begin by demonstrating how to organize ideas for a given topic, how to structure an opening paragraph, and how to develop the remaining ideas in logical sequence. During strategy training, students are typically taught to use self-questioning and self-instruction to assist with the process of planning, evaluating, and improving a written assignment (Harris & McKeown, 2022). Emphasis is placed on the metacognitive aspects of the writing process (self-monitoring, checking for clarity, and self-correction). Students can also be given a checklist or rubric to help them evaluate and revise their written work. For example, a checklist might contain the following items:

- Did you begin with an interesting sentence that holds a reader's attention?
- Are your points easy to understand and presented in the best sequence?
- Did you give examples to help readers understand your points?
- Is your material interesting? If not, how might you make it more interesting?
- Have you used paragraphs?
- Have you checked spelling and punctuation?

Many low-achieving students tend to write very little during times set aside for writing. This is part of the vicious circle which begins: 'I don't like writing so I don't write much, so I don't get much practice, so I don't improve...' Use of strategies such as 'LESSER helps me write MORE' can help reduce the problem of limited output. The strategy guides students thinking and can result in a longer and more interesting assignment than they would otherwise produce.

L = List your ideas.
E = Examine your list.
S = Select your starting point.
S = Sentence 1 will tell us about this first idea.
E = Expand on this first idea with another, related sentence.
R_3 = Read what you have written. Revise if necessary. Repeat for the next paragraph.

It is always necessary to maximize the possibility that a strategy taught during a lesson will generalize beyond the lesson into students' everyday writing. This may be supported by (1) continuing with instruction and practice until students have thoroughly internalized the strategy and can use it without prompting and (2) frequently reminding students to consider where a particular strategy can be used.

Digital technology and writing

Students today have easy access to digital technology through tablets and smartphones, and most spend many hours a week playing games online or communicating with friends. At school and at home, they can also use technology to search for information to enrich their projects and compositions when they are writing on particular topics for assignments. Over the past decade, many new apps have been created to assist students in developing their writing skills (e.g., Quinn & Bliss, 2021). Links to some of these apps can be found on the "Online" list in the "Resources" section.

Teachers have reported that the use of technology in writing lessons enables them to motivate and engage students and also differentiate aspects of a writing activity for students who have a learning difficulty or disability (Lim & Lee, 2019; Murnan & Cornell, 2023; Regan et al., 2019). Often, working with technology results in these students increasing the number of sentences written, number of ideas expressed, and spelling accuracy (Pacheco & Huertas, 2022). Software or web-based tools and apps can be used to assist students to think and plan before writing—for example, by creating a map of ideas (graphic organizer) as the first step (Flanagan, 2023). Story maps of this type are described later.

The most common form of technology that students use for assignment work in classrooms and at home is word processing. Undoubtedly, the arrival of word processors heralded a new opportunity for students of all levels of ability to enter the realm of writing and composing with more enthusiasm and enjoyment. Students with learning difficulties can gain confidence in creating, editing, erasing, and publishing their own unique material through a medium that holds attention and is infinitely patient. Using a word processor makes the task of writing less arduous, and the writer receives immediate corrective feedback.

A new concern emerged in 2024 as teachers expressed alarm that artificial intelligence (AI) apps such as ChatGPT (released in 2022) could be used by students to produce an essay on almost any given subject. The concern is that students would have no incentive to become proficient and creative writers, because ChatGPT would do the job for them (Miller, 2024). The task for schools and universities now is to determine how to use AI productively to supplement other study skills (Stornaiuolo et al., 2024) and how to detect its improper use in assignments and research (Perkins et al., 2024). It will then be necessary to provide relevant in-service professional development on this topic for teachers (Hays et al., 2024).

When many schools were closed during the Covid-19 pandemic, digital technology proved to be a boon for teachers to communicate with their students, setting them online assignments and providing individualized feedback on their writing. Schools are still benefitting from the effects of having to make much greater use of technology for teaching and learning during the pandemic.

Teachers' expertise

Some students struggle with writing at Tier 1, and many teachers lack the necessary expertise for helping them. Troia (2014, p. 10) has written:

Younger writers and those who struggle with writing will require greater explicitness, more practice, and enhanced scaffolding (e.g., repetitive modelling, graphic aids, checklists, incremental goals, expectations) than older writers and those who do not struggle with writing.

Unfortunately, it seems that too many universities and colleges responsible for pre-service training of teachers are still tending to present student-centred process writing as the only recommended approach for use in primary and secondary schools; the skills-based approach is rarely mentioned. This probably accounts for the finding that many teachers are not confident in how to teach writing and to help students who find writing very difficult (Brenner & McQuirk, 2019; Cohen, 2023; Gardner & Kuzich, 2022; Givler, 2022). There is an obvious need to include more guidance during pre-service teacher education courses on how best to teach writing (Carter et al., 2022; Gardner & Kuzich, 2022; Spiker, 2023).

Considerations for Tier 2 and Tier 3 interventions

Students who exhibit difficulties in writing fall into one of two categories, but their instructional needs overlap. The first group comprises students who have learning difficulties of a cognitive, sensory, or physical nature, or a learning disability, that impairs their ability to write. The second group comprises reluctant and unmotivated students who have the ability to write but do not like to do so.

In order to assist students with learning difficulties or disabilities, there is a need to structure every writing task carefully and then provide appropriate support. Students need help at two stages of the writing process: (i) planning what to write and (ii) revising and polishing the final product. The revising stage should involve the teacher covering topics such as how to combine short sentences into longer sentences to improve the flow of the text, how to expand an idea with more examples, how using more adjectives and adverbs bring colour and detail to a story, and the way to check for grammatical or spelling errors. The teaching at each stage should embody basic principles of effective instruction, namely demonstration by the teacher of the steps involved, followed by guided practice with feedback, and ultimately students engaging in independent practice and application.

Reluctant and unmotivated students have usually encountered negative or unrewarding experiences during the early stages of becoming writers and may have acquired what has been termed *writing apprehension*. This state of anxiety begins in the primary school but can last into adulthood, with many individuals trying to avoid the task of putting pen to paper or using a keyboard. Their avoidance leads to habitually low levels of practice and productivity, so in school the teacher's challenge is to find ways of helping these students regain lost interest and re-build their confidence. An atmosphere that encourages students to experiment with their writing without fear of failure is a very necessary condition for struggling writers; but in many cases, simply creating the supportive atmosphere is not enough, particularly for students with a long history of bad experiences with writing. At Tier 2 and Tier 3, much more than the ordinary amount of scaffolding and encouragement from the teacher will be needed. Small booklets devoted to one topic or one story are usually better than thick exercise books for students who are reluctant writers. The opportunity to make a fresh start every week is far better than being faced with the accumulated evidence of past failures which accrue in an exercise book. For students of all ages, a loose-leaf folder with work samples and computer printouts is a useful replacement for the traditional exercise book.

At Tier 2, maximum attention needs to be given to teaching students effective strategies for planning what they intend to write and for evaluating and revising their work as they progress (Ralli et al., 2023). They need specific guidance on how to begin their writing, how to develop an idea, and how to complete the task. Students with difficulties who lack confidence benefit from (1) talking through the topic first, to think around the main theme and a generate a sequence of related ideas; (2) noting down some key vocabulary; and (3) drawing a graphic organizer (story map) to show how ideas will be linked.

The first important step in improving students' writing skills is to allocate sufficient time for writing within every school day. When writing occurs daily, there is much greater likelihood that skills, motivation, and confidence will all improve. In a group tutoring situation, it is essential to assign an appropriately stimulating subject about which students have reasonable depth of knowledge and experience. The students must see a purpose in transferring ideas to paper or computer and should perceive the task as worthwhile. In the early stages, it is important not to place undue stress on perfect accuracy in spelling or grammar since this can stifle a student's attempts to write freely. If the student is using a word processor, it is best not to stop to check spellings until the writing is complete, so that the student's full attention can be devoted to composing content and sequence.

The following sections describe various activities and frameworks that can be used with struggling writers at Tier 2 and Tier 3. All the suggestions are designed to structure the task demands for writing and at the same time motivate a reluctant student to complete the work successfully. In most cases, the use of a word processor will help with motivation and has an important element of control by the learner and immediate feedback. Studies have indicated that interventions that target writing, particularly those involving direct teaching and self-regulated strategy development, do result in improvement in students' writing fluency (Datchuk et al., 2020; Rodgers & Loveall, 2023).

The skeleton story

Getting started is the first obstacle faced by many students who find writing difficult. To address this problem, some teachers use writing frames (templates) and rubrics designed to scaffold the task of composing. One version is to provide a few stem sentences that must be completed using the students' own ideas and words. Students find it very much easier to complete a story when the demands for writing and sequencing are reduced in this way and when a structure has been provided.

> **Example:**
>
> Something woke me in the middle of the night.
> I heard ....
> I climbed out of the bed quietly and ....
> To my surprise, I saw ....
> At first, I ....
> I was lucky because ....
> In the end, ...

Simple frameworks of this type can be used with an individual student in a tutorial session or can be used as a group activity involving collaborative effort to complete a version of the story on the whiteboard or screen. Each student is then given a sheet with the same sentence beginnings, but he or she must write a different story. These stories are later shared in the group.

Story web

A story web is a form of graphic organizer that provides writers with a starting point for generating ideas for writing. The web is created by writing the main topic or title for the story in the middle of the paper (or whiteboard), then using spokes branching off from the main idea into different types of information—for example, the setting for the story, the characters involved, the type of action that takes place, and the outcome. In a group, students brainstorm for ideas that might go into the story, and these are added to the web. Digital technology has proven useful as a tool for helping students with learning difficulties construct such a graphic organizer (e.g., Brady et al., 2022).

- Prompts and cues can be used to stimulate students' thinking as the web is constructed.
- The class then reviews the ideas and decides upon an appropriate starting point for the story. Number 1 is written against that idea.

- How will the story develop? The students determine the order in which the other ideas will be used, and the appropriate numbers are written against each spoke.
- Some of the ideas may not be used at all and can be erased. Other ideas may need to be added at this stage and numbered accordingly.

The students now use the bank of ideas on the story web to start writing their own stories. Brief notes can be elaborated into sentences, and the sentences gradually extended into paragraphs. By preparing the draft ideas and then discussing the best order in which to write them, the students have tackled two of the most difficult problems they face when composing: planning and sequencing. This approach has much in common with the self-directing strategy known as POW (*Pick idea - Organise notes - Write and say more*) (Ögülmüs, 2021).

Think it. Say it. Write it. Read it.

This commonsense strategy for improving students' writing has been available for many years but is still taught too infrequently in primary schools. The strategy can be incorporated into most of the thoughtful-planning-before-writing approaches described here. As the title indicates, students are encouraged to think carefully about each sentence they want to use, then say it aloud before writing or typing it, and finally reading aloud what is written. The teacher or tutor first demonstrates (models) this procedure, and students try to use the same steps when writing their own topic. They could have a partner to provide feedback. What has been written is then modified if necessary to increase clarity and cohesion.

For details of the strategy and sample resources, see the "Online" list in the "Resources" section.

Expanding an idea

Informative or narrative writing can be expanded beyond simple statement. The teacher demonstrates the following procedure, incorporating ideas from the group. Students are then given guided practice and further modelling over a series of lessons, each time using a different theme.

- Begin by writing a short, declarative sentence.
  We have too many cars coming into our school parking area.
- Next, write two or three sentences that add information to and are connected with the first sentence. Leave a space between each statement.
  We have too many cars coming into our school parking area.
  -
  -
  The noise they make often disturbs our lessons.

-

-

The cars sometimes travel fast and could knock someone down.

-

What can we do about this problem?

-

• Now write more sentences in the spaces.

We have too many cars coming into our school parking area.
It is becoming very annoying.
The noise they make often disturbs our lessons.
The drivers rev the engines. Sometimes I can't even hear what our teacher is saying.
The cars travel fast and could knock someone down. I saw a girl step out behind one car yesterday. She screamed when it reversed suddenly.
What can we do about this problem?
Perhaps there should be a sign saying 'NO CARS ALLOWED'. They might build some speed humps or set a speed limit.

Finally, edit the sentences into appropriate paragraphs and combine some short statements into longer, complex sentences. Use of a word processor makes these steps much faster and the process of editing and checking spelling easier.

Writing a summary

Students with learning difficulties often have problems when required to write a summary of something they have just read. Specific help is needed in this area, and one or more of the following procedures can be helpful to such students. It can be used with an individual in a tutorial session (Tier 3) or with a group of students at Tier 2.

• After students have read the text together or independently, the teacher provides a written set of 'true/false' statements based on information in the text. The statements are presented on a sheet in random order. Students must read each statement and place a tick against those that are true. They then decide the most logical sequence in which to arrange these true statements to form a logical summary when copied into an exercise book.
• A different approach is the teacher providing some sentence starters in a sequence that will provide a framework for writing the summary. The student completes the unfinished sentences and in doing so writes the summary.

For example:

The first thing the three travellers noticed when they arrived at the airport was ...
   When they travelled by taxi to the city, they noticed ...
   They begin to wonder if ...
   In the end, they discovered that ....

- Alternatively, the teacher provides a summary with key words or phrases omitted. This is often referred to as preparing a *cloze passage*. Students must provide the missing words. At the simplest level, the words required may be presented below the passage in random order, or clues may be given in terms of initial letters of word required. The student completes the cloze passage by supplying the missing words.
- Simple multiple-choice questions can be presented. The questions may deal with the main ideas from the text and with supporting detail. By selecting appropriate responses and writing these down, the student creates a brief summary.

The following chapter provides information on spelling and how to address the needs of students who have difficulty in mastering this important skill. Many of the suggested strategies and methods for improving spelling can also be integrated into most of the interventions for writing described above.

Resources

Online

- Lost for Words *(TV Documentary Series)*. https://www.sbs.com.au/ondemand/tv-series/lost-for-words
- *Think it. Say it. Write it. Read it.*
  - Details of the strategy: https://receptionowls.weebly.com/uploads/1/9/8/1/19811075/thinkit_say_it_write_it_read_it_posters.pdf
  - Sample resources: https://www.cgpplus.co.uk/primary/ks1/english/e1wat223-think-it-say-it-write-it-check-it
- Karakus, G. (2023). Systematic review of studies on writing in elementary school. *Research in Pedagogy*, 13(1), 146-176. Online: https://eric.ed.gov/?q=teaching+writing&id=EJ1393135
- Descriptions of online apps to motivate students and teach writing skills can be found at https://www.splashlearn.com/blog/writing-apps-for-kids/ or at https://www.weareteachers.com/writing-apps-for-kids/

- Russell, D. (2024). *What is explicit instruction?* https://www.teacher magazine.com/au_en/articles/teaching-resource-what-is-explicit-instruction?utm_source=CM&utm_medium=Bulletin&utm_campaign=16April
- Issues associated with difficulties in writing are discussed online by Dr Mel Levine at: https://www.pbs.org/wgbh/misunderstoodminds/writingdiffs.html
- For information on a range of strategies for helping struggling writers, see

  - https://www.teachwriting.org/blog/2017/6/14/12-strategies-to-support-struggling-writers-in-elementary
  - https://www.readingandwritinghaven.com/14-ways-support-struggling-writers-build-confidence-increase-success/

- Kelly, K. *8 tools for kids with dysgraphia.* https://www.understood.org/en/articles/8-tools-for-kids-with-dysgraphia
- *Great apps for struggling readers/writers.* https://keystoliteracy.com/blog/great-apps-for-struggling-readerswriters/
- *Basic writing disabilities in children.* https://www.verywellfamily.com/what-are-basic-writing-disabilities-2162445

Print

Biays, J.S., & Wershoven, C. (2019). *Along these lines: Writing sentences and paragraphs* (7th ed.). New York: Pearson.

Clements, J. (2022). *On the write track: A practical guide to teaching writing in primary schools.* London: Routledge.

Graham, S., Collins, A.A., & Ciullo, S. (2024). Evidence-based recommendations for teaching writing. *Education 3–13*, 52(7), 979–992.

Graham, S., MacArthur, C.A., & Fitzgerald, J. (2019). *Best practices in writing instruction* (3rd ed.). New York: Guilford Press.

Smith, A. (2023). *Simplify your writing instruction: A framework for a student-centered writing block.* Indianapolis, IN: Jossey-Bass-Wiley.

Young, R. (2020). *Real-world writers: A handbook for teaching writing with 7 -11year olds.* London: Routledge.

Chapter 12

Difficulties with spelling

The ability to spell (encode) words is a basic skill needed by everyone in order to communicate effectively. Unfortunately, many students across the age and ability range find learning to spell a major problem. Poor spelling is a common phenomenon even in the adult population. It is reasonable to question why this is so.

Learning to spell

Learning to spell can be challenging for anyone, because the English language contains a number of words that are impossible to spell by a simple translation of sounds to single letters. Many of these 'irregular' words have been absorbed centuries ago from foreign languages, particularly from old German and Norman French. Learning the spelling of these irregular words does require practice and memorization. It is important to stress, however, that irregularities in English spelling are greatly overestimated, and English is not the 'unruly writing system' described by Kearns and Borkenhagen (2024). In reality, only about 15 per cent of English words have irregular spellings, and only 4 per cent have no connection at all with letter-to-sound correspondences. Some 85 per cent of words are therefore predictable and encodable if the writer knows not only all single letter–sound correspondences but also all the consonant blends such as str-, bl-, and cr-; the digraphs such as th-, wh-, ch-, and ph-; and certain common orthographic units such as -ough, -ight, and -ious. If, over time, young students can master these sound-to-letter correspondences, they can attempt to spell (and read) almost all words within their current vocabulary (Ehri, 2023a). It is important that teaching basic phonic knowledge should begin early in kindergarten and extend into first years of primary school (McNeill et al., 2023).

Another reason for some students' difficulties in learning to spell is that too little attention has been devoted to the systematic teaching of phonics and spelling in schools because of a misguided belief that spelling skill will be acquired incidentally if students simply engage in writing every day. Systematic teaching of spelling ceased to feature prominently in the primary school

DOI: 10.4324/9781003598671-13

curriculum for several decades from the 1970s, due mainly to the influence of whole-language approach to literacy. Teachers were encouraged to accept 'invented' spellings in order to focus on creativity and expression rather than transcription aspects of writing. This immersion approach was deemed to be a 'natural' way of acquiring spelling ability and therefore regarded as preferable to any form of direct teaching. The reality was that the immersion approach proved totally inadequate for many students, and they failed to become proficient spellers. Without explicit instruction, many students develop their own strategies for spelling difficult words, but usually these strategies are unreliable and they create ongoing problems.

More recently, systematic teaching of spelling has enjoyed something of a renaissance due to the 'standards agenda' and an increased acceptance that accurate spelling is actually important. Students will not necessarily become adequate spellers if they are left to discover spelling principles for themselves. Research suggests that students learn the most effective strategies for encoding words when they are given explicit instruction in how to analyze the sounds within a word, to note and remember any irregularities, and given abundant opportunities to practice (Conrad et al., 2019; Neilson, 2019; Vadasy & Sanders, 2021). The current view is that a systematic approach to spelling and word study is absolutely essential and leads to measurable improvement in spelling ability. Current teaching approaches aim to help students become more independent and more capable of detecting and correcting spelling errors. Guidelines for national curriculum in the US, Britain, and Australia now require that due attention be given to ensuring that all students can spell and can use appropriate resources to obtain and check the spelling of complex words.

Best practices in spelling instruction

Research studies in recent years have confirmed that best practice in spelling at Tier 1 involves teaching all students knowledge, skills, and strategies that are useful for tackling unfamiliar words they may require when engaged in authentic writing (Cordewener et al., 2018; Ehri, 2022). In the early stages, this teaching should involve clear modelling by a teacher, imitation and practice by students, and corrective feedback from the teacher. Students also need to learn efficient methods for remembering irregular words and for proofreading and self-correction.

There are specific principles that should guide a classroom approach to teaching spelling to students at Tier 1:

- In the primary school years, allocate adequate time for instruction and practice; this is recommended to be 15 minutes daily working with words.
- Arouse students' genuine interest in words and pride in producing accurate spelling.

- Teach a core vocabulary of commonly needed irregular words.
- Match spelling activities to students' stage of development.
- In upper primary school and above, teach effective cognitive strategies for proofreading and self-correcting.
- Make classroom self-help spelling resources readily available: dictionaries, common core word lists, topic-specific word lists, word walls, electronic spell checkers, and computer access.

Developmental stages

It is important to recognize that acquisition of spelling ability has identifiable stages of development, and teaching must take these stages into account when selecting words and strategies to be taught to a particular age group of students. The stages have been described in the following way – although the name for each stage has differed among various researchers (e.g., Bissex, 1980; Ehri, 2023b; Scharer & Zutell, 2003; Templeton, 2020).

Stage 1: Prephonetic. This stage represents the first tentative step towards invented spelling as a component of emergent writing. In the kindergarten years, preschool children pretend to write words in imitation of the writing they have seen from others, often using a mix of capital and lowercase letters. There is no connection between these scribbles and real words, but studies have indicated that if developmentally appropriate feedback is provided to children during this stage, they begin to pay closer attention to associations between oral and written language.

Stage 2: Phonetic. At this stage, children draw upon their increasing awareness of sounds within spoken words through incidental learning and begin to gain basic knowledge of letter-to-sound correspondences. The spellings that children invent at this stage are often quite recognizable because they are based on phonic principles.

Towards the end of the phonetic stage, approximations of words move much nearer to regular letter-to-sound correspondences, as in 'sed' (said), 'becos' (because), or 'wotch' (watch). Sometimes, a phoneme may be equated incorrectly with a letter *name* rather than the sound—as in 'rsk' (ask), 'yl' (while), and 'lfnt' (elephant). Some children still have difficulty identifying the second or third consonant in a letter string and may write 'stong' (strong) or 'bow' (blow); or they may fail to identify correctly a phoneme in a spoken word, so they write incorrect letters as in 'druck' (truck), 'jriv' (drive), 'sboon' (spoon), and 'dewis' (juice). These inaccuracies are normal slips on the way to proficiency.

It should be noted that the majority of individuals with poor spelling have reached this phonetic stage but have not progressed beyond it. Their tendency is to be over-dependent on phonics and therefore write all irregular words as if they have regular letter-to-sound correspondences. In order to move to the next stage, students need to be taught how to use different strategies—such as more carefully checking the visual image of the target word or writing the word several times.

Stage 3: Transitional. At this stage, there is clear evidence of a more sophisticated understanding of word structure, and more caution is applied when attempting unfamiliar words. Students become more aware of within-word letter strings and syllable junctures. Activities involving word analysis are useful for helping students recognize letter patterns within words (orthographic units) (Bear et al., 2020). Common letter sequences such as *str-*, *pre-*, *-ough*, *-ious*, *-ea-*, *-ai-*, *-aw-*, and *-ing* are used much more automatically and reliably. The process of building up orthographic images in memory is also facilitated by study of word families with common letter sequences—for example, *gate*, *date*, *late*, *fate*, and *mate*. Students who gain mastery over spelling at this stage also start to use words they know already in order to spell words they have never written before (spelling by analogy).

Stage 4: Independence. At this stage, students have gained mastery of quite complex grapho-phonic principles and also use visual memory more effectively when writing words. Flexible use is made of a wide range of spelling, proofreading, and self-correcting strategies. A growing awareness of the meaning of root words, prefixes, suffixes, and derivations also signals increased control over spelling.

In general, spellings produced by students provide a window not only to their developmental stage but also to their current thought processes related to encoding written language. Examination of the written work produced by students with difficulties can reveal a great deal about their existing skills and their specific needs for instruction in spelling. This type of assessment should be the starting point for planning any intervention. Some experts suggest that when an individual is receiving Tier 3 intervention for a significant problem in learning to spell, it is often useful to analyze the types of error he or she makes (Daffern & Fleet, 2021; Henbest & Apel, 2021). However, while spelling error analysis has a place in Tier 3 intervention, the procedure is not widely used by classroom teachers. It is very time-consuming, the procedure requires collection of many work samples from the student before even tentative conclusions can be drawn, and judging the errors is rather subjective.

Spelling as a complex behaviour

Spelling can be regarded as a very complex behaviour because it involves coordination of eye, ear, hand, brain, and speech (through the accurate pronunciation of words). The strategies used to teach spelling to all students should be based on the potential contribution of each of these five modalities. For many years, teachers regarded the correct spelling of words as a predominantly *visual* skill. If students were fortunate enough to receive any guidance at all in spelling, they were taught the 'look-cover-write-check' strategy, as discussed later. Much less importance was attached to careful listening (auditory processing) because it was argued that too many words in English are not written with perfect letter-to-sound translation. However, as indicated previously, it should be noted that a high percentage of English words can be encoded 'as they sound' if attention is given not just to single letters but to *letter clusters* (e.g., *-ei-, -ie-, thr-, -ough, -tion*, and *-ength*).

Auditory skills and phonic knowledge

The basic knowledge upon which successful spelling develops depends upon grasping the concept that spoken words can be broken down into smaller units of sound (phonemes) and that these sounds can be represented by letters (Rice et al., 2024). It is now accepted that carefully listening to words as they are pronounced enables young children to relate the sequence of phonemes they can hear to the single letters or groups of letters needed to represent those sounds in the written form. Later, at the transitional stage, children learn to encode using letter clusters rather than just single letters, and they are able to spell much more efficiently. They will not always arrive at the perfect spelling of a tricky word, but they will come to a close approximation.

One group of students where the influence of auditory perception on spelling negatively affects their ability is those with significant hearing impairment. Evidence suggests that, for these students, visual exposure to word-forms through reading still provides the main influence for developing orthographic awareness, backed up with phonic knowledge where possible (Sabatier et al., 2024; Wass et al., 2019). Working with 'word families' comprising words that have a common letter sequence is also helpful (e.g., *sight, tight, fight, light,* and *right*).

Visual skills

Of course, visual skills are also vitally important for learning and remembering the orthographic patterns of words. Proficient spellers make great use of visual images stored in memory when they check words they have written or typed to detect errors. For example, *brekfirst* should be recognized by the student as an incorrect visual image for the word *breakfast*—it doesn't 'look right'. The effective use of visual perception in learning to spell helps students build a memory bank of common letter clusters, and these images can be called upon whenever the student attempts to write an unfamiliar word. Over time, most students develop *orthographic awareness*, which means they recognize groups of letters that occur frequently within English words (e.g., *-ate* or *un-*); and equally important, they realize that certain combinations of letters rarely or never occur in English (e.g., *vt, chk,* or *tz*). Increasingly, this awareness guides them when selecting certain letter clusters and rejecting others when writing a tricky word.

Learning strategies that involve visual imagery, such as look-say-cover-write-check, are very effective for learning irregular words. It is necessary to examine the word very carefully, with every intention of trying to commit its configuration to memory. As this process of close scrutiny of words does not come naturally to students, it is important that they be given the necessary direction and practice. By implication, this means devoting specific time for word study, over and above the help given to individuals as they write. It is most unlikely that such an important skill as word analysis could be adequately developed through incidental learning alone.

Spelling by hand

In addition to combining visual and auditory skills, spelling is a manual skill. The physical act of spelling of a word by writing or keyboarding involves muscle memory (*kinaesthetic memory*). The ease with which a competent speller encodes a very familiar word in print supports this view. The frequent action of writing or keyboarding is a powerful way of establishing and maintaining the stock of word images and letter strings in long-term memory. Poorly executed handwriting and uncertain letter formation inhibit easy development of spelling at an automatic response level. It is essential that an easy style of writing be taught and practised thoroughly from the early years of schooling (James & Beringer, 2019). Most experts now recommend that cursive (joined) handwriting has benefits over manuscript style (in which each letter is written separately). Handwriting appears to facilitate spelling, and the advantage of cursive style is that each written word consists of a continuous pattern with all elements flowing together. For Tier 3 intervention, it is usually important to assess a student's handwriting skill along with spelling ability (Downing & Caravolas, 2024).

Spelling and the brain

The human brain plays the executive role in thinking about words and in generating and checking plausible spelling alternatives. The learning of new words and the analysis of unfamiliar words are both brain-based (cognitive) activities. The brain coordinates various sources of perceptual information to help determine the spelling of a word. It is also the brain that makes the decision whether to apply auditory, visual, or some other strategy to encode the word. The ability to recall and apply spelling rules and strategies, or to recognize when a word is an exception to a rule, reflects a cognitive aspect of spelling. Working out the most probable way to spell an unfamiliar word may also require the writer to consider the meaning of the word and the separate *morphemes* (small units of meaning such as prefixes, suffixes, and plural endings) that make up the word.

Pronunciation

Accurate pronunciation of a word plays an important role in spelling. This issue is particularly relevant when teaching English as a second language, but it also applies to students from restricted language backgrounds, those using a strong regional dialect, and students with hearing impairment. In cases of serious spelling difficulty, it is always wise to check if the student is actually hearing and saying a target word correctly. For example, you are unlikely to spell *library* or *escape* correctly if you say *'libry'* and *'excape'*. In the early years, children benefit from guided experience in listening carefully to words, stretching words out and segmenting them into pronounceable sub-units.

Teaching spelling

The majority of students do not become good spellers simply by being immersed in reading and writing activities—specific time must be devoted to spelling instruction, particularly in the primary school years. The starting point for enhancing spelling development is arousal of a student's genuine interest in words, and this requires that teachers and tutors display personal enthusiasm for all forms of word study.

Effective instruction at Tier 1 does not set out to teach students how to spell each and every word they may need at some time in their writing. Students make most progress when they are explicitly taught strategies for working out how to learn new words and how to construct words by utilizing the multiple linguistic influences that underpin English spelling. Students with spelling difficulties will always need more individualized attention, systematic error correction, and more frequent practice. Often, it is necessary to create spelling-ability groups within the inclusive classroom so that the amount of teacher support can be differentiated and session content adjusted (Broughton, 2023). For students with the most significant learning difficulties at Tier 3, it is often helpful to include methods that involve multisensory input such as finger-tracing over a word or repeated writing or typing on a keyboard (Cerni & Job, 2024).

Learning to spell obviously involves the integration of phonic, alphabetic, orthographic, and morphemic knowledge (Hennenfent et al., 2022; McMurray, 2020). In the sections below, descriptions are provided for several Tier 1 general approaches that can be used singly or in combination to facilitate development in these dimensions. The approaches can also be used at Tier 2 and Tier 3 if differentiated and adapted to meet the specific needs and abilities of the students.

Applying a visual approach

A visual approach is most appropriate for the learning of irregular words. A visual approach requires students to memorize and retain the correct sequence of letters in long-term memory rather than attending only to sounds and syllables within the word. One of the best-known methods is called 'look-say-cover-write-check', or simply 'copy-cover-compare' (Nelson & Eckert, 2024). This approach gives a student an independent system that can be applied at any time to the learning of irregular or very unfamiliar words.

Look-say-cover-write-check involves the following steps:

- Look very carefully at the target word.
- Say the word clearly while looking closely at the left-to-right sequence of letters.
- Cover the word so that it cannot be seen.
- Write the word from immediate memory, pronouncing it quietly as you write.
- Check your version of the word with the original; if it is not correct, go back through the steps again until you can produce the word accurately.
- For some students with severe problems, tracing over the word with a finger at steps 1 and 2 may help with attention to detail and retention of the letter sequence.
- Check for recall a week later.

The simplest aid to make and use is the flashcard. The word is pronounced clearly, and attention is drawn to any particular features in the printed word that may be difficult to recall later. The student is encouraged to make a 'mental picture' of the word and examine it. Some teachers say: 'Use your eyes like a camera. Take a picture of the word. Close your eyes and imagine you can still see the word.' With eyes closed, the student is then told to trace the word in the air. After a few seconds, he or she writes the word from memory, articulating it clearly as it is written. The word is then checked against the flashcard. The rapid writing of the whole word using cursive style avoids the inefficient letter-by-letter copying habit that some students have developed.

It is important that a student have sufficient practice and application over a period of time to fully internalize this strategy and can then use it without prompting or reminders. Evidence suggests that this level of independence can be achieved and maintained after explicit teaching (Nelson & Eckert, 2024).

Applying a phonological approach

Using the phonological approach for spelling should be an integral part of systematic phonics teaching for reading. In a comprehensive literacy programme, decoding and encoding processes are taught together and writing and spelling are as much a focus of attention as reading. A phonological approach encourages students to attend carefully to sounds and syllables within words and to write the letters most likely to represent these sounds (McMurray, 2020). As indicated already, the phonic knowledge necessary for effective spelling goes well beyond simply knowing each single letter. Students also needs to use letter clusters (orthographic units) with vowels and consonants (e.g., -tion, -ail, pre-, and ought). When students can function at this level, they are able to write correctly most of the 85+ per cent of words they may need to use.

Applying a morphemic approach

Morphology is the study of word structure as it relates to meaning. A knowledge of morphological structure of words provides students with new insight on spelling patterns, because relating meaning to parts of words helps make spelling more predictable (Levesque et al., 2021). It has been found that when students understand how meaning influences the structure of a word, they have a better appreciation of the logic that governs English spelling (Breadmore et al., 2023; Wolter & Dilworth, 2014). Evidence suggests that even young children in the early grades of primary school can use awareness of meaning to help with spelling of words (Grigorakis & Manolitsis, 2021). There is clearly value in including attention to meaning and morphemes in interventions for students with literacy skills problems (Brady & Mason, 2024).

In a morphemic approach, students are taught to recognize and apply knowledge of sub-units of meaning within a word. The smallest unit of meaning is termed a 'morpheme', and the written equivalent of a morpheme is known as a 'morphograph'. For example, the word *throw* contains only one morpheme, but *throwing* contains two. The word *unhappiness* (un-happ[y]-ness) contains three morphemes—and this example also illustrates a common rule (changing y to i) when combining certain morphemes. These rules need to be taught and practised when using a morphemic approach. To facilitate study, students can be helped to compile 'word families' (e.g., *certain, uncertain, certainly, uncertainty, certainty*, and *ascertain*). A dictionary is an easy resource to identify such words. Morphological awareness is one of the main topics addressed with students in typical Tier 1 'word study' sessions (see below).

The best-known commercial programme using a morphemic approach is *Spelling Through Morphographs* (Dixon & Englemann, 2006). The materials are appropriate for students from Year 4 upwards and can also be used with adults. In 140 lessons, the students learn all the key morphographs and the basic rules of how they can be combined in the spelling system. *Spelling Through Morphographs* has proven particularly valuable for students with learning difficulties. The same publishing house also produces *Spelling Mastery* for students in grades 1 to 6. This programme includes visual, phonological, and morphologic learning strategies. An evaluation of *Spelling Mastery* by What Works Clearinghouse concluded that the programme can have positive effects for students with learning disabilities (Institute of Education Sciences, 2014). For a very comprehensive and helpful 2024 description of *Spelling Mastery*, see the "Online" list in the "Resources" section at the end of the chapter.

Digital technology

There has been a noticeable increase in the use of technology to teach spelling, and this has proven very useful for students with learning difficulties (Ault et al., 2017; Elimelech & Aram, 2019). The concern expressed a few years ago that technology in the form of spell checkers would result in declining spelling standards has not turned out to be true. Rather than proving to be detrimental to spelling, technology has given us programmes and apps that can be used effectively for learning to spell and for deeper studying of words (Dreyer, 2023). When used with young students just beginning primary school, the effectiveness of age-appropriate apps seems to depend on their prior knowledge of words in print (Boggio et al., 2023). Several computer programmes designed to develop spelling skills using a visual approach are available, and studies have indicated that these can be quite effective. Any online search under 'spelling software' will yield details of a range of existing programmes and apps.

When using digital technology to teach or practice spelling, teachers should ensure that the way in which words are presented on the screen causes a student to attend carefully to the left-to-right sequence of letters and requires the student to type the *complete word* from memory each time. Programmes that focus too much attention on unscrambling jumbled words, spelling letter-by-letter, or inserting missing letters into spaces are far less effective.

Word study

Activities used in word study sessions are designed to help students analyze words more deeply by finding within-word letter patterns, identifying syllables and affixes, and attending to meaning. The actual processes involved in word study are described as examining, manipulating, comparing, and categorizing words to reveal the logic within written language.

Findings from research support the belief that clear instruction in word analysis can successfully reveal connections between phonological, morphological, and orthographic features within words (Caines, 2022). It is believed that this type of word study helps all students achieve a better standard in spelling (Broughton, 2023) and is of particular help for students with language disorders, learning difficulties, and those learning English as a second language.

One activity involving word study for all students at Tier 1 is *Word Sorting*. This approach represents an investigative and active way to help students discriminate among orthographic features within and across words. Comparing and contrasting words in this way helps older students (including adults) discover basic some spelling rules.

Students are provided with a set of cards containing the words to be studied and compared. The words might be *sock, black, back, truck, lock, dock, rack, luck, trick, track, block, lick, sack, stick, flock, flick,* and *suck*. The students are asked, 'What is the same about some of these words?' The response might be that the words all end with /ck/. The words might now be categorized in other ways by sorting the cards into groups (e.g., words ending in /ock/ or words ending in /ack/). At a more advanced level, *Word Sorts* can involve words grouped according to the meaning–spelling connection, as discussed above under the morphemic approach—for example, *played, playfully, replay, player, playground, horseplay,* and *playback*.

Spelling rules

Some experts advocate teaching spelling rules to students as a key part of the classroom spelling programme; but students with learning difficulties find most rules too obscure to be of help when they are faced with a particularly tricky word to spell. In many cases, rather than drilling complex rules, it is easier to help students spell the specific word they need for their immediate writing but also to teach them effective strategies to use to master that word for future use.

Learning spelling rules may, however, be of some value for older students and students of above average intelligence. This is particularly the case if rules are incorporated into the morphemic approach described above (Burton et al., 2021). Intelligent students can often understand the rule and can apply it appropriately. Rules taught should be simple and have few exceptions (e.g., 'i' before 'e' except after 'c': *receive*; words ending with 'e', drop the 'e' when adding an ending that begins with a vowel: *hope, hoping*; words ending in a single vowel must double the consonant before adding an ending that begins with a vowel: *stop, stopped, stopping*).

Dictation

The regular use of dictation has fallen out of favour in many schools, although it is suggested that dictation can develop listening skills and concentration and at the same time gives spelling practice with words in context (Marsh, 2023; Rippel, 2024). Dictation still enjoys an accepted place in teaching English as a second or additional language.

When dictation is used for teaching rather than testing, the material at an appropriate level of difficulty should first be presented for students to study *before* it is dictated. In this way, there is an opportunity to clarify meaning of certain unfamiliar words and to point out any potentially difficult spellings. The passage is then dictated for students to write, and they are given a period of time to proofread and self-correct any words that they think are incorrect. The teacher checks the work and can observe two aspects of the student's performance. First, it is useful to look at the words the student has been able to self-correct (or at least knows to be wrong). Second, the teacher can record words that were in fact wrong but were not noticed by the student. If these are common words that should be known by the student, activities can be devised that will help the student master them.

Spelling lists

The National Curriculum in England specifies core spelling lists for each year level in primary school, and there are many other resources that also provide general-purpose word lists. A quick online search will yield many links to list that can be downloaded. However, it is widely believed by teachers that rote learning of words from lists does not usually result in any sure retention and transfer to everyday writing. The limitation of formal lists is that having one common word list for all students in the class ignores the fact that students are at different stages of spelling development and therefore have different learning needs (Esposito et al., 2023). There is, however, a place for judicious use of spelling lists if they are tailored to students' interests and writing needs.

From the point of view of the weakest spellers, the most useful list will be one compiled according to everyday writing needs, and the words that are often incorrect in the student's writing. A copy of this self-help list can be kept in the back of the exercise book or folder and used when he or she is writing a rough draft or proofreading a final draft of a piece of work.

Other lists might contain words grouped by visual, phonemic, or morphemic similarity (word families). The value of lists comprising word families is that they represent yet another way of helping students establish awareness of commonly occurring orthographic units. This awareness enables a student to use a more rational approach to tackling an unfamiliar word—for example, by using *analogy* to move from the known to the unknown. The decision to use such lists with an individual student or group of students must be made in the light of their specific learning needs.

Word Walls represent one excellent method of ensuring that the words students need in their daily writing in any subject area are readily to hand. Words are written in blackboard-size writing on poster sheets on the classroom wall so that students can locate and use them as necessary. Vocabulary is added regularly to the *Word Wall* as each new curriculum topic is introduced. This approach applies in secondary schools as well as primary schools. Students may not need to learn all the words on such a list, but they can refer to it when writing. It is often recommended in secondary schools, as part of a 'across the curriculum' policy on literacy, that specialist subject teachers should provide their students with a list of core terms frequently used in that subject.

Developing strategic spellers

Students become truly independent in spelling when they can look at an unfamiliar word and select the most appropriate strategy for learning and remembering that word. For example, they need to be able to look at a word and decide for themselves whether it is phonemically irregular or regular. For an irregular word, they may need to apply the look-cover-write-check strategy, coupled perhaps with repeated writing of the word. If the word is phonemically regular, they recognize that they can spell it easily from its component sounds. When students can operate at this level, the shift is from rote learning to an emphasis on approaching words rationally.

This level of independence does not come easily, and many students need to be taught how to learn and remember new spellings. Some students, if left to their own devices, fail to develop any systematic approach—or they may just look at the word and recite the spelling alphabetically—or they may copy letter-by-letter rather than smoothly writing the whole word—or they may use no particular strategy at all, believing that learning to spell the word is beyond them.

Where a student has no systematic approach, it is essential that he or she be taught one. Any serious attempt to help students with spelling difficulties must first involve observing how they set about learning any new group of words. Then, the teacher replaces the student's inefficient system of operating with a more effective way of mastering the correct spelling of a word. Cognitive and metacognitive approaches are designed to teach students self-regulatory strategies to use when learning new words or when checking spelling at the proofreading stage of writing. Explicit teaching of cognitive strategies has been found to be effective with students with a learning disability (Atmaca & Yildiz-Demirtas, 2023).

A typical strategy to teach to weaker spellers involves them asking themselves the following questions:

- What sounds can I hear in this word?
- Do I know any other words that sound like this word?
- Can I write this word correctly after a quick glance?
- How many syllables do I hear in this word?
- Do I have the right number of syllables in what I have written?
- Does this word look correct? I'll try it again.
- Does this look better?

Intervention for Tier 2 and Tier 3

In addition to the general teaching strategies described above, several specific approaches have been developed to help struggling spellers. The paragraphs below describe some of the most useful that have survived the passage of time. Most of these intervention approaches involve intensive one-to-one instruction (Tier 3).

Simultaneous Oral Spelling

Simultaneous Oral Spelling (SOS) was developed by Gillingham and Stillman (1956), and it has been applied very successfully for remediation of spelling problems in individual tutorial settings. Note that the letter *name*, not its common sound, is used. This makes the method particularly appropriate for older students or adults who may be embarrassed by 'sounding out' a word using phonics.

The SOS approach involves these steps:

- A target word is selected—perhaps a word that is a persistent spelling error.
- Teacher or tutor pronounces the word clearly and checks that student can also pronounce it accurately.
- Student then segments the word by saying each syllable (e.g., *re-mem-ber*) or, in the case of a single-syllable word, saying the onset and rime units (*s-un; b-et*).
- Student then *names* the letters in the word in sequence, twice.
- Without reference to the model, the student then writes the word *while naming each letter.*
- Check against the original spelling—correct, if necessary, and repeat.

Repeated writing

Writing a word several times is one way in which a kinaesthetic image of the word can be more firmly established in long-term memory. Only a few words (*no more than three*) should be practised in any one session. Repeated writing can easily be incorporated as the last step in the SOS strategy described above.

Repeated writing of a target word that the student is trying to master can be very helpful indeed if (i) the learner has every intention of trying to remedy an error and (ii) he or she is attending fully to the task. However, if the student is thinking of other things or is distracted while carrying out the repeated writing, the procedure is of little or no value. It simply becomes a mechanical performance that can be carried out without conscious effort, and the words are not remembered later.

Old Way/New Way method

Lyndon (1989) suggested that the reason for the difficulty many students have in 'unlearning' an incorrect spelling they have in memory is due to *proactive inhibition* (or proactive interference). This term refers to a situation where previously stored information interferes with one's ability to acquire a new correct response. What the individual already knows is inwardly protected from change. Lyndon's approach called 'Old Way/New Way' uses a student's error as the starting point for change, and memory of the old way of spelling of the word is used later to activate an awareness of the new (correct) way of spelling the word.

The following steps and procedures are used:

- Student writes the word in the usual incorrect form.
- Teacher and student agree to call this the 'old way' of spelling that word.
- Teacher shows student a 'new way' (correct way) of spelling the word.
- Attention is drawn to the similarities and differences between the old and the new forms: *"You used to write 'biter', with only one 't'. In the new way you spell it with 'tt'. Bitter."*
- Student writes word again in the old way.
- Student writes word in the new way and explains aloud the difference: *"Now I write it with two tts.* Bitter."
- Repeat five such writings of old way, new way, and statement of differences.
- Students may be asked to write five different sentences using the word in its 'new' form.
- Revise the words taught after a week.
- If necessary, repeat this procedure every two weeks until the new response is firmly established in long-term memory.

Tutoring individual students

When planning an individualized programme in spelling, keep the following points in mind:

- First determine the developmental level at which the student is already functioning in spelling; study some samples of the student's written work and use appropriate spelling tests to discover existing skill level and areas of weakness; note any common errors that need to be remedied.
- Set clear objectives for learning; discuss these with the student.
- In secondary schools, talk with the student's subject teachers to collect a list of subject or topic words frequently needed by the student in writing in their subject: for example, *ingredients, temperature, chisel, theory, science, hydrochloric, equation,* and *gymnasium.*

- Use this list for regular study, review, and assessment.
- Within each tutorial session, work on specific words misspelled in free writing lessons as well as on more general word lists or word families.
- When making a correction to a word, the student should rewrite the whole word, not merely erase the incorrect letters; where relevant, apply Old Way/New Way strategy and repeated writing.
- Repetition and overlearning are important, so aim to achieve high levels of practice through a range of exercises, games, word puzzles, and computer tasks to reinforce spelling of important words.
- Daily attention will be needed for the least able spellers, with weekly revision and regular testing for maintenance.
- Requiring a student to spell words aloud without writing them down and seeing them is of no value for weak spellers—although it is traditionally used in 'spelling bees'.
- A neat, careful style of handwriting that can be executed swiftly and easily is an important factor associated with good spelling.
- Smooth use of keyboard is also important for spelling.

Partner spelling

There is evidence that just as working with a partner when writing can assist with composing and editing skills, peer assistance can lead to growth in spelling ability in the primary school (Lundberg et al., 2023). One partner can rehearse the other to correctly spell words that were incorrect in a written assignment and can provide feedback and encouragement. The pair can also assist with proofreading of each other's assignments.

In the next chapter, attention turns to developing important numeracy skills. Often, students with learning difficulties find working with numbers and solving mathematical problems even more challenging than learning literacy skills.

Resources

Online

- *Spelling Mastery.* https://www.goodtogreatschools.org.au/spelling masteryguide/
- Ankucic, M. *The complete and exhaustive guide on how to teach spelling.* https://www.3plearning.com/blog/how-to-teach-spelling/
- BBC: *Spelling.* https://www.bbc.co.uk/teach/skillswise/articles/z6c6d6f
- Casey, M. *8 strategies for teaching spelling in primary schools.* https://bedrocklearning.org/literacy-blogs/teaching-spelling-in-primary-school/
- *How to teach spelling so words stick.* https://www.twinkl.co.uk/blog/how-to-teach-spelling-so-words-stick

- Institute of Education Sciences. *Students with learning disabilities: Spelling Mastery*. What Works Clearinghouse™. https://files.eric.ed.gov/fulltext/ED544745.pdf

Print

Brady, S., & Mason, L.H. (2024b). A literature review of morphological awareness interventions and the effects on literacy outcomes. *Learning Disability Quarterly*, 47(1), 16–29.

Helman, L., Bear, D.R., Templeton, S., Invernizzi, M., & Johnston, F.R. (2023). *Word study with multilingual learners: Phonics, spelling, and vocabulary instruction* (2nd ed.). Upper Saddle River, NJ: Pearson.

Hennenfent, L., Johnson, L.J., Novelli, C., & Sharkey, E. (2022b). *Intensive intervention practice guide: Explicit morphology instruction to improve overall literacy skills in secondary students*. Washington, DC. Office of Special Education Programs, US Department of Education.

Ittner, A.C., Frederick, A., Kiernan, D., & Bear, D.R. (2023). *Word study for literacy leaders: Guiding professional learning*. New York: Guilford Press.

Westwood, P. (2023b). *Developing spelling skills across the age range*. Macquarie Park, NSW: MTU Press.

Chapter 13

Numeracy and basic mathematical skills

The importance of numeracy has not decreased in this era of digital technology and continues to rank alongside literacy. When students leave school with a poor standard of numeracy, this can have devastating impact on career and economic prospects. Poor numeracy skills are known to affect a range of everyday competencies such as the ability to manage money, understand basic statistics and graphs in daily news reports, and comprehend details in medical reports, accounts, and invoices that one may receive. It is therefore acknowledged that in the current economic, scientific, and technological environment, there is a need to ensure that students leave school and enter adult life with a good standard of numeracy.

In several countries around the world, there has been growing concern that numeracy standards are falling well below those required for the 21st century (e.g., Lu, 2022; Picken, 2023; Poulter, 2023; Savage, 2023). To combat this situation, schools need to provide much more effective teaching of numeracy at all year levels and to provide early intervention for any students who are not progressing well. This chapter addresses the difficulties faced by many students in becoming fully numerate and presents some appropriate teaching methods to help overcome learning difficulties.

Mathematics teaching at Tier 1

Student-centred approach

Reforms in mathematics education that began in many countries in the late 1980s encouraged schools to implement what is known as a *constructivist approach*—often referred to as student-centred problem-based mathematics. Teachers were expected to create learning situations that provide opportunities for students to investigate mathematical concepts and discover number relationships for themselves by engaging in real problem-solving. This was deemed to be a more motivating and insightful way of learning rather than receiving traditional teacher-directed instruction and practice in arithmetic

DOI: 10.4324/9781003598671-14

skills. This constructivist approach is still advocated by the National Council of Teachers of Mathematics (NCTM) and is also implicit in the methodology recommended for implementing national curricula in Australia, the UK, and the US.

The constructivist approach places most emphasis on students developing deeper understanding of mathematical concepts while avoiding the rote learning of poorly understood calculation procedures. It was said that, too often in the past, students have been expected to remember algorithms, rules, and facts without grasping the underlying principles on which they are based. Currell (2018, p. 1) has written:

> During my schooling, math was a matter of following procedures and rules, and involved endless practice. I could follow and apply the steps as required, but understand little of it in a deeper, interconnected way.

Constructivist approaches have much to offer, but the notion that all students can learn mathematics entirely by immersion in problems has been challenged. Currently, there is concern that, under a constructivist approach, the reduced attention given to practising basic arithmetic skills to the point of mastery means that too many students do not develop essential fluency and automaticity (Poast et al., 2021; Nelson et al., 2018). There is little doubt that students with learning difficulties make much better progress in mathematics, particularly in the early stages of learning, when they are directly taught and then given time to practice each skill to an automatic level (Doabler & Fien, 2013; Flores & Hinton, 2022; Lu, 2022).

Teacher-led instruction

Critics have suggested that an extreme constructivist approach makes unreasonable assumptions concerning students' ability to discover, understand, and remember mathematical relationships—and this is certainly not the way that mathematics is taught in countries that rank highest in achievement (Japan, Korea, China, Singapore, Finland). In these countries, teachers use a much more teacher-led but interactive approach that integrates student participation with teacher instruction within a carefully sequenced and structured programme. Clear standards of achievement are specified, and the most effective teachers provide systematic instruction and constant questioning of students to ensure that understanding accompanies mastery of number skills and problem-solving. For example, what has become known as *Singapore Math*® recognizes that it is essential to spend as much time as is needed for students to master each concept before moving on. When introducing and developing new concepts, *Singapore Math*® always respects a teaching sequence of Concrete to Pictorial to Abstract (CPA). The goal is always to construct meaning in mathematics but not through the medium of unguided activity. The emerging perspective is that effective teaching and learning of mathematics require a well-orchestrated combination of investigative activities *and* teacher-directed explicit instruction and practice.

Using groupwork

The use of a direct teaching approach at Tier 1 does not mean that teachers abandon the use of groupwork and collaborative learning in the classroom. Lessons within a well-balanced programme include some time spent in teacher-led whole-class activity and some time devoted to group activities and independent practice. The groups are closely monitored and guided by the teacher to maintain a high success rate and strengthen students' motivation. Tasks involving students in discussion and sharing of ideas help them negotiate a deeper understanding of key concepts and processes that have already been more directly taught. Groupwork also allows for some degree of differentiation of curriculum content according to students' ability levels and rate of learning.

Digital technology

At Tier 1, use can be made of online and computer-based activities as part of groupwork, paired assignments, or differentiated individualized learning in the mathematics lesson (Kaczorowski et al., 2019; Serhan & Almeqdadi, 2020). Most recently, attention has been given to designing online math programmes that provide each student with immediate personalized correction, prompting, and feedback (Liu et al., 2024). In primary schools, much more use should be made of digital apps for practice in arithmetic operations (Dyrvold, 2022). At home and in school, mobile devices have increased significantly the opportunities for practice, revision, and developing automaticity in basic number skills (Urquhart et al., 2024).

Learning difficulties in mathematics

Students' level of achievement in numeracy is affected by many factors, including gender, socioeconomic family background, parents' level of education, and (most importantly) quality of instruction in school. While many students find mathematics a difficult subject to study, it is suggested that some 7 per cent of students have very significant problems in learning even the most basic concepts and skills (Nelson & Powell, 2018). A few of these students may have a specific learning disability related to mathematics (*dyscalculia*) (Hughes et al., 2023), but most have simply encountered difficulty in the early stages and have lost confidence in their own ability. They quickly develop a poor attitude towards the subject, and this destroys their future motivation.

The major factors associated with learning difficulty in mathematics include

- students falling behind and becoming discouraged
- little or no differentiation of learning activities or assessment tasks to match students' current abilities
- too little structuring of activity-based math, with students failing to learn anything
- teacher's use of overly complex language when explaining mathematical relationships or when posing questions
- students' weak reading skills contributing to difficulties in understanding math problems or printed explanations
- too little direct teaching time devoted to ensuring that students do achieve conceptual understanding.

Many difficulties can also be traced to poor teaching that has involved (1) abstract symbols being introduced too early in the absence of concrete materials and real-life or pictorial examples; (2) larger numbers involving complications of place-value being introduced before students have grasped simple relationships in numbers to 20; and (3) too little time spent developing automaticity with basic number facts, leading to slowness and inaccuracy in calculations.

One of the negative affective outcomes from difficulty in learning mathematics is a high level of anxiety in situations where competency needs to be demonstrated. The anxiety begins during the early school years but then remains during adolescence, preventing school-leavers from taking a career path that might have to involve dealing with numbers.

Math anxiety is now a well-recognized phenomenon and has attracted much research interest. High anxiety not only is emotionally draining but also leads to avoidance of all mathematics learning situations (Song et al., 2023). Students who display this anxiety usually require therapeutic counselling as well as intensive math intervention at Tier 3. The main challenge for teachers is to present the subject in such a way that students begin to succeed and enjoy the work rather than fail. One way of stimulating interest of students with learning difficulties is to avoid making textbook and whiteboard exercises the only medium used in lessons. Greater use should be made of engaging and authentic topics and materials from outside the classroom (e.g., sports results in the television news, data in newspaper reports, poll results, holiday planning and costings from online advertisements, and air fares).

Tier 2 and Tier 3 programmes

Several intervention programmes exist that focus on fundamental skills of counting, numeral recognition, grouping, solving simple addition and subtraction problems, and understanding place value. A meta-analysis of math intervention studies has yielded a very positive overall effect size of 1.02, a clear indication of benefits from such intervention (Rojo et al., 2023). Useful programmes include the following examples:

- *Mathematics Recovery* (Wright, 2003): Involves 30 minutes a day of individualized assessment-based instruction for low-achieving children ages 6 to 7 years.
- *QuickSmart Numeracy* (Bellert, 2009): Targets students in the middle-school years and is effective in building up fluency and confidence in basic arithmetic and in strategy use.
- *Numeracy Recovery* (Dowker, 2005): Targets 6- to 7-year-old children and involves 30 minutes of instruction per week over a period of about 30 weeks.
- *GRIN (Getting Ready in Numeracy)* (Kalogeropoulos et al., 2020): This small group or individual tutoring programme involves 15- to 25-minute sessions delivered at least three times per week. The purpose is to prepare primary and secondary school students who are weak at math for the upcoming mathematics lessons in their main classroom. The classroom math teacher communicates details of the content of future digital lessons in advance to the tutor.
- *DreamBox Math* (DreamBox Learning Inc., 2023). This is a concept-based computerized mathematics intervention for pre-K to grade 8. The programme adapts its feedback to the needs and performance of the individual learner. For more details, see the "Online" list in the "Resources" section at the end of the chapter.

Tier 3 individualized intervention

It is important that students with learning difficulties in mathematics should be identified early and given appropriate support. Individual support may come from the teacher, a classroom assistant, or a peer.

The most important features of intervention at Tier 3 include:

- providing direct guidance that is matched to the student's current level of understanding
- giving abundant additional practice opportunities that achieve mastery and automaticity in using basic facts and procedures
- sequencing curriculum topics carefully and controlling difficulty level
- encouraging the use of concrete or graphic materials where necessary and helpful
- using cue cards to display the steps to take in carrying out a specific process
- reading word problems aloud to the student to avoid any reading difficulty
- providing extended time to complete assignments and to work on problems
- encouraging use of a calculator to check an answer.

What should be taught?

In recent years, the content of mathematics courses in the UK and Australia has generally been delineated in guidelines that accompany national curricula. Similarly, in the US, the *Common Core State Standards* describes the mathematical skills and concepts that must be mastered from kindergarten through to high school. In 2017, Education Scotland also provided examples of specific standards (benchmarks) for numeracy (see "Resources"). In these countries, it is agreed that at Tier 1 all students need to develop problem-solving skills and that to achieve this goal it is important also that they acquire fluency in mental arithmetic and written calculation through the use of effective evidence-based methods. It is acknowledged that to achieve this outcome, adjustments and differentiation often need to be made to the learning activities, resource materials, and objectives for students with learning difficulties. For some students, additional teaching and re-teaching will be required at Tier 2 and Tier 3.

Traditionally, students with learning difficulties were placed in the lowest-ability group and given a modified version of the mainstream math curriculum. Sometimes (particularly in special schools and secondary special classes), an alternative math curriculum would be developed with a focus on teaching 'survival math,' involving much practice in basic addition, subtraction, multiplication and division, and applications to counting money, giving change, budgeting, paying bills, and simple linear measurement. It was thought that a functional approach geared to everyday life was more likely to enhance students' motivation and engagement and would also increase the likelihood that skills taught would generalize beyond the school setting. Now inclusive education policies generally recommend that, as far as possible, these students should be helped to engage in the same Tier 1 mathematics curriculum as all other students, with extra help for some at Tier 2 or Tier 3.

A diagnostic approach

There are three levels at which diagnostic work in mathematics can be conducted—*concrete, semi-concrete*, and *abstract*. During diagnostic work with a student, the teacher may move up or down within this continuum from concrete to abstract in an attempt to discover the level at which the student can succeed with each concept or process. At the *concrete level*, the student may be able to solve a problem or complete a process correctly if allowed to use real objects or counters. At the *semi-concrete level*, pictorial representation of objects, together with tally marks, will provide sufficient visual information to ensure success. At the *abstract level*, a student can work mentally with numerals, signs, and symbols.

The first step in intervention at Tiers 2 and 3 should be to ascertain what the student can already do in each area of the appropriate math curriculum. The next step is to locate any gaps in knowledge and skills and determine precisely what he or she needs to be taught next. The teacher is really finding answers to the questions: 'What can the student do independently in mathematics?' and 'What can he or she do if given a little help and guidance (scaffolding)?' It is also essential to gain an impression of the student's level of confidence or anxiety.

The first question can be answered by conducting some informal testing and examining the student's workbooks to determine the level at which he or she is functioning. A student's errors tend to reveal much about their current knowledge and skills and can help identify faulty procedural knowledge, gaps in understanding, and misconceptions. Appropriate follow-up testing can then be used. For this purpose, teachers usually construct their own informal 'mathematical skills inventory' containing items covering key concepts, knowledge, and processes presented in earlier years, together with essential material from the current curriculum. Observing a student working through the items can indicate what the student can do, what he or she is not sure about, and how confident he or she is in tackling math problems.

Assessment should not be confined to the four arithmetic processes but should also include age-appropriate word problems to be solved. Observing how a student goes about solving a problem can reveal much about his or her flexibility in thinking, underlying knowledge, and number skills proficiency. When a student explains or demonstrates how he or she tackles a problem, the teacher can identify the exact point of confusion and can intervene from there.

Teachers usually check the following capabilities when appraising problem-solving.

Can the student…

- detect what is called for in a problem?
- identify relevant information?
- select and perform correct procedure?
- estimate an approximate answer?
- compute the solution?
- check the answer and, if necessary, self-correct?

By referring to any items the student fails to solve in a test or during deskwork, the teacher should consider the following: (1) *Why* did the student get this item wrong? (2) Can he or she carry out the process if allowed to count on fingers or use a number line or calculator? (3) Can the student work through an example step by step, explaining aloud each action. At what point does the student misunderstand or forget the next step?

Teaching at concrete and semi-concrete levels

Having used a diagnostic approach to discover what a student can already do, and having planned an intervention, the teacher should consider age-appropriate methods and activities for Tiers 2 and 3. The following pages identify some issues to consider.

Real and structural materials

When working with young or intellectually disabled children, the teacher should at first use real objects to illustrate quantitative relationships. However, in Tier 2 and Tier 3 remedial teaching contexts, real objects can be supplemented or replaced by materials such as counters, picture cards, Multibase Arithmetic Blocks, Cuisenaire Rods, or Unifix. These can be used to illustrate concepts such as conservation of number, grouping and re-grouping, place value, multiplication, and division. Blocks can also be used to visually represent the quantities referred to within a word problem (e.g., 6 cars and 3 trucks; 14 girls and 4 boys). This is particularly important for students with learning difficulties, as it helps them store *visual representations* of number relationships in memory. It must be recognized, however, that a student must not rely for too long on having blocks or counters but must progress to the next stage of processing number relationships mentally. In recent years, digital technology and virtual reality have created several resources that depict blocks that can be manipulated on a screen (Park et al., 2022).

Counting

Counting is the most fundamental of all early number skills and underpins most of the basic number concepts and processes required in early learning (Gripton & Rawluch, 2021; Westwood, 2023). Counting must be recognized as a very important foundation for numeracy development, and counting strategies used by preschoolers are highly predictive of their later mathematics achievement. This essential skill includes rote counting (reciting the number names in correct order), counting on fingers, accurate counting of small groups using one-to-one correspondence, and using more advanced counting strategies such as 'counting on' from a given number, counting back, and counting by 2s, 5s, and 10s. In the beginning stages, physically counting items in a set helps the youngest children reinforce the important concept of number conservation—the understanding that no matter how items in a group are rearranged, the number of items does not change unless you put more in or take some out.

If a young or severely disabled child has not acquired accurate counting of real objects, the skill must be taught by direct instruction and practice (Greer & Erickson, 2019). The problem is often that these students can rote-count but, when counting an actual group, fail to make a correct one-to-one correspondence between the spoken number word and each object touched in a sequence. Teachers should take every opportunity during any school day to have preschool children count with one-to-one correspondence—for example, when walking up steps, when counting out books, and when counting children into groups. Counting activities using pictorial material and animations can now be presented also on a computer screen, to supplement any hands-on concrete counting activities (Mutflu & Akgün, 2019).

Recognition and writing of numerals

Alongside counting, the ability to recognize instantly the numerals from 1 to 10 (and later from 11 to 20, etc.) is an important step in increasing a preschool child's number system. It is helpful that numerals are very frequently on display in preschool children's educational television programmes and picture books, with the cardinal value of number symbols related to a wide variety of objects. At home and in preschool, games provide a very natural and effective way of practicing both counting and numeral recognition (Lange et al., 2021). Number games also have a role to play in Tier 2 and Tier 3 intervention for young students with intellectual disability.

Activities that can help to establish numeral recognition include

- numeral-to-group matching games—for example, the numeral 11 on a card to be matched with 11 birds, 11 kites, 11 cars, 11 dots, and 11 tally marks
- lotto cards with a selection of number symbols (1 to 10; 1 to 20; or 25 to 50, etc.)—when the teacher holds up and says a number, the child covers the numeral on the lotto card and, at the end of the game, must read each number aloud to the teacher
- The same lotto cards can be used for basic addition and subtraction facts, the numerals on the cards now representing correct answers to some simple oral question from the teacher ('5 add 4 = …' 'The number 1 less than 8 is …').
- Numeral cards can also be devised for students to sort and arrange in correct sequence from one to ten, one to twenty, and so on.
- Basic items from Unifix can also be helpful at this stage (e.g., inset pattern boards, number indicators, and number line one-to-twenty).

At this stage, correct writing of numerals should also be taught as part of normal handwriting instruction. Correct formation of numerals should be established thoroughly to reduce the incidence of reversals of certain figures like 3, 5, 9 in written recording. A tendency to reverse a figure or place value needs to be remedied before it becomes stored in muscle memory as an incorrect motor habit.

As students move through the grades, it is also important that they can *correctly read aloud* the printed numbers involving tens, hundreds, and thousands that they encounter in school and elsewhere (Shalit & Dotan, 2024).

Number facts

Number facts are those familiar associations that can instantly be retrieved from memory (e.g., $5 + 2 = 7$; $3 \times 2 = 6$; up to $9 + 9$ and 9×9). Such facts are always involved within sub-routines carried out in all calculations, and for this reason they need to be recalled with a high degree of automaticity. Being able to recall number facts easily is important because it makes calculation faster. Knowing number facts is partly a matter of learning through repetition (constant exposure and practice) and partly a matter of grasping a rule and developing insight (e.g., that zero added to any number does not change it: 3 + 0 = 3, 13 + 0 = 13, etc.; or if 7 + 3 = 10, then 7 + 4 must be 'one more than ten', etc.). Number facts become automatic only after a great deal of practice. Many students with learning disabilities have difficulty recalling number facts and tables, so they require extra attention devoted to this key area.

Using a number line

A number line or number track is a linear representation of numbers placed in correct visual sequence. This line is a very useful aid for supporting students' counting skills and for making clear processes of simple addition (counting on from a given number) and subtraction (counting back) (Sutherland et al., 2024). The number line can also be used to teach 'interval counting' in twos, fives, and tens.

Many students discover the value of a number line for themselves without formal instruction; and even older students will often be seen using calibrations on a ruler to count forward or back as an aid to mental calculation. In primary school, teachers can use a number line to demonstrate basic operations such as multiplication and division or as an aid to problem-solving. Unifix has a 1-to-100 number track divided into 10-unit sections. In kindergarten, one would use only the section for 1 to 10 or 1 to 20. In primary school, the sections from 20 to 100 can be added and students can place blocks in the track to model operations such as 22 + 13, 45 + 17, 21 x 3, 26 ÷ 4, etc.

Teaching computation skills

Computation skills are those used in applying routine procedures involved in addition, subtraction, multiplication, and division. Students with learning difficulties often experience problems in becoming proficient in these essential skills (Rojo & Wakim, 2023). Once young students are ready to learn conventional ways of recording number operations, they must be taught how to encode vertical and horizontal forms of computation. For example, a student should be able to watch as a 'bundle of ten rods and two extra ones' (12) are added to a set already containing a 'bundle of ten rods and three extra ones' (13) and then write the operation as

$$12 + 13 = 25$$

or

$$12 + 13 = 25$$

When students are first learning a new algorithm, it is usual practice to teach them 'self-instructions' for carrying out each step in a particular calculation. An example is provided below for a subtraction item (HTU) using the *decomposition method*.

$$5_7 \cancel{8}_1 1 - 1\ 3\ 9$$
$$\overline{4\ 4\ 2}$$

The student would be taught to verbalize the steps in some way similar to the wording below. Practice in applying this mental 'script' is essential (Powell et al., 2023), but once mastered, the procedure becomes automatic and verbalizing is unnecessary.

The student says:

Start with the units. I can't take 9 from 1, so I must borrow a ten. Cross out the 8 tens and write 7 tens.
Write the borrowed ten next to the 1 to make 11.
Now I can take 9 from 11 and write 2 in the answer space.
Under the 10's column: 7 take away 3, leaves 4 tens.
In the 100's column: 5 take away 1, leaves 4. Write 4 in the answer space.
My answer is 442.

A support teacher, tutor, or parent who attempts to help a student in this area of school work should liaise with the class teacher in order to find out the precise 'self-talk' that is used in teaching the four arithmetic processes, so that exactly the same directions are used in the Tier 2 or Tier 3 remedial programme to avoid confusion.

With the advent of the constructivist approach, teaching these verbal scripts fell into disrepute. It was argued that mindlessly following a memorized script may represent nothing more than rote learning. It is also felt by some experts that learning to use scripts may inhibit the mathematical thinking of more-able students and may prevent them from devising insightful methods of calculation. However, without such verbal cues in the early stages, lower-ability students are likely to remain totally confused and frustrated.

Calculators

The most common form of technology in the mathematics classroom is, of course, the calculator. This handheld device has proven to be a boon for many students, allowing them to complete more work and spend more time on problem-solving. Calculators are of particular value for students of high ability, enabling them to tackle some very complex and challenging problems and to explore mathematical ideas more deeply.

Calculators have an important role that is far more than simply acting as a tool to avoid tedious calculations by hand. For students with special needs, a calculator provides a means of temporarily bypassing computation weaknesses. In math tutoring at Tier 2 and Tier 3, calculators can certainly be used to add variety to lessons and help develop important self-help skills for everyday use.

In the Australian Curriculum, guidelines state that from Year 3 onwards students should be able to use a calculator to check the solution and reasonableness of an answer. By Year 7, they should be able to investigate problems with digital technologies; and beyond Year 7, calculators are recommended to support graphical, computational, and statistical aspects in mathematics lessons. Guidelines within the revised National Curriculum in the UK suggest that calculators should be a regular tool only in later stages of Key Stage 2 (age about 10 years). In the primary school years, students still need to develop sound and reliable skills in mental and written calculation without relying on a calculator.

Developing problem-solving skills and strategies

The whole purpose of learning mathematics is to acquire knowledge, skills, and strategies that enable an individual to solve problems they may encounter during school time, working life, at home, and during leisure. From the learner's perspective, solving a real-life problem involves much more than simply applying a pre-taught algorithm. Non-routine problems need to be analyzed carefully, and procedures selected must be suitable for purpose. Instructing students in problem-solving is more difficult than teaching them basic arithmetic processes. However, there is evidence that all students can be helped to become more proficient at solving math problems if adequate time is devoted to this important aspect of mathematics.

Mathematical problem-solving is particularly challenging for students with learning difficulties because it often involves close reading of a word problem, interpreting and integrating information, selecting an appropriate computation process, performing the calculation, and checking the result obtained. These students commonly display confusion and anxiety when faced with complex mathematical problems in printed form (Passolunghi et al., 2019). They may begin by having difficulty reading the words and comprehending the exact meaning of specific terms. Next, they do not really understand what they are being asked to find out, and this uncertainty compounds their difficulty in selecting a process to use. Their constant lack of success with math problems leads to loss of confidence and undermines self-esteem and motivation.

Most students with these difficulties need to be directly taught a range of problem-solving strategies. A few online e-books are beginning to make use of 'personalized prompting' to help a student move step by step through a problem (Lee et al., 2024b). The aim is to show how to process the information in a problem thoughtfully and sequentially—and without feeling helpless. Students need to be able to sift the relevant from the irrelevant information and impose some degree of structure on the problem.

It is clear that students can understand problems much more easily if the subject matter relates closely to real-life situations and to their own direct experience (Ma & Xin, 2024). There are apps available now that can help create such problems for use in teaching (e.g., *Realistic Mathematics Education Strategies Mobile App*: Sanal & Elmali, 2024). It is generally accepted now that there are teachable steps through which an individual must pass when solving mathematical problems. These steps can be summarized as

- interpretation of the problem
- identification of processes and steps needed
- translation of the information into an appropriate algorithm or algorithms
- careful calculation
- checking of the result
- self-correction when necessary.

While working through a problem, a student needs to think

- what needs to be worked out here? (identify the problem)
- can I picture this problem in my mind? Can I draw it? (visualization)
- how will I do this? (select a process or strategy)
- perform relevant calculations
- is this calculation producing a reasonable result? (self-monitoring)
- check if my final solution is correct (reflection, reasoning, evaluation)
- do I need to correct any error and try again? (self-correction)

The sequence for teaching problem-solving to students with learning difficulties begins with direct teaching, followed by guided practice, and ending with independent control. Once students have been taught a particular strategy, they must have many opportunities to apply the strategy themselves under teacher guidance and with corrective feedback. Finally, they must be able to use the strategy independently and generalize its use to other problem contexts.

An example

A problem-solving strategy might use a particular mnemonic to aid recall of the procedure. For example, in the mnemonic 'RAVE CCC', the word RAVE can be used to identify the first four possible steps to take:

R = Read the problem carefully.

A = Attend to words that may suggest the process required (*share*, *altogether*, *less than, how many*).

V = Visualize the problem and perhaps make a sketch, diagram, or table.

E = Estimate the possible answer.

The letters CCC suggest what to do next:

C = Choose the numbers to use.

C = Calculate the answer.

C = Check the answer against your estimate.

Additional teaching points to consider when improving the problem-solving abilities of students with learning difficulties include

- deliberately linking math problems to the students' life experiences
- pre-teaching any difficult vocabulary associated with a specific word problem, so that comprehension is facilitated
- providing cues (such as directional arrows) in the early stages to indicate where to begin calculations and in which direction to proceed
- providing more examples than usual, to establish and strengthen the application of a particular strategy
- giving students experience in setting their own problems for others to solve
- stressing the value of self-checking and self-correction
- using appropriate computer-aided instruction or specifically designed apps.

Students with specific talents in mathematics

Students who possess extremely high aptitude for mathematics can be regarded as having 'special educational needs' in that they require a curriculum that is far deeper and more demanding than that usually offered in the mainstream. In inclusive classes, it is all too easy for these students to become bored and frustrated in math lessons where the material is pitched at the average standard and the pace is too slow. It is vital to identify these students quickly and intervene with some form of differentiation that provides greater intellectual challenge and enrichment (Budínová, 2024; Çayir & Balci, 2023). Such differentiation is achieved by modifying curriculum content, creating non-routine problems, and using a variety of higher-level resource materials (including computer software). Investigative projects that require talented students to use initiative, creativity, and mathematical reasoning must become the norm. Some schools have also found it valuable to offer extra-curricular activities with a focus on mathematics and to find mentors who can work with gifted students to advance their mathematical reasoning and skills.

A few students who are gifted in mathematics may not necessarily be gifted in other subjects; conversely, not all gifted students have a high aptitude for mathematics (Paz-Baruch et al., 2022). As a contrast to students with a high aptitude for mathematics, there are a few gifted students who may achieve highly in most school subjects but exhibit a specific learning disability (*dyscalculia*) in the area of mathematics (Holman, 2023). These students usually require Tier 3 intensive support and are known to learn best when teachers use explicit instruction, with lesson content broken down into achievable steps and instructional scaffolding provided. They may also need personal therapeutic counselling if their dyscalculia is causing them chronic anxiety. There are now many computer programmes and apps for mobile devices that can be used by students with dyscalculia to help practice basic computation processes.

The remaining two chapters provide additional information on teaching methods that are known to produce the most effective outcomes and on how teaching methods, learning materials, and assessment can be adapted for students with learning difficulties and disabilities.

Resources

Online

- *DreamBox Math.*   https://apps.apple.com/us/app/dreambox-math/id675354945
- Department for Education and Skills (UK). *National standards for adult literacy and numeracy.*
- https://management-ui.excellencegateway.org.uk/sites/default/files/National%20standards%20Eng%20and%20Maths.pdf
- National Numeracy Organization (UK). *The essentials of numeracy.* https://www.nationalnumeracy.org.uk/what-numeracy/essentials-numeracy
- New Zealand Ministry of Education (2024). *NCEA Numeracy in your classroom.* https://ncea.education.govt.nz/ncea-numeracy-your-classroom
- Development and Research in Early Math Education (DREME). Stanford University. *What children know and need to learn about counting.* https://prek-math-te.stanford.edu/counting/what-children-know-and-need-learn-about-counting
- Education Scotland. (2017). *Benchmarks: Numeracy and mathematics (e.g., Savage, 2023).* https://education.gov.scot/media/s5edgtvx/numeracyandmathematicsbenchmarks.pdf

Print

Dole, S., & Geiger, V. (2019). *Numeracy across the Curriculum: Research-based strategies for enhancing teaching and learning.* New York & London: Routledge.
Ferguson, S., & Polojac-Chenoweth, D.L. (2024). *Implementing problem-based instruction in secondary mathematics classrooms.* New York: Teachers College Press.

NSW Department of Education (2024). *Numeracy guide: Years 3 to 8.* Sydney, Australia: NSW Department of Education.

Skills You Need Ltd. (2021). *Fundamentals of numeracy.* Witney, UK: Skills You Need Ltd.

Westwood, P. (2021b). *Teaching for numeracy across the age range: An introduction.* Singapore: Springer.

Chapter 14

A taxonomy of teaching methods

There is no single method that is superior to all other methods for all teaching purposes. One specific method cannot possibly be appropriate for all areas of the curriculum or for all ages and abilities of students. Methods must be selected according to their suitability for a given purpose with a specific age group. A teacher's decision to select an approach for use at a particular time must depend upon the nature of the lesson content to be taught, the learning objectives, and the salient characteristics of the students in the group. Selection of approach should also be based on hard research evidence that the method is the most effective. When an inappropriate teaching approach is used, learning difficulties are created or exacerbated.

An example of inappropriate teaching is the use of an informal immersion method for the beginning stages of learning to read and write. Under this approach, the role of the teacher is regarded not as that of an instructor but as that of a 'facilitator and creator of opportunities for students to learn for themselves.' Against such an approach for teaching literacy and numeracy skills is research evidence showing conclusively that young children make significantly better progress when directly taught in the beginning stages. Over many decades, this research has provided evidence that direct and active teaching appears to be the most powerful method for introducing any new knowledge or skills in many areas of the curriculum and particularly for addressing the needs of students with learning difficulties and disabilities (Brophy & Good, 1986; Gage & Giaconia, 1981; Gillon et al., 2020; Spooner et al., 2019; Witter & Hattie, 2024). It has also been suggested that teacher-directed learning for all students in the early stages is the best preparation for students later to become efficient self-regulated learners (Tan, 2018).

Despite the evidence supporting teacher-directed methods, pre-service teacher education courses in the US, Britain, New Zealand, and Australia are tending to advocate only methods almost entirely based on the *constructivist theory* of learning—meaning that that all lessons must be student-centred and inductive rather than teacher-directed and instructive. Decades after the important teacher-effectiveness studies were conducted, one of those key researchers has remarked: 'Despite the potential value of this research, it has

DOI: 10.4324/9781003598671-15

largely been ignored by policy makers, and when used, has been misused' (Good, 2024, p. 111).

Tier 1 teacher-led approaches

It is relevant to begin by exploring Tier 1 methods that are teacher-directed and structured. As indicated above, the effectiveness of these approaches has been strongly supported by evidence. This teacher effectiveness also depends upon the teacher managing the behaviour of the class well and establishing a good working relationship with the students (Berger et al., 2023).

Direct and active teaching

Direct teaching is the term applied to all forms of active teacher-led instruction that attempt to take students through the curriculum in a reasonably structured and systematic manner. Direct teaching is characterized by having precise learning objectives, clear demonstrations, explanations and modelling by the teacher, guided practice for students, corrective feedback, and finally independent practice and application by the students. The approach is sometimes referred to as 'I do. We do. You do' (Bauml, 2023). Learning is assessed at very regular intervals, and re-teaching is provided if necessary. Direct and active teaching can be thought of as the complete opposite of 'immersion methods' that simply expose students to learning situations with the minimum of guidance.

This form of teaching can be used across the curriculum when introducing any new topic to a class, when clarifying a concept, when providing important information, when setting out the steps in a new procedure or process, and when consolidating or reviewing content at the end of a lesson or series of lessons. In reality, no teacher would use direct and explicit instruction as his or her *only* approach for all purposes—but the ability to teach essential curriculum content and skills explicitly, *when necessary*, should be part of all teachers' classroom expertise. In the course of a single lesson a teacher may switch several times between teacher-directed input and student guided and independent study.

Explicit instruction

Explicit instruction is an important feature of direct teaching and involves presenting any new information clearly and directly to learners in language and a form they can access and understand (Agarwal & Bain, 2019; Michaud & Ammar, 2023; Stratton, 2023). Explicitness in teaching core curriculum subjects involves clarity, and logically sequencing lesson content organized into manageable units. The approach involves teachers in the classroom informing, demonstrating, explaining and narrating. The same principles also need to be implemented in the design of any online teaching programmes that present new information in a clear and systematic manner. Explicit instruction has proven to be of particular importance for students with learning difficulties and disabilities and also for those learning English as a second language (Colovic-Markovic, 2019; Ennis & Losinski, 2019; Lantolf, 2024). Countries where explicit teaching is the dominant approach for academic subjects are also the countries that are found to have the highest student achievement levels (e.g., China, Korea, Singapore, and Japan). It is fair to assume that this relationship is not a coincidence.

Explicit instruction is not simply a passive 'transmission' approach that attempts to fill up 'empty brains' of students with information; good explicit instruction involves a great deal of interaction between teacher and students—particularly when teachers use questioning effectively. More is said later on this important role of questioning. The approach can be greatly enhanced by appropriate use of visual and technological support, such as interactive whiteboards, graphic organizers, on-screen PowerPoint material, pictures, models, illustrated textbooks, and web-based resources.

The most essential skill for a teacher to possess for explicit instruction is the ability to explain things simply and clearly. This skill depends partly on the teacher's ability to view a new topic from the perspective of a student learning it for the first time, partly on the ability to organize information into sequential, teachable, and learnable units, and partly on the ability to express ideas in plain language that can be understood by learners of that age and ability. According to Serki and Bolkan (2024), clarity in instructions and in teaching materials facilitates easy access, maintains students' motivation, and increases their rate of learning.

It is important always to recognize that when used in inclusive classes, teacher-led lessons need to take account of individual differences among students, such as their prior knowledge and skills, language background, literacy level, attention span, and motivation. Some students will require more explanations, more reteaching, and more correction than others. Chapter 15 provides practical advice on differentiating instruction and support.

Interactive whole-class teaching

Interactive whole-class teaching combines teacher-led instruction with very high levels of active participation and responses from the students (Slater & Chambers, 2024). The lesson operates through a two-way process in which the teacher (or computer app) presents and explains new information to students, then asks questions that challenge students' thinking and invite responses. The students offer their ideas and suggestions, explain their thinking, express their opinions, and ask questions of the teacher and each other (Sherry, 2019). The activities the teacher designs for use within a lesson are intended to encourage and maintain this type of dialogue.

Inclusive teaching strategies often incorporated into interactive whole-class teaching include *unison responding* (answering together) (Barbetta & Morales, 2022; Thompson et al., 2019) and the use of *response cards* (Gulboy, 2023). Unison responding simply involves all (or several) students answering a question or repeating information together rather than the traditional method of asking them to raise a hand and then calling upon one student. When response cards are used, the teacher provides all students in the class with a set of blank cards at the beginning of the session. At certain times during the lesson, the teacher asks the students a particular question and every student immediately writes his or her response on the card and holds it up for the teacher to check. Both unison responding and response cards ensure a high rate of active participation by all students and have been shown to produce positive learning outcomes.

In Britain, interactive whole-class teaching is advocated as an approach for improving literacy and numeracy standards in primary schools and is regarded as much more productive than individual programming or unstructured group work. It is claimed that effective use of interactive whole-class teaching helps to close the learning gap that usually appears between higher-achievers and lower-achievers when 'work at your own pace' methods are used.

Some points to consider concerning interactive whole-class teaching include (1) the teacher needs to be skilled at drawing all students into discussion, otherwise some students will not participate actively in the lesson; (2) some teachers, particularly those who believe strongly in informal methods, appear to find this often fast-paced, interactive approach difficult to implement and sustain; (3) if the pace of the lesson is too brisk, students with learning difficulties tend to fall behind and opt out.

Direct Instruction

The most formal and structured version of teacher-led method has the capitalized name Direct Instruction (DI). It is usually implemented for teaching reading, spelling, and arithmetic as a small-group Tier 2 intervention for students with learning difficulties or for students with mild intellectual disability. In the US, DI has also been used as a Tier 1 booster approach with young students in very socio-economically disadvantaged schools.

DI delivered to small groups of early primary school students was first developed by Engelmann and others at the University of Oregon (e.g., Adams & Engelmann, 1996; Engelmann, 1999). The commercial material associated with that form of DI usually comprises a scripted manual of pre-planned lessons for the teacher and workbooks for students. In a typical DI lesson, about six to eight students are seated in a semi-circle facing the teacher. The teacher gains and holds their attention and then follows the teaching script with steps clearly set out. This ensures that all input and questions in the planned teaching sequence are followed. Unison responding by the whole group is used as a strategy for maximizing participation. This form of DI has been very well researched over many years, with a diverse range of students with special needs and disadvantages (e.g., Engelmann, 1999; Mason & Otero, 2021; Thompson et al., 2019). DI of this type has proven very effective indeed in raising achievement levels in basic academic skills in students with learning difficulties and those with intellectual disability.

Since DI is highly effective, one would expect to find the method being widely used for teaching the foundation stages of basic literacy and numeracy; but this is not the case. While DI has enjoyed some popularity in special education settings, it has had limited impact in mainstream schools where primary and early childhood teachers prefer to use methods that encourage children to learn at their own rate and in their own way. These teachers react very negatively towards DI, claiming that it is too highly structured, too rapidly paced, and allows no creativity on the part of teachers. It is also clear that most teacher education institutions in the past thirty years have tended to omit coverage of DI in their methodology courses, instead devoting their full attention to methods that are child-centred and guided by constructivist learning theory.

The following points need to be considered when deciding to use DI: (1) it is not appropriate to pick and choose certain parts to be used and to omit others; published DI programmes must be implemented exactly as the designer has prescribed; (2) the fact that DI must be implemented on a daily basis, using small group instruction rather than a whole-class teaching can cause problems in scheduling and staffing.

In contrast to teacher-led instruction, the approaches described below endeavour to place learning more in the hands of the students. Descriptions are provided of discovery learning, project-based learning, resource-based learning, inquiry-based and issues-based learning, and situated learning.

Tier 1 teaching approaches based on constructivist principles

Constructivist, student-centred inductive methods such as discovery learning and activity-based approaches are highly appropriate for areas if the curriculum that require investigation and that encourage curiosity and creativity. However, there is very little research evidence to support superiority of inductive methods over teacher-led instruction for beginning to learn basic information and entry skills in a new subject. This is particularly the case with entry into beginning literacy and numeracy. A main concern is that when used inappropriately, these inductive methods tend to maximize the *cognitive load* placed on a learner when attempting to process simultaneously many different sources of information in unstructured tasks or problems (Gorbunova et al., 2023). A very different situation occurs in teacher-led instruction, because overloading of short-term memory processes is avoided by the teacher presenting information clearly to learners in manageable and sequential steps (Serki & Bolkan, 2024). *Cognitive load theory* (Sweller, 1988, 2023) suggests that we need to provide direct teaching and teaching materials that do not overload a learner's short-term memory processing capacity.

Discovery learning

Discovery learning (DL) draws upon the constructivist theory that believes students construct knowledge about a topic or concept best through their own engagement with it and by accessing whatever human, technological, and other resources they require. All variations of DL place emphasis on students being active investigators, rather than passive recipients of information delivered to them by a teacher, textbook, or computer programme.

DL has been in use in schools and universities for many generations, and its popularity ebbs and flows according to the prevailing beliefs about learning. DL has spawned several offshoots such as *inquiry-based learning, problem-based approach* and *guided discovery*. The guided or assisted discovery approach recognizes that some degree of input from a teacher or an online programme can greatly enhance the discovery process (Dunn, 2022; Großmann & Wilde, 2019; Lee & Yeung, 2022). In unstructured discovery situations, learners are given very little direction from the teacher and must decide for themselves the appropriate way to investigate a given topic or problem.

This unstructured approach is often used in secondary school science and mathematics and sometimes for topics in social studies. The outcome is not always good, particularly for students with poor literacy or numeracy skills and difficulties with inductive reasoning. In order to participate successfully in open discovery activities, learners must have adequate inductive reasoning ability to recognize principles or cause-effect relationships emerging from their observations. Some students can develop serious misconceptions and become very confused and frustrated in unstructured discovery activities. Guided or assisted discovery has much tighter structure, and teachers have found that learning is more successful when the investigative process is explicitly taught and the students have the prerequisite understandings. The teacher (or the online programme) sets clear objectives, provides initial explanation to help students begin the assignment efficiently, and may offer suggestions for a step-by-step procedure to find the target information or to solve the problem.

The major benefits of DL include

- learners are actively involved in the process of learning and the topics studied are usually intrinsically motivating
- activities used in authentic discovery contexts are usually more meaningful than classroom exercises and textbook study

- it is claimed (but is by no means certain) that learners are more likely to remember facts and concepts if they discover them
- DL builds on learners' prior knowledge and experience
- DL encourages independence in learning because learners acquire new investigative skills that can be applied in many other contexts
- DL requiring collaboration among students can foster positive group-working skills.

The following points must be considered when using DL:

- DL processes can be a very time-consuming, often taking much longer for concepts to be 'discovered' and understood than would occur with direct teaching
- DL relies on learners having adequate literacy, numeracy and independent study skills
- students may learn little of value from discovery activities if they lack adequate prior knowledge for interpreting their discoveries accurately
- 'activity' does not necessarily equate with 'learning'—learners may appear to be actively involved but may still not understand or recognize underlying concepts, rules or principles
- students with learning problems often have difficulty forming opinions, making predictions and drawing conclusions based on evidence
- teachers are not always good at creating and managing DL activities, and poor outcomes occur.

Project-based learning

The project approach has also been used in primary and secondary schools for many years. It lends itself easily to curriculum areas such as social studies, environmental education, geography, history, civics, science, mathematics and the languages, enabling students to apply and extend their knowledge. Project-based learning for individuals and groups has also become very commonplace in universities and vocational colleges.

Project work can help students integrate ideas, information and skills from different subject areas. It has also been found that the collaborative activities that are typically involved in classroom project work can enhance motivation and the working relationship between students and their teachers. All teacher education programmes should equip trainee teachers with the knowledge and skills necessary to design and use project-based learning effectively in their subject areas (Grossman et al., 2019).

Information technology can be fully utilized in project work, resulting in students gaining both information and communication technologies (ICT) skills and specific curriculum content knowledge simultaneously. The extended timeframe usually provided for project work allows students to plan carefully, revise, and reflect more deeply upon their learning. Currently, it is suggested that projects should adopt a 'Five E's' framework with attention to student engagement, exploration, explanation, elaboration, and evaluation (Rodriguez et al., 2019).

Based on research to date, the effects of project-based learning have been mixed. Some studies have found no advantage over other approaches, while others have found positive impacts in science and social studies. Some schools have also pointed to positive effects of project work on students' engagement, motivation, and self-efficacy (Bergeron, 2021; Saavedra & Rapaport, 2024).

There are many potential benefits from project work:

- It is an inclusive approach in that all learners can participate to the best of their ability.
- Projects promote meaningful learning and can connect new information to students' experience and prior knowledge.
- Generic processes involved in gathering and processing data can transfer easily to other topics and situations.
- Students become better both at self-direction and at working as a member of a team.
- Undertaking a project encourages decision-making and allows for student choice.
- In addition to acquiring facts, learners use higher-order thinking and planning abilities.
- Preparing the project helps students apply basic reading, writing, and ICT skills.
- Assessment can be performance-based.

Important points to consider when using project-based learning include

- Some students lack adequate independent study skills for researching, collating, and interpreting information and will need to be well supported.
- When working on projects, some students may give the outward impression of productive involvement but may in fact be learning and contributing very little.
- When projects involve the production of posters, models, charts, recordings, photographs, and written reports for display, there is a danger that these are actually 'window dressing' that hides a fairly shallow investigation and poor overall understanding of the topic.
- When different aspects of a topic are given to different group members to research, there is a likelihood that individual members never really grasp a deep *overall understanding* of the whole topic. The teacher needs to spend adequate time bringing together, summarizing, and consolidating the various products.

Resource-based learning

Resource-based learning (RBL) is also underpinned by constructivist learning principles and is closely associated with project work and guided discovery. RBL can be used across the curriculum but currently is mainly applied in social studies, history, geography, science, and environmental studies. RBL is an approach that can be used in differentiated programmes, where the resources are carefully matched or adapted to students' different levels of ability and special needs. In this respect, digital technology in the form of web-based learning resources has increased exponentially the range of materials that students can access at home and in school (Kyriakos, 2023). Online materials proved to be a boon during the Covid-19 pandemic.

The main aim of RBL is to foster students' autonomy in learning by providing opportunities to work individually or collaboratively while utilizing appropriate resources, such as books, community publications, photographs, reports, recordings, and online information, to investigate authentic topics. Students obtain information they must then interpret and collate before organizing their findings into an appropriate form for presentation. The use of authentic resources and tools in a meaningful context makes the approach interesting and motivating for a wide ability range.

Typically, in RBL situations, the teacher introduces a topic or problem to be investigated through the use of a variety of relevant resources. The teacher and students together clarify the nature the task and set goals for inquiry. In some cases, it may be necessary to pre-teach researching skills such as online searches, locating print information, extracting relevant data, summarizing, locating websites, and taking notes. The students then work individually or in groups to carry out the required investigation over a series of lessons.

Advantages claimed for RBL include the following:

- Use of print, electronic media, and other authentic resources motivates students and encourages self-directed learning.
- Students learn from their own active interpretation and collation of information.
- Study skills are strengthened and extended in ways that easily generalize to other learning contexts.
- RBL topics can stimulate higher-order thinking, problem-solving, reasoning, and critical evaluation.
- RBL can increase students' academic engagement time.

Points to consider when using RBL:

- RBL requires a resource-rich learning environment, including easy access to reference books and digital media.

- Effective engagement in RBL depends on students having adequate literacy and numeracy skills and also demands motivation, initiative, and self-management.
- Care must be taken to guard against students simply using a copy-and-paste approach to recording and collating information without fully understanding the material.
- Students with learning difficulties may need to be placed with a supportive partner or group in order to participate successfully.

Problem-based, inquiry-based, and issues-based learning

These closely related approaches are widely recommended in many official guidelines for school curricula, and they are considered particularly useful in programmes for gifted students. Currently, problem-based learning (PBL) is still not widely used as a main approach in primary and lower secondary schools but has become very popular in senior school and in higher education. PBL is now seen as the method of choice in training programmes for many professions (e.g., medicine, law, sciences, and engineering).

In problem- and issues-based learning, students are presented with a real-life situation or issue that requires investigation and a decision leading to action. With older learners, the problems are often intentionally 'messy' (ill-defined) in the sense that not all of the information required for solution is provided in the problem, and there is no clear path or procedure to follow. It is believed that through tackling the complex issue students will acquire new skills and insights.

It is claimed that inquiry-based and problem-based teaching can lead to better knowledge acquisition than traditional methods for most learners (Kožuchová et al., 2023). However, many students with special needs find engaging in the inquiry and problem-solving process difficult because of their weaker literacy and study skills. There is a danger that, when faced with a challenging topic, they opt out of making much effort, so become marginalized in group activities. It is suggested that instead of presenting them with topics or problems that are totally unstructured, a teacher should provide more step-by-step guidance using what is termed *learner-centred scaffolding* (LCS). The use of such scaffolding over time plays an important role in ultimately improving students' own self-directed learning (Kim et al., 2019).

The advantages of these inquiry and problem-solving approaches include the following:

- Learning objectives are authentic and can link school learning with the real world.
- The process of tackling problems and identifying, locating, and using appropriate resources can be motivating for learners.

- Participating in the approaches involves active construction of new knowledge and usually requires the integration of information and skills from different disciplines.
- Knowledge obtained is likely to be retained and can be transferred to other situations.
- These methods encourage self-direction in learning and prepare students to think critically and analytically.
- Investigating problems or issues usually requires teamwork and thus can enhance communication and collaborative skills.

Considerations when applying problem-based, inquiry-based, and issues-based learning include the following:

- The problem or issue to be studied must be of genuine interest and significance to the students.
- The school needs to have the appropriate resources to support and facilitate students' investigations.
- Students need to have (or be provided with) adequate prior knowledge to make sense of the topic or content of the problem.
- Students must possess the prerequisite independent study skills to engage successfully with the problem or issue, or they need to have adequate support through direction and input from the teacher.
- Students with learning difficulties will usually require much more individual scaffolding to achieve successful outcomes.

Situated learning

Situated learning is an attempt to combat criticism that much of the teaching that goes on in schools is artificial because it is not presented in a real-life context and often learners do not recognize the social and functional value of what they are taught. Whenever possible, teachers should make use of authentic tasks in real-life contexts for teaching information, skills, and strategies (D'Souza & Clare, 2018). Situated learning places students in a physical and social setting that is real (or close to real) where the knowledge and skills will be applied in real life. Examples might be a supermarket, bus station, airport, workshop, or kitchen. Within that setting, a range of teaching methods may be used, including discovery, problem-solving and enquiry, and direct teaching. This type of *in situ* teaching and learning has long been a feature in special schools for students with intellectual disability, where students need reality-based learning.

The advantages of situated learning include the following:

- It represents a motivating and participatory approach to learning.
- Opportunities are provided for learning and practising in real or simulated contexts where skills can be acquired for immediate use.

- Experts or mentors are available to provide learners with support; instructional scaffolding and direct coaching are provided as necessary.
- Students are more likely to become confident and independent thinkers.
- Learning is likely to generalize more easily to new contexts.
- Collaboration among learners can be encouraged.

Issues to consider when providing situated learning in school contexts include the following:

- Arranging and maintaining real-life learning situations (often off campus) add considerably to teachers' workload.
- Technical expertise is often required by the teacher for developing or assembling situated resources.
- Some teachers are not confident in teaching in unusual and unpredictable settings and without clear lesson structure.
- Class size can be a major obstacle to organizing sessions off campus.

Computer-based instruction and computer-aided learning

There are at least a dozen different terms currently in circulation related to the use of computers and handheld devices for educational purposes. In most cases, the differences in meaning are almost negligible. For the purposes of this chapter, the preferred terms are *computer-based instruction* (CBI) and *computer-aided learning* (CAL). The use of CBI and CAL in the classroom has increased very rapidly in the past decade, with positive effects reported for students' academic achievement and for increased motivation, engagement, and students' self-esteem. It is relevant to note that these benefits apply equally to students with special needs (Burt et al., 2022; de Barros & Ganimian, 2024; Simmons et al., 2023; Stultz, 2017). In the case of students with behaviour problems or with attention-deficit/hyperactivity disorder, working at a computer can significantly improve on-task engagement and productivity.

CBI is the broad term applied to all forms of instruction where a computer is used to present curriculum content. Usually, the student responds to material displayed on screen and followed up with embedded questions or problems. The computer programme often monitors the learning that is taking place as the student works through the material, and it may provide corrective feedback and re-teaching of key points. CBI can be used as a starting point for studying a new topic independently or later for extension and application work once a topic has been introduced by other methods such as explicit teaching and class discussion.

CBI embodies the basic principles of any form of effective instruction, namely very clear presentation of information, careful sequencing of steps, embedded practice, feedback, and applications. These programmes normally contain on-screen text, graphics, sound, and video and are very effective in gaining and holding students' attention and participation. CBI programmes often provide direct links to other web-based resources and can greatly increase students' access to information.

CAL is the term usually applied to the planned integration of computer materials to supplement or reinforce other forms of teaching. Often, one-to-one programmes are designed to provide additional practice exercises or new problems or may present additional examples to enrich the content taught during face-to-face lessons. Immediate corrective feedback to the learner is always a strong feature of CAI, and usually the programme does not move ahead until the student has mastered current content. According to Hattie and Yates (2014), use of a computer to supplement traditional teaching produces stronger results than using CBI alone as a total alternative.

CAL has proven useful for students with learning difficulties and disabilities, and they frequently display a positive attitude towards using a computer. Students with learning difficulties usually require more time and direction than others in the early stages in order to develop confidence and competence in basic computer skills.

CBI and CAL have both played an important role in the current trend to move away from traditional models of teaching to a more technology-based and independent learning approach. This is most clearly evident in the notion of the 'flipped classroom', currently used principally in higher education settings but also appearing in schools, particularly during the Covid-19 pandemic (Wang & Jou, 2023; Maycock, 2019; Verdonck et al., 2024). 'Flipped' in this context means a reversal of the conventional sequence where a teacher first presents new information through a formal lesson, and then students work on related class exercises and homework. In the flipped classroom, new curriculum topics are first studied by the students via digital programmes and other forms of print and on-line resources. After this period of student-centred learning, the students come together with the teacher to use the knowledge they have gained by engaging in work that requires application, discussion, and expansion of what they know. The teacher monitors this in-class work, corrects any misconceptions, sets follow-up activities, and acts as a supportive tutor when individual students require help or direction. The teacher's role is to consolidate and expand upon concepts and skills the students have acquired independently, regularly assess their progress, and provide appropriate feedback. The approach has been suggested as particularly appropriate for academically gifted learners.

CBI and CAI have the following benefits:

- Mode of presentation ensures that learners make active, self-initiated responses and are in charge of the learning situation.
- Software can be matched to students' ability level and rate of learning and is therefore one valuable way of differentiating instruction.

- Learners usually gain immediate knowledge of results after every response they make, so reinforcement and corrective feedback can be provided efficiently.
- Students move towards greater independence and self-regulation in learning.
- CBI and CAL provide a private method of making errors and self-correcting.
- Learners can engage in extra practice and overlearning to master basic skills.
- Most (but not all) students enjoy working at a computer more than using textbooks and print resources.
- Students can extend their computer competencies, now regarded as essential life skills.
- Teaching subjects such as science, social studies, mathematics, environmental education, and the arts can be enhanced by documentary or simulation programmes and by giving access to Internet resources.

Issues to consider in relation to CBI or CAL: (1) students with literacy problems may have difficulty comprehending text displayed on the screen; programmes and apps with voice input as accompaniment can help; (2) technical failures occur, resulting in lost time and frustration; and (3) a few students actually prefer group interactions with peers and teacher rather than using technology.

E-learning

O'Neill (2024) has identified 15 unique definitions of e-learning, but they all tend to cover forms of digital online and web-based teaching and learning. The availability of online learning has proven to be a boon for students who are unable to attend school for reasons such as living in a remote region, having a severe disability or chronic illness, home schooling, or due to school closure during a pandemic or crisis. These forms of technology are enriching the quality of educational programmes and can greatly enhance students' motivation and participation.

This additional mode for teaching and learning is still developing at an exponential rate and has much to offer students at all levels of ability. However, issues surround the online ready availability of what is termed 'generative artificial intelligence' (Gen AI). AI can create original text on request, such as an essay or speech (Bradley, 2024). The fear is that students will use AI to complete assignments, solve mathematical problems, or prepare model answers for examinations instead of engaging cognitively themselves with the tasks.

E-learning is being incorporated increasingly into the education of students with special needs (Abed, 2018; Mølster & Nes, 2018; Smith et al., 2013; Young & Donovan, 2022). Combining e-learning and CAL with other forms of teaching has proven to be an effective blended approach with students with a variety of disabilities. Naturally, aspects of e-learning can be problematic for students with hearing or vision impairment, and Lee and Oh (2017) have suggested that to improve accessibility of e-materials for these students it is usually necessary to provide additional in-built supports in the form of online guidance and assistance.

Effective use of e-learning and technology relies entirely on a teacher's pedagogical judgement and skills to determine how, when, and where to integrate it effectively into the curriculum. The term *blended teaching* is often used now to describe the mixing of face-to-face instruction with the use of CAL and web-based resources (Seage & Türegün, 2020). Pre- and in-service professional training for teachers needs to provide more guidance in how best to utilize e-learning and other technologies as an integral part of a differentiated approach in inclusive classrooms.

The final chapter provides information and suggestions for adapting or modifying some of the methods described here, to make them more inclusive of a wider range of students. The main theme of Chapter 15 is differentiation of methods, materials, and curriculum content.

Resources

Online

- An overview of teacher-led and student-centred methods can be found at https://teach.com/what/teachers-know/teaching-methods/
- *What is inductive method of teaching: Pros & cons* (2024). https://www.splashlearn.com/blog/inductive-method-of-teaching/
- Utah State Board of Education. (2020). *Instructional approaches: Explicit and inquiry-based instruction.* Salt Lake City, UT: Utah State Board of Education. https://www.schools.utah.gov/curr/elaelementary/_eleelementary_/Explicit%20an%20Inquiry%20Based%20Instructional%20V2%20-%20ADA%20COMPLIANT.pdf
- Benjamin, Z. (2024). *Cognitive load theory: A practical guide and tips for teachers.* https://thirdspacelearning.com/blog/cognitive-load-theory/
- A list of evidence-based teaching strategies can be found at https://teaching.utk.edu/evidence-based-teaching-strategies/
- An overview of the advantages and disadvantages of E-learning can be found at https://www.academia.edu/4052785/Advantages_and_Disadvantages_of_e_Learning

Print

Cole, F. (2024). *An educator's guide to project-based learning: Turning theory into practice*. Independence, KY: David Fulton Publishers.

Ferguson, S., & Polojac-Chenoweth, D.L. (2024). *Implementing problem-based instruction in secondary mathematics classrooms*. New York: Teachers College Press.

Hall, T.E., Robinson, K.H., & Gordon, D. (Eds.). (2024). *Universal Design for Learning in the classroom: Practical applications for K-12 and beyond* (2nd ed.). New York: Guilford Press.

Proctor, J. (2022). *Teaching methods and practices*. Minnesota, MN.: University of Minnesota.

Scanlon, D.M., Anderson, K.L., Barnes, E.M., & Sweeney, J.M. (2024). *Early literacy instruction and intervention: The interactive strategies approach* (3rd ed.). New York: Guilford Press.

Chapter 15

Differentiating the curriculum and adapting instruction

Inclusive schooling has brought with it the urgent need to adapt aspects of Tier 1 teaching so that students with special learning needs or disabilities could participate successfully in the mainstream curriculum. The term *differentiation* is now used to describe these adjustments to classroom environment, teaching method, curriculum content, and teaching materials (Roiha & Polso, 2021). In simple terms, differentiated instruction can be regarded as the fine-tuning of classroom teaching procedures and learning activities to address important differences evident among learners. An important aspect of this differentiation is teachers making choices about how they distribute their time and support during a lesson (van Vijfeijken et al., 2023).

Adaptations and differentiation

Meeting students' special educational needs successfully in inclusive classrooms usually requires that subject matter, learning activities, teaching procedures, resource materials, methods of assessment, and patterns of classroom organization *at times* be adapted or modified. It is claimed that for many students it is often differentiation during whole-class teaching at Tier 1 that makes the difference between success and failure. There will still be some students with special needs (including gifted learners) who may require additional teaching, tutoring, or intervention beyond that given through differentiation at Tier 1 (Gilson & Lee, 2023; Mays, 2020).

In the UK, curriculum guidelines and the *Special educational needs and disability code of practice* (DfE, 2015) have endorsed a differentiated approach as a necessary component for inclusive education to give almost all learners access to the National Curriculum. The guidelines also state that teachers have an obligation to plan lessons to include successful participation by students who are low achievers or who come from disadvantaged backgrounds. This indicates clearly that a differentiated approach does not simply target students with disabilities but includes students with other special needs. Some students will require consolidation of what they have been taught, while others, such as gifted learners, will need to deepen their understanding. Data collected from

DOI: 10.4324/9781003598671-16

UK schools and students indicate that teachers are indeed endeavouring to adapt their teaching and make other adjustments that enable students with special needs to participate in the curriculum, but much more still needs to be done (Ofsted, 2021).

Similarly, the Australian Curriculum Assessment and Reporting Authority (ACARA, 2024) offers specific guidance on how the Australian Curriculum can accommodate the diverse learning needs of students with disabilities and learning difficulties, gifted and talented students, and students with English as an additional language or dialect. As is the case in the UK, Australian schools also need to do much more in terms of differentiation within classroom teaching.

In the US, the expectation is also that teaching methods and curriculum will be differentiated to ensure that as many as possible students can achieve the required level in the *Common Core State Standards* (Tomlinson & Imbeau, 2014; Tomlinson & Imbeau, 2023). It is recommended that if a student with special needs requires an individual education plan (IEP), the goals for that programme should connect as far as possible with the published Common Core Standards.

The small amount of evaluation research that has been carried out suggests that teachers find differentiation very difficult to plan and maintain and that differentiated teaching as provided in schools at the moment may have only a slightly positive effect on students' overall achievement.

Guiding principle: Keep it simple

Sustaining a differentiated approach in inclusive classes invariably places heavy demands on teachers' ingenuity and organizational skills. It is no simple task to manage a class in which many different activities and levels of work are occurring simultaneously and where individual students are requiring different amounts of guidance and direct support. So, from the beginning, it is essential to stress that there are many occasions every day when all students can engage successfully in the same activity, so make adaptations and modifications only when it is essential to do so. Whenever possible, a student with special needs should be helped to use the same learning materials and participate in the same learning activities as all other students. Differentiation should be less about drastically changing the content of the curriculum for some individuals and more about providing differentiated amounts of direct support to individual students during the lesson. In this way, all students are included when working towards a common goal in a particular curriculum topic.

Starting points for differentiation

An appropriate place to begin planning differentiated instruction is by identi-fying essential core information, concepts, or skills associated with the curriculum topic to be taught. All students in the class will be expected to master this core content to the best of their individual abilities. Differentiating the topic then becomes a process of creating different ways that students with difficulties can achieve this goal through engaging in a variety of coherent experiences matched to their abilities. As a general rule, all students in the group will learn best if provided with a variety and combination of activities and pathways.

Planning needs to include consideration of strategies for delivering additional help to certain students during the lesson (e.g., via peer assistance, a learning-support assistant, or from the teacher or digital resources). It is also important to consider how students will be grouped and how the available time will be used most effectively. When planning differentiated objectives for a lesson, you may find it helpful to keep in mind the three stem statements:

- All students will...
- Some students will...
- A few students may...

In other words, *all students* will be expected to master the essential core knowledge and skills in a lesson but possibly through engaging in different learning activities. *Some students* will achieve more than this core, and *a few students* may achieve one or two higher-order objectives through extension and enrichment activities.

Typical adjustments that can be made include the following examples. Many of these adaptations and accommodations are explained in more detail later:

- providing alternative teaching materials for some curriculum topics (e.g., simplified reading material with more illustrations, graded worksheets, concrete materials and visual aids for math, Braille texts, captioned videos, and computer apps that match a student's ability level)
- when necessary, using more direct and explicit teaching, more modelling by the teacher of skills and cognitive strategies, more frequent guided practice, and more personalized support and re-teaching for some students
- scaffolding students' learning through more prompting, guidance, feedback, and correction
- varying time allocation for classroom tasks to take account of students' differing learning rates
- providing alternative ways for students to demonstrate their learning (e.g., oral rather than written assignments and tests; assistive technology; and augmentative and alternative communication systems)
- improving access to learning activities and resources (e.g., seating arrangements; wider aisles for wheelchair access; modified furniture; and assistive technology)

- organizing flexible groupings of students and facilitating more peer assistance and peer tutoring
- making any necessary accommodations for certain students during tests and examinations (e.g., allowing an adult to read questions aloud and then write the student's responses; giving more time to complete a test; presenting the test via computer rather than paper-and-pencil; and larger writing on the whiteboard)
- utilizing additional support personnel such as classroom assistants (paraprofessionals), parents, and volunteer helpers to work with groups or individuals
- adjusting the timetable to accommodate out-of-classroom therapy sessions for students with a physical disability or speech disorder or for accommodating a behaviour modification programme for a student with a conduct disorder.

It can be seen that manageable differentiation and adaptations are usually associated with adjustments to learning activities, instructional materials, and student support strategies.

Adapting curriculum content and learning activities

Differentiation of curriculum usually means that for some students, the content to be studied may be increased or decreased in terms of quantity, depth, and complexity while still ensuring that core concepts and skills are covered. Differentiation is most easily implemented where it does not involve drastic changes to curriculum content.

In many countries, recommended modifications to curriculum are indicated in a student's IEP. The IEP may also suggest alternative activities and provision of additional services such as counselling, speech therapy, or a behaviour change intervention. In the UK, much the same function is embodied in the *Education, Health and Care Plan* (*EHCP*) (Council for Disabled Children, 2017).

Modifying curriculum content usually implies that students with learning difficulties will cover activities or exercises that are a little easier to accomplish and perhaps involve smaller steps in learning or with more repetition. In the case of gifted students, the reverse would be true—lesson content would be made more challenging, and students would cover content in greater depth, often through independent computer-based and online studies.

Learning activities represent the main way in which learners engage actively with curriculum content. Activities can be presented and engaged in via different methods (e.g., responding to a computer programme, tackling a textbook exercise, watching a video, and manipulating objects). It is important that activities and tasks set for students with special needs not be simply 'busy work' that is less demanding and less interesting.

One approach to differentiating activities and tasks is termed *tiered assignments*, with work on a topic provided at three or four levels of challenge (Magableh & Abdullah, 2022). Students are first allocated tasks at a level that matches their own ability and rate of learning; they can progress to higher levels over time.

For more information on using tiered assignments that can be found online, see the "Online" list in the "Resources" section at the end of the chapter. In addition, Hodgson (2013) presented some excellent examples of tiered reading comprehension and writing activities around the theme of 'motor-cycles'. These examples have the great advantage of using a format that does not immediately label the worksheets (in the eyes of the peer group) as being for a specific ability level. Students do not like to be given simplified materials, because this marks them out as different and undermines their status in the peer group. Adolescents in particular are acutely sensitive to peer-group reactions and deeply resent being overtly treated as if they are lacking in ability. Teachers can use various ways of grouping students within the class to allow for different tiered activities to take place, under differing amounts of teacher direction. At various times, the classroom can be set up to support individualized projects or for cooperative group-work, and use may be made of learning centres, computer-aided instruction, or resource-based learning.

Obviously, greater adjustments to the curriculum are always required for students with moderate intellectual disability. Often, there is a greater necessity to help these students acquire essential everyday living skills and greater autonomy rather than study traditional subject matter (Amir & Guskey, 2024; Rochford, 2016). This represents one of the most serious and unresolved challenges for inclusive schools: how to provide a really relevant curriculum for students with significant cognitive impairment.

Several potential problems exist when modifying the curriculum and the associated activities; for example, reducing the complexity and demands of tasks and setting easier objectives for some students may sound like very good advice, but watering down the curriculum in this way can have the long-term effect of increasing the achievement and knowledge gap between students with learning difficulties and other students (Westwood, 2024). By reducing the demands placed on students of lower ability, we may be exaggerating the effect of individual differences and perpetuating inequalities among students. The ideal to be aimed for is that all students experience basically the same curriculum a far as possible but receive varying amounts and types of additional support to ensure success.

Homework assignments

Differentiated homework assignments are an important way of meeting the needs of gifted and able students as well as those of students with difficulties

(Vatterott, 2018). Some students may be given homework that involves additional practice at the same level of difficulty, while others may have extension tasks involving more challenging applications, critical thinking, and reflection. It is often helpful to discuss with students the exact purpose of a homework assignment so that they can appreciate its relevance for their overall progression. Parents of students with mild intellectual disability can benefit from practical advice on how to help and motivate their child to engage in simple homework (Payne & Swanson, 2023).

Adapting instructional materials

Instructional materials and learning resources represent another area where modifications can be made to improve access to the curriculum. A variety of texts and materials at various levels of complexity and readability should be available for students to use. The resources within a lesson (worksheet exercises, whiteboard notes, computer software, and captioned videos) will need to be carefully selected to match a student's ability level, and additional equipment (e.g., assistive technology; calculator with audio output for a student with impaired vision; modified keyboard; and touch screen) may need to be provided for some students.

Listed below are suggestions for preparing instructional materials for students with poor literacy skills. Often, these simple adjustments enable a student to access text without the need for further assistance.

When preparing print materials (worksheets, assignment cards, study notes, and independent learning contracts), a teacher may

- pre-teach recognition and meaning of key terms and important new vocabulary
- simplify information and instructions by using short sentences and substituting simple words for difficult terms
- modify sentences to facilitate comprehension——active voice is easier to process than passive voice: *The teacher reads the story* rather than *A story was read by the teacher.*
- present information in small blocks of text rather than as dense paragraphs
- use bullet points and lists rather than dense paragraphs
- improve legibility of print and layout; if necessary, enlarge the size of print
- highlight important information by using underlining or printing the words in bold type or colour
- provide supporting illustrations or diagrams where possible
- give cues or prompts where written responses are required from the students; for example, provide the initial letter of the answer or use dashes to show the number of words required in the answer.

Differentiating products from lessons

Often, the output from a lesson will be tangible products, such as written work, graphics, or models, but sometimes the product is another form of evidence of learning, such as an oral report, a physical demonstration, a group presentation, active participation in discussion, or the answering of oral questions. Digital technology has increased the range of options that students can utilize when presenting their evidence of learning.

Differentiating the products of learning may mean that

- each student is not expected to produce exactly the same amount or quality of work as every other student
- a student may be asked to produce work in a different format—for example, an audio recording, a drawing or poster, scrapbook, or a multiple-choice exercise—rather than a formal essay
- individual students may negotiate what they will produce and how they will produce it in order to provide evidence of their learning in a particular topic
- encourage the use of varied types of resources and formats in preparing products
- provide product assignments at varying degrees of difficulty to match student readiness.

The potential danger in setting out from the start to accept less work from some students or of a lesser quality is that this strategy represents a lowering of expectations that can result in a self-fulfilling prophecy—a student produces less and less, and the teacher in turn expects less and less of them. A different perspective suggests that teachers need to help students achieve more by working on the same product as other students *but with more guidance and support.* Differentiation of product should never be seen as offering certain students a soft option; and it should never lead to a student consistently managing to avoid tasks he or she does not like to complete.

Adapting teaching strategies

Teachers tend to be much better at using modifications to teaching processes than they are at modifying curriculum content. They appear to find teaching modifications more 'natural' and easier to accomplish within their personal teaching approach. For example, skilled teachers are observant and already provide additional help and re-teaching to students when necessary and use prompting and guidance. They also differentiate the level of their questioning, and they make greater use of targeted praise, encouragement, and rewards during lessons. These are all strategies that can be applied while the teacher is still following a common curriculum with the whole class——for this reason, they are regarded as the most feasible adaptations for teachers to make. As indicated already, the most natural way that teachers manage student diversity in their class is to vary the amount of direct help given to individuals during a lesson. They may also encourage peer assistance and collaboration among students and may use the services of a classroom assistant or volunteer helper to give extra individual assistance to students.

When teaching procedures and processes are differentiated, some of the following strategies may be used:

- make full use of explicit and direct forms of instruction at Tier 1 when introducing new topics and when re-teaching small groups at Tier 2
- re-teach information to some students using simpler language and more examples
- use effective tactics to gain and maintain the interest of poorly motivated or distractible students
- ask questions at different levels of difficulty and targeting different individuals
- monitor the work of some students much more closely throughout the lesson and provide more guidance and encouragement when needed
- give corrective feedback and descriptive praise, with more detail or less detail according to the students' needs
- provide extra practice for some students, often via differentiated homework assignments
- to the most-able students, allocate more demanding extension work requiring independent study, investigation, and application
- use tiered activities with different degrees of challenge
- establish and equip small learning centres (or interest centres) in the classroom to enable students to explore certain topics independently.

General areas in which teachers can adapt their teaching approach include varying the pace of instruction and the use of additional support to individuals. The rate at which new information is presented and activities carried out during lessons can be varied. The speed at which students are required to complete tasks, answer questions, and produce outputs can be adjusted to individual capabilities. The nature of learning tasks set for students will be matched to their learning rate and abilities, and some tasks will take longer to complete than others.

Adapting assessment

Assessment refers to any process used to determine what learners already know and how much new learning has occurred for each student in the class. Outcomes from assessment highlight anything that may need to be taught again to all students, revised, or given additional practice time for some students. Assessment thus provides an indication of how effective a particular episode of teaching has been.

Differentiation of assessment procedures may often be necessary for any students with a disability, because these students may have problems revealing what they know or can do in typical tests and examinations. Their difficulties are magnified when an assessment method requires proficient literacy, numeracy, or motor skills at a level they have not yet achieved. Modifications to assessment processes are therefore necessary to enable equal access for students with special needs. Typical modifications include

- simplifying the instructions for tests and for questions embedded within assessment tasks
- shortening tests and tasks
- allowing longer time for these students to complete the work
- allowing a student with special needs to have some assistance in completing the test (e.g., questions read aloud to the student; student dictating answers to a scribe)
- enabling the student to carry out the work in a different format (e.g., notes rather than an essay; oral answers; computer printout).

Classroom tests are one of the ways in which teachers routinely assess progress of their students. These teacher-made tests may require modification to format for students with special needs. Modification to formats may involve

- enlarging the print
- leaving more space for the student to write an answer
- using different types of questions (e.g., short answer, multiple-choice, sentence completion, gapped paragraphs, and matching-items format)
- writing instructions in simpler language and highlighting key points
- keeping directions brief and simple
- providing prompts such as *Begin the problem here* and *Answer in one sentence only.*

Modifications to test administration procedures include

- using oral questioning and accepting oral answers
- using a scribe to write down a student's answers
- giving short rest breaks during the test
- allowing extra time to complete the test
- avoiding penalties for poor spelling or handwriting
- allowing a student to use a laptop to undertake the test
- giving credit for providing supporting drawings if these will help to indicate that the student knows the concept or information
- administering the test in a quiet environment other than the classroom to reduce distractions for some students (e.g., social worker's office, withdrawal room).

In the UK, the *Rochford Review* (Rochford, 2016) provided valuable guidelines for carrying out assessment with students who have severe disabilities and for whom a mainstream subject-based curriculum is inappropriate. The Review suggests that assessment for these students should focus on acquisition of daily living skills and development of the attributes that enable them to engage in learning: attention, responsiveness, curiosity, persistence, initiation, and investigation. These attributes are seen as pre-requisites for possibly progressing to a more subject-specific curriculum.

Accommodations for students with disabilities

The specific needs of students with disabilities are usually identified within their IEP, and the IEP should be seen as the main source of advice for the types of differentiation and adaptation needed. The term *accommodation* usually conveys the notion of making allowances to ensure that students with disabilities can participate fully or partially in the common curriculum. This accommodation for most students with special needs is achieved (as described above) by varying the type of activities or the method of instruction, providing additional human and technical support, modifying the ways in which the student can respond, or adapting the classroom environment.

Many students with disabilities will also need assistive technology such as modified keyboard, computer with a visual display and touch screen or with voice synthesizer, audio books with text-to-speech features, simple predictive spelling apps, Braillers for blind students, enlarged text on computer screen for a student with partial sight, and radio-frequency hearing aids for students with impaired hearing. Less sophisticated aids might include basic communication boards for students without speech (Redford, 2019). It is beyond the scope of this book to discuss assistive technology in great detail, but some basic information was provided in Chapters 4 and 5. The use of assistive technology has increased greatly over the past four decades and, in addition to helping students in inclusive settings, has improved the quality of life for adults with disabilities (Piekema et al., 2024).

Universal Design for Learning

In recent years, much has been written about the notion of Universal Design for Learning (UDL) as a model for providing differentiated pathways to studying a common curriculum. The assumption behind UDL is that it should be possible to prepare and present information and skills to students in multiple ways that match their aptitudes and enable them to express themselves and demonstrate their learning. In principle, UDL caters for the needs of all students, ranging from those with difficulties to those with gifts and talents and from school-age students to adults. Under this principle, it should be possible for students of differing abilities in any classroom or in any online learning situation to have equal access to the curriculum and to achieve the planned learning objectives by taking different pathways tailored to their abilities and needs (Cumming & Gilanyi, 2023; Lohmann et al., 2023; Murawski & Scott, 2019).

The three essential features of UDL that must be incorporated when designing curricula are (1) *multiple means of representation* (e.g., print medium, Braille, video, audio, information and communication technology, concrete materials, diagrams, and simulations), (2) *multiple means of engagement* (looking, listening, hands on, participating, discussing, individual, group, independent, collaborative, interacting, and peer tutoring), and (3) *multiple means of expression* (e.g., oral, written, photographic illustration, art, and creative performance) (Gargiulo & Metcalf, 2022). It is suggested that digital formats and e-learning tend to be flexible enough to incorporate many of these features in ways that can adapt to individual differences among learners. Digital technology can utilize many variations in modes of presentation, engagement, and response, thus relieving the teacher of the massive burden of designing multiple pathways in advance. UDL obviously has much in common with differentiated instruction in the sense that barriers to learning are reduced by offering multiple pathways to achievement.

Unfortunately, so far, UDL has been largely an unfulfilled ideal and remains a practice more written about than implemented. There is a need for more research to indicate whether UDL initiatives can improve learning outcomes for a wide ability range and, importantly, whether the typical teacher can sustain the model on a daily basis.

The way ahead

Most teachers are experimenting now with ways of addressing individual differences, such as by making more effective use of technology, multi-media kits, peer tutoring, flexible grouping, and tiered assignments. Similarly, designers of e-learning software are becoming increasingly skilled at producing multi-level motivating and interactive programmes. School systems are experimenting with ways of meeting students' special needs through various tiered models of intervention. Much has been achieved, but there is still much to do and to learn. It is hoped that the chapters in this book have given teachers additional understandings and skills necessary to achieve inclusive teaching expertise.

Resources

Online

- Tiered assignments. https://teachers-blog.com/guide-to-implementing-tiered-assignments-in-classrooms/

- Adaptive teaching: A practical step-by-step guide. https://thirdspacelearning.com/blog/adaptive-teaching/
- A teacher's guide to using effective differentiation in teaching. https://thirdspacelearning.com/blog/differentiation-in-teaching/
- Moving from differentiation to adaptive teaching. https://educationendowmentfoundation.org.uk/news/moving-from-differentiation-to-adaptive-teaching
- Differentiated instruction. https://ctl.stanford.edu/differentiated-instruction
- Adapting materials for mixed-ability classes. https://www.teachingenglish.org.uk/article/adapting-materials-mixed-ability-classes
- Differentiation of student products. https://www.lessonplanet.com/article/gifted-and-talented-education/differentiation-of-student-products

Print

Amir, A.S.F., & Guskey, T.R. (2024b). *Life skills for all learners: How to teach, assess, and report education's new essentials.* Alexandria, VA: ASCD.

Blevins, W. (2024). *Differentiating phonics instruction for maximum impact: How to scaffold whole-group instruction so all students can access grade-level content.* Thousand Oaks, CA: Corwin.

Murawski, W.W., & Scott, K.L. (Eds.). (2019b). *What really works with Universal Design for Learning.* Thousand Oaks, CA: Corwin.

Roberts, J.L., & Inman, T.F. (2023). *Strategies for differentiating instruction: Best practices for the classroom* (4th ed.). Austin, TX: Prufrock Press.

Tomlinson, C.A., & Imbeau, M.B. (2023b). *Leading and managing a differentiated classroom* (2nd ed.). Alexandria, VA: ASCD.

Westwood, P. (2024b). *Inclusive and adaptive teaching: Meeting the challenge of diversity in the classroom* (3rd ed.). London: Routledge.

References

Abed, M.G. (2018). Teachers' perspectives surrounding ICT use amongst SEN students in the mainstream educational setting. *World Journal of Education*, 8(1), 6–16.

Abu, N.K., Akkanat, Ç., & Gökdere, M. (2017). Teachers' views about the education of gifted students in regular classrooms. *Turkish Journal of Giftedness and Education*, 7(2), 87–109.

ACARA (Australian Curriculum, Assessment and Reporting Authority), (2024). *Student diversity*. https://www.australiancurriculum.edu.au/resources/student-diversity/

ACER (Australian Council for Educational Research). (2013). *Literacy and numeracy intervention in the early years: A report to the NSW Ministerial Advisory Group on Literacy and Numeracy*. Melbourne: ACER.

Adamecz, A., Henderson, M., & Shure, N. (2024). Intergenerational educational mobility: The role of non-cognitive skills. *Education Economics*, 32(1), 59–78.

Adams, G.L., & Engelmann, S. (1996). *Research on Direct Instruction: 25 years beyond DISTAR*. Seattle, WA: Educational Achievement Systems.

Adams, R. (2019). Children with special needs are marginalized, says NAO. *The Guardian*, 11 September 2019. https://www.theguardian.com/education/2019/sep/11/children-with-special-needs-are-marginalised-at-school-says-nao

Adams, R.E., Lampinen, L., Zheng, S. Sullivan, V., Taylor, J.L., & Bishop, S.L. (2024). Associations between social activities and depressive symptoms in adolescents and young adults with autism spectrum disorder: Testing the indirect effects of loneliness. *Autism: The International Journal of Research and Practice*, 28(2), 461–473.

ADCET (Australian Disability Clearinghouse on Education and Training). (2024). *Physical Disability*. https://www.adcet.edu.au/inclusive-teaching/specific-disabilities/physical-disability

Agarwal, P.K., & Bain, P.M. (2019). *Powerful teaching: Unleash the science of learning*. San Francisco, CA: Jossey-Bass-Wiley.

Alberto, P.A., Troutman, A.C., & Axe, J. (2021). *Applied behavior analysis for teachers* (10th ed.). Upper Saddle River, NJ: Pearson.

Alqahtani, S.S. (2023). iPad text-to-speech and repeated reading to improve reading comprehension for students with SLD. *Reading & Writing Quarterly*, 39(1), 1–15.

Altintas, E., & Özdemir, A.S. (2015). The effect of differentiation approach developed on creativity of gifted students: Cognitive and affective factors. *Educational Research and Reviews*, 10(8), 1191–1201.

Amir, A.S.F., & Guskey, T.R. (2024). *Life skills for all learners: How to teach, assess, and report education's new essentials*. Alexandria, VA: ASCD.

APA (American Psychiatric Association). (2013). *Diagnostic and statistical manual of mental disorders (DSM-5)*. Arlington, VA: American Psychiatric Association.

APA (American Psychiatric Association) (2024). *What is a specific learning disorder?* https://www.psychiatry.org/patients-families/specific-learning-disorder/what-is-specific-learning-disorder

Argyropoulos, V., Paveli, A., & Nikolaraizi, M. (2019). The role of DAISY digital talking books in the education of individuals with blindness: A pilot study. *Education and Information Technologies*, 24(1), 693–709.

Arias, V.B., Arias, B., Burns, G.L., & Servera, M. (2019). Invariance of parent ratings of attention deficit hyperactivity disorder symptoms for children with and without intellectual disability. *Journal of Applied Research in Intellectual Disabilities*, 32(2), 288–299.

Arrow, A., Neville, A., Denston, A., & Nicholson, T. (2022). Investigating the number and type of literacy assessments and interventions in Aotearoa New Zealand primary schools. Australian Journal of Learning Difficulties, 27(2), 185–199.

Atmaca, F., & Yildiz-Demirtas, V. (2023). Does cognitive training affect reading and writing skills of students with specific learning disabilities? *Learning Disability Quarterly*, 46(2), 106–119.

Ault, M., Baggerman, M.A., & Horn, C.K. (2017). Effects of an app incorporating systematic instruction to teach spelling to students with developmental delays. *Journal of Special Education Technology*, 32(3), 123–137.

Australian Alliance for Inclusive Education. (2020). *All means all: Submission to the Review to Achieve Educational Excellence in Australian Schools.* https://www.education.gov.au/system/files/documents/document-file/2020-12/all-means-all-the-australian-alliance-for-inclusive-education

Azano, A.P., Missett, T.C., Tackett, M.E., & Callahan, C.M. (Eds.) (2017). The CLEAR curriculum model. In C.M. Callahan & H.L. Hertberg-Davis (Eds.). *Fundamentals of gifted education*. London: Routledge.

Bahr, M.W., Edwin, M., & Long, K.A. (2023). Development of a brief measure for multi-tiered systems of support sustainability. *Assessment for Effective Intervention*, 48(2), 90–99.

Baker, E.R., Huang, R., Battista, C., & Liu, Q. (2023). Head Start children's moral reasoning predicts aggressive forms and functions. *Early Childhood Education Journal*, 51(3), 443–455.

BANA (Braille Authority of North America). (2022). *The Nemeth Braille Code for Mathematics and Science Notation*. https://www.brailleauthority.org/sites/default/files/2024-02/Nemeth2022.pdf

Barbera, M. (2023). *Is lack of pointing a sign of autism?* https://marybarbera.com/lack-of-pointing-sign-of-autism/

Barbetta, P.M., & Morales, M. (2022). Three low-tech active student responding strategies for inclusive online teaching. *TEACHING Exceptional Children*, 54(5), 346–353.

Barlow-Brown, F., Barker, C., & Harris, M. (2019). Size and modality effects in braille learning: implications for the blind child from pre-reading sighted children. *British Journal of Educational Psychology*, 89(1), 165–176.

Barna, J., Arter, P., & Arban, K. (2024). Evidence-based strategies to reduce anxiety in students with autism spectrum disorder. *Intervention in School and Clinic*, 59(4), 236–242.

Baser, D., & Arsian-Ari, I. (2023). Assistive technology education: Experiences of pre-service special education teachers within an instructional material development project. *Journal of Special Education Technology*, 38(3), 340–354.

Bauml, M. (2023). I do, we do, you do: Teaching map skills in early grades. Social Studies and the Young Learner, 36(2), 28–32.

Beal, C.R., & Rosenblum, L.P. (2018). Evaluation of the effectiveness of a tablet computer application (app) in helping students with visual impairments solve mathematics problems. *Journal of Visual Impairment & Blindness*, 112(1), 5–19.

Bear, D.R., Invernizzi, M.A., Templeton, S.R., & Johnston, F.R., Flanigan, K., Townsend, D.R., Helman, L. & Hayes, L. (2020). *Words their way®: Word study for Phonics, Vocabulary, and Spelling Instruction* (7th ed.). Boston: Pearson.

Bellert, A. (2009). Narrowing the gap: A report on the *QuickSmart* mathematics intervention. *Australian Journal of Learning Difficulties*, 14(2), 171–183.

Berger, N., Holmes, K., & Mackenzie, E. (2023). *Instructional clarity, classroom disorder, and student achievement in mathematics: An exploratory analysis of TIMSS 2019.* Mathematics Education Research Group of Australasia: Paper presented at the *Annual Conference of the Mathematics Education Research Group of Australasia (MERGA)* (45th, Newcastle, Australia, July 2–6, 2023).

Bergeron, H. (2021). *Project-based learning and student engagement in elementary school.* ProQuest LLC, Ed.D. Dissertation, Northeastern University. ERIC Document ED642347.

Bernstein, B., Lubinski, D., & Benbow, C.P. (2021). Academic acceleration in gifted youth and fruitless concerns regarding psychological well-being: A 35-year longitudinal study. *Journal of Educational Psychology*, 113(4), 830–845.

Berridge, S., & Hutchinson, N. (2021). Staff experience of the implementation of intensive interaction within their places of work with people with learning disabilities and/or autism. *Journal of Applied Research in Intellectual Disabilities*, 34(1), 1–15.

Beschorner, B., & Hall, A. (2021), Building inclusivity and empathy through Writers' Workshop. *Reading Teacher*, 74(5), 631–634.

Betts, G.T., Carey, R.J., & Kapushion, B.M. (2021). *Autonomous Learner Model Resource Book.* London: Routledge.

Bibro, M.A., & Zarów, R. (2023). The influence of climbing activities on physical fitness of people with intellectual disabilities. *International Journal of Disability, Development and Education*, 70(4), 530–539.

Bissex, G. (1980). *GYNS AT WRK: A child learns to write and read.* Cambridge, MA: Harvard University Press.

Black, A. (2019). Future secondary schools for diversity: Where are we now and were could we be? *Review of Education*, 7(1), 36–38.

Blankenship, A.P., & Canto, A.I. (2018). Traumatic brain injuries and special education services in the schools. *Exceptionality*, 26(4), 218–229.

Boggio, C., Zaher, A., & Bosse, M. (2023). ECRIMO, an app to train first graders' spelling: Effectiveness and comparison between different designs. *British Journal of Educational Technology*, 54(5), 1332–1350.

Bondebjerg, A., Dalgaard, N. T., Filges, T., & Viinholt, B. C. A. (2023). The effects of small class sizes on students' academic achievement, socioemotional development and well-being in special education: A systematic review. *Campbell Systematic Reviews*, 19, e1345. https://doi.org/10.1002/cl2.1345

Borton, L.D., & Herzberg, T.S. (2023). Using constant time delay to teach final-letter group signs in Braille. *Journal of Visual Impairment & Blindness*, 117(6), 491–497.

Bradburn, S.M., Ryan, M.C., & Leung, W. (2024). Factors influencing children's attitudes toward their peers with disabilities. *Journal of Physical Education, Recreation & Dance*, 95(3), 56.

Bradley, A. (2024). Integrating AI into the curriculum. *Teacher Magazine* 24 April (Online. Not paginated). teacherbulletin@acer.org

Bradley, R.L., & Noell, G.H. (2018). The effectiveness of supplemental phonics instruction employing constant time delay instruction for struggling readers. *Psychology in the Schools*, 55(7), 880–892.

Brady, K.K., Evmenova, A.S., Regan, K.S., Ainsworth, M.K., & Gafurov, B.S. (2022). Using a technology-based graphic organizer to improve the planning and persuasive paragraph writing by adolescents with disabilities and writing difficulties. *Journal of Special Education*, 55(4), 222–233.

Brady, S., & Mason, L.H. (2024). A literature review of morphological awareness interventions and the effects on literacy outcomes. *Learning Disability Quarterly*, 47(1), 16–29.

Breadmore, H.L., Côté, E., & Deacon, S.H. (2023). The timing tells the tale: Multiple morphological processes in children's and adults' spelling. *Scientific Studies of Reading*, 27(5), 408–427.

Brenner, D., & McQuirk, A. (2019). A snapshot of writing in elementary teacher preparation programs. *New Educator*, 15(1), 18–29.

Brimo, D., Nallamala, K., & Werfel, K.L. (2023). Writing errors of children with developmental language disorder. *Topics in Language Disorders*, 43(4), 302–316.

Brock, M.E., Dueker, S.A., & Barczak, M.A. (2018). Brief report: Improving social outcomes for students with autism at recess through peer-mediated pivotal response training. *Journal of Autism and Developmental Disorders*, 48(6), 2224–2230.

Brophy, J., & Good, T. (1986). Teacher behaviour and student achievement. In M. Wittrock (Ed.) *Handbook of research in teaching* (3rd ed, pp. 328–375), New York: Macmillan.

Broughton, S. (2023). Differentiated spelling: Using small group instruction. *Networks: An Online Journal for Teacher Research*, 24(1), 2.

Brown, K.M. (2018). *Scaffolding and Lucy Calkins writers' workshop: A case study in first grade*. ProQuest LLC, DEd. Dissertation, Capella University. ERIC Document ED588005

Budínová, I. (2024) Risks in identifying gifted students in mathematics: Case studies. *Open Education Studies*, 6(1), 20220218.

Burns, H. (2024). Imagining imagination: Towards cognitive and metacognitive models. *Pedagogy, Culture and Society*, 32(2), 515–534.

Burt, D., Graham, L. & Hoang, T. (2022). Effectiveness of computer-assisted vocabulary instruction for secondary students with mild intellectual disability. *International Journal of Disability, Development and Education*, 69(4), 1273–1294.

Burton, L., Nunes, T., & Evangelou, M. (2021). Do children use logic to spell logician? Implicit versus explicit teaching of morphological spelling rules. *British Journal of Educational Psychology*, 91(4), 1231–1248.

Caines, A. (2022). An instructional approach to teaching spelling: Word study. *BU Journal of Graduate Studies in Education*, 14(4), 4–12.

Calvert, E., Olszeswki-Kubilius, P., Cross, T.L., & Cross, J.R. (2023). Project OCCAMS: A five-year, collaborative intervention of an online intensive, accelerated, two-year language arts program designed to address systemic disparities among high ability middle school students. *Gifted Child Today*, 46(3), 159–167.

Carey, E., Ryan, R., Sheikhi, A., & Dore, L. (2023). Exercising autonomy: The effectiveness and meaningfulness of autonomy support interventions engaged by adults with intellectual disability. *British Journal of Learning Disabilities*, 51(3), 307–323.

Carlberg, C.G., & Kavale, K.A. (1980). The efficacy of special versus regular class placement for exceptional children: A meta-analysis. *Journal of Special Education*, 14, 295–309.

Caron, V., Barras, A., van Nispen, R.M.A., & Ruffieux, N. (2023). Teaching social skills to children and adolescents with visual impairments: A systematic review. *Journal of Visual Impairment & Blindness*, 117(2), 128–147.

Carter, E.W., Tuttle, M., Asmus, J.M., Moss, C.K., & Lloyd, B.P. (2024). Observations of students with and without severe disabilities in general education classes: A portrait of inclusion? *Focus on Autism and Other Developmental Disabilities*, 39(1), 3–13.

Carter, H., Abbott, J., & Landau Wright, K. (2022). Preservice teachers' preparedness to teach writing: Looking closely at a semester of structured literacy tutoring. *Journal of Writing Research*, 14(1), 77–111.

Carter, J. (2023a). Supporting preservice teachers to become informed teachers of reading through one-to-one tutoring in an English initial teacher education setting. *Education 3–13*, 51(4), 543–556.

Carter, S. (2023b). Snoezelen: A multi-sensory therapeutic approach. https://www.montessori-theory.com/snoezelen-a-multi-sensory-therapeutic-approach/

Çayir, A., & Balci, E. (2023). The effect of differentiated instruction on gifted students' critical thinking skills and mathematics problem solving attitudes. *Educational Research and Reviews*, 18(12), 392–398.

Cerni, T., & Job, R. (2024). Spelling processing during handwriting and typing and the role of reading and visual-motor skills when typing is less practiced than handwriting. *Reading and Writing: An Interdisciplinary Journal*, 37(1), 205–237.

Cerveny, L.D. (2016). *Evaluation of the effectiveness of a preference-based teaching approach with children with developmental disabilities*. Psychology Master's Thesis, State University of New York. https://digitalcommons.brockport.edu/psh_theses/13

Child Mind Institute (2023). *Children's friendship training*. https://childmind.org/care/areas-of-expertise/autism-clinical-center/childrens-friendship-training/

Childress, T. (2015). For all students everywhere: Technology means independence in a beautiful digital world. *Odyssey: New Directions in Deaf Education*, 16, 56–59.

Chodkiewicz, A.R., & Boyle, C. (2016). Promoting positive learning in Australian students aged 10- to 12-years-old using attribution retraining and cognitive behavioral therapy: A pilot study. *School Psychology International*, 37(5), 519–535.

Chow, J.C., & Wehby, J.H. (2019). Profiles of problem behavior in children with varying language ability. *Journal of Emotional and Behavioral Disorders*, 27(2), 110–118.

Chua, B.Y.E., & Poon, K.K. (2018). Studying the implementation of PECS in a naturalistic special education school setting. *Educational & Child Psychology*, 35(2), 60–75.

Clement, G. (2023). Meeting students' needs through MTSS; A case study of an inner Melbourne primary school. *Learning Difficulties Australia Bulletin*, 55(1), 24–25.

Cohen, L. (2023). *Third- to fifth-grade teachers' training and their confidence in teaching writing*. ProQuest LLC, Ph.D. Dissertation, Walden University. ERIC document: ED639030

Coleman, H., Hume, K., Fanning, L., & Scott, S. (2022). Examining the feasibility and fit of family implemented TEACCH for toddlers in rural settings. *Journal of Early Intervention*, 44(1), 58–77.

Collins, K.H., Roberson, J.J., & Piske, F.H.R. (2023). *Underachievement in gifted education: Perspectives, practices, and possibilities*. Florence, KY: Prufrock Press.

Cologon, K. (2022). Is inclusive education really for everyone? Family stories of children and young people labelled with 'severe and multiple' or 'profound' 'disabilities'. *Research Papers in Education*, 37(3), 395–417.

Colovic-Markovic, J. (2019). 'The class changed the way I read': The effects of explicit instruction of academic formulas on ESL writers. *Applied Language Learning*, 29(1–2), 17–51.

Condliffe, E. (2023). "Out of sight, out of mind": An interpretative phenomenological analysis of young people's experience of isolation rooms/booths in UK mainstream secondary schools. *Emotional & Behavioural Difficulties*, 28(2–3), 129–144.

Connelly, A., & Doyle, J. (2023). Speech to text, text to speech: Support for deaf and hard of hearing students. *Odyssey: New Directions in Deaf Education*, 23, 64–67.

Conrad, N.J., Kennedy, K., Saoud, W., Scallion, L., & Hanusiak, L. (2019). Establishing word representations through reading and spelling: Comparing degree of orthographic learning. *Journal of Research in Reading*, 42(1), 162–177.

Cooney, P., Tunney, C., & O'Reilly, G. (2018). A systematic review of the evidence regarding cognitive therapy skills that assist cognitive behavioural therapy in adults who have an intellectual disability. *Journal of Applied Research in Intellectual Disabilities*, 31(1), 23–42.

Cordewener, K.A., Hasselman, F., Verhoeven, L., & Bosman, A.M. (2018). The Role of instruction for spelling performance and spelling consciousness. *Journal of Experimental Education*, 86(2), 135–153.

Council for Disabled Children [UK]. (2017). *Education, Health and Care Plans: Examples of good practice*. https://councilfordisabledchildren.org.uk/help-resources/resources/education-health-and-care-plans-examples-good-practice

Counihan, C., Humble, S., Gittins, L., & Dixon, P. (2022). The effect of different teacher literacy training programmes on student's word reading abilities in government primary schools in northern Nigeria. *School Effectiveness and School Improvement*, 33(2), 198–217.

Cranmer, S. (2020). Disabled children's evolving digital use practices to support formal learning: A missed opportunity for inclusion. *British Journal of Educational Technology*, 51(2), 315–330.

Crawford, M. (2018). Acceleration for gifted girls facilitated by multiplicity and flexibility of provision and practices. *Australasian Journal of Gifted Education*, 27(2), 28–39.

Cueli, M., Cañamero, L.M., Rodriquez, C., & González-Castro, P. (2024). What different education professionals know about ADHD and their attitudes towards it. *European Journal of Special Needs Education*, 39(1), 33–47.

Cumming, T.M., & Gilanyi, L. (2023). "Our classes are like mainstream school now": Implementing Universal Design for Learning at a special school. *Australasian Journal of Special and Inclusive Education*, 47(2), 63–77.

Cuncic, A. (2024). *An overview of social skills training*. https://www.verywellmind.com/social-skills-4157216

Currell, J. (2018). Understanding relational and instrumental mathematics. Retrieved from: https://mathsnoproblem.com/understanding-relational-and-instrumental-mathematics/

CYDA (Children and Young People with Disabilities Australia). (2019). *Media release: Aussie schoolkids with disability excluded, segregated, bullied and robbed of education*. www.cyda.org.au

Daffern, T., & Fleet, R. (2021). Investigating the efficacy of using error analysis data to inform explicit teaching of spelling. *Australian Journal of Learning Difficulties*, 26(1), 67–88.

Daniel, J., Barth, A., & Ankrum, E. (2024). Multicomponent reading intervention: A practitioner's guide. *Reading Teacher*, 77(4), 473–484.

Danniels, E., & Pyle, A. (2023). Teacher perspectives and approaches toward promoting inclusion in play-based learning for children with developmental disabilities. *Journal of Early Childhood Research*, 21(3), 288–302.

Dart, E.H., Radley, K.C., Helbig, K.A., & Salvatore, C. (2024). Reframing social skills practices for autistic students: A responsive framework for assessment and intervention. *Journal of Educational and Psychological Consultation*, 34(1), 44–70.

Datchuk, S.M., Wagner, K., & Hier, B. (2020). Level and trend of writing sequences: A review and meta-analysis of writing interventions for students with disabilities. *Exceptional Children*, 86(2), 174–192.

de Barros, A., & Ganimian, A.J. (2024). Which students benefit from computer-based individualized instruction? Experimental evidence from public schools in India. *Journal of Research on Educational Effectiveness*, 17(2), 318–343.

De Smedt, F., Graham, S., & Van Keer, H. (2020). "It takes two": The added value of structured peer-assisted writing in explicit writing instruction. *Contemporary Educational Psychology*, 60, 101835.

Dean, R., & Gibbs, S. (2023). Teacher collective efficacy and the management of difficult behaviour: The role of student-teacher relationships. *Educational Psychology in Practice*, 39(3), 273–293.

Debenham, L. (2018). *Non-verbal learning disabilities.* https://www.aboutlearningdisabilities.co.uk/nonverbal-learning-disabilities.html

Del Bigio, M.R. (2010). Neuropathology and structural changes in hydrocephalus. *Developmental Disabilities Research Reviews*, 16(1), 16–22.

Dennis, L., Eldridge, J., Wade, T., Robbins, A., Larkin, M., & Fundelius, E. (2024). The effects of practice-based coaching and scripted supports on teachers' implementation of shared book reading strategies. *Child Language Teaching and Therapy*, 40(1), 77–95.

DeSipio, B.E., & Pallotti, C. (2024). Sex communication: The new consent education. *Journal of Student Affairs Research and Practice*, 61(2), 295–308.

Desmet, O.A., Crimmins, D.M., Flewellen, G., & Seigfried-Spellar, K.C. (2023). Students' Perceptions of a Cyber Enrichment Program. *Gifted Child Today*, 46(4), 266–272.

DfE (Department for Education: UK). (2015). *Special educational needs and disability code of practice: 0 to 25 years.* London: Department of Education & Department for Health.

DfE (Department for Education: UK). (2023). *Special educational needs and disability: An analysis and summary of data sources.* Assets Publishing Service, Govt.UK.

DfE (Department for Education: UK). (2024). *Promoting and supporting mental health and well-being in schools and college.* London: DfE. https://www.gov.uk/guidance/mental-health-and-wellbeing-support-in-schools-and-colleges

Diaz-Garolera, G., Pallisera, M., & Fullana, J. (2022). Developing social skills to empower friendships: Design and assessment of a social skills training programme. *International Journal of Inclusive Education*, 26(1), 1–15.

Dillon, M.B., Radley, K.C., Tingstrom, D.H., Dart, E.H., & Barry, C.T. (2019). The effects of tootling via ClassDojo on student behavior in elementary classrooms. *School Psychology Review*, 48(1), 18–30.

Dixon, A.M. (2022). *Multisensory phonics instruction in struggling readers.* ProQuest LLC: Ed.D. Dissertation, University of South Carolina. ERIC document ED637159.

Dixon, R. & Englemann, S. (2006). *Spelling through morphographs: Teacher's guide.* Colombus, OH: McGraw Hill.

Doabler, C. & Fien, H. (2013). Explicit mathematics instruction: What teachers can do for teaching students with mathematics difficulties. *Intervention in School and Clinic*, 48(5), 276–285.

Dominquez-Reyes, R., Moreno, L., Munoz-Sanchez, A., Ruiz, M., & Savoini, B. (2023). Modular 3D-printed education tool for blind and visually impaired students oriented to net structures. *IEEE Transactions on Education*, 66(1), 55–61.

Doremus, W.A. (2023). *Prevention and intervention of bullying and cyberbullying in schools. Revised position statement.* Silver Spring, MD: National Association of School Nurses.

Dorn, B. (2019). The changing role of teachers of students who are deaf or hard of hearing: Consultation as an increasing part of the job. *Journal of Educational and Psychological Consultation*, 29(2), 237–254.

Doumas, D.M., & Midgett, A. (2023). Witnessing cyberbullying and suicidal ideation among middle school students. *Psychology in the Schools*, 60(4), 1149–1163.

Dowker, A. (2005). Early identification and intervention for students with mathematics difficulties. *Journal of Learning Disabilities*, 38(4), 324–332.

Downing, C., & Caravolas, M. (2024). Evaluating the Spelling and Handwriting Legibility Test (SaHLT): A tool for the concurrent assessment of spelling and handwriting. *Reading and Writing: An Interdisciplinary Journal*, 37(1), 147–172.

DreamBox Learning Inc. (2023). *DreamBox Math.* https://www.dreambox.com/summer

Dreyer, V. (2023). *The digital influence on beginning writers: A basic qualitative study.* ProQuest LLC, Ed.D. Dissertation, American College of Education. ERIC document ED640875.

Drushlyak, M., Semenikhina, O., Kharchenko, I., Mulesa, P., & Shamonia, V. (2023). Effectiveness of digital technologies in inclusive learning for teacher preparation. *Journal of Learning for Development,* 10(2), 177–195.

D'Souza, D.A.C., & Clare, A.C. (2018). Effect of situated learning model on critical problem-solving skills among higher secondary pupils. *Journal on School Educational Technology,* 14(1), 27–34.

Dunn, L.M. (1968). Special education for the mildly retarded. Is much of it justifiable? *Exceptional Children,* 35, 5–22.

Dunn, R.J. (2022). Utilizing guided discovery to promote transfer of responsibility values in young children. *Journal of Teaching in Physical Education,* 41(2), 242–251.

Duplenne, L., Bourdin, B., Fernandez, D.N., Blondelle, G., & Aubry, A. (2024). Anxiety and depression in gifted individuals: A systematic and meta-analytic review. *Gifted Child Quarterly,* 68(1), 65–83.

Dymond, S.K., & Orelove, P. (2001). What constitutes effective curriculum for students with severe disabilities? *Exceptionality,* 9(3), 109–122.

Dyrvold, A. (2022). Missed opportunities in digital teaching platforms: Under-use of interactive and dynamic elements. *Journal of Computers in Mathematics and Science Teaching,* 41(2), 135–161.

Earp, J. (2024). [Infographic]. Classroom disciplinary climate: Global comparisons. *Teacher Magazine,* 14 March, 2024. https://www.teachermagazine.com/au_en/articles/infographic-classroom-disciplinary-climate-global-comparisons

Ebrahim, M.T. (2019). Effectiveness of a pivotal response training programme in joint attention and social interaction of kindergarten children with autism spectrum disorder. *International Journal of Psycho-Educational Sciences,* 8(2), 48–56.

EEF (Education Endowment Foundation). (2019). *Metacognition and self-regulation.* https://educationendowmentfoundation.org.uk/evidence-summaries/teaching-learning-toolkit/meta-cognition-and-self-regulation/

Ehri, L.C. (2022). What teachers need to know and do to teach letter-sounds, phonemic awareness, word reading, and phonics. *Reading Teacher,* 76(1), 53–61.

Ehri, L.C. (2023a). Roads travelled researching how children learn to read words. *Australian Journal of Learning Difficulties,* 28(1), 55–71.

Ehri, L.C. (2023b). Phases of development in learning to read and spell words. *American Educator,* 47(3), 17–18.

Elimelech, A., & Aram, D. (2019). A digital early spelling game: The role of auditory and visual support. *AERA Open,* 5(2), 1–11.

Elliott, A., Reddy, L.A., Lekwa, A.J., & Fingerhut, J. (2024). Teacher stress and supports, classroom practices and student outcomes in high poverty urban elementary schools. *Psychology in the Schools,* 61(1), 29–42.

Engelmann, S. (1999). The benefits of direct instruction: Affirmative action for at-risk students. *Educational Leadership,* 57(1), 77–79.

Ennis, R.P., & Losinski, M. (2019). Interventions to improve fraction skills for students with disabilities: A meta-analysis. *Exceptional Children,* 85(3), 367–386.

Erickson, C., & Maricle, D.E. (2021). Cerebral palsy: What school psychologists should know. *Communique,* 49(5), 20–22.

Erskine, M., Ferguson, C., & Ayre, K. (2023). "I don't want to come back now": Teacher directed violence. *Issues in Educational Research,* 33(3), 920–936.

Esposito, C., Affuso, G., Miranda, M.C., & Bacchini, D. (2021). A new dimensional measure of antisocial behaviour evaluation (ASBE). *European Journal of Developmental Psychology,* 18(2), 257–270.

Esposito, R., Herbert, E., & Sumner, E. (2023). Capturing variations in how spelling is taught in primary school classrooms in England. *British Educational Research Journal*, 49(1), 70–92.

Ewing, E.L., Khatri, S.M., Irsheid, S.B., & Castleberry, L.Y. (2022). "They don't have the right to be touching girls": Understanding middle school students' consent scripts. *Teachers College Record*, 124(12), 3–34.

Fallon, L.M., & Kurtz, K.D. (2019). Coaching teachers to implement the Good Behavior Game: A direct training approach. *Teaching Exceptional Children*, 51(4), 296–304.

Fava, L., & Strauss, K. (2010). Multi-sensory rooms: Comparing effects of the Snoezelen and the stimulus preference environment on the behavior of adults with profound mental retardation. *Research in Developmental Disabilities: A Multidisciplinary Journal*, 31(1), 160–171.

Fishstrom, S., Capin, P., Fall, A.M., Roberts, G., Grills, A.E., & Vaughn, S. (2024). Understanding the relation between reading and anxiety among upper elementary students with reading difficulties. *Annals of Dyslexia*, 74(1), 123–141.

Flanagan, S.M. (2023). Map it out! Using technology-based concept mapping for written expression. *TEACHING Exceptional Children*, 55(3), 220–223.

Fleming, J.I., Grasley-Boy, N.M., Gage, N.A., Lombardo, M., & Anderson, L. (2024). Effects of tiered SWPBIS fidelity on exclusionary discipline outcomes for students with disabilities: A conceptual replication. *Journal of Positive Behavior Interventions*, 26(1), 3–13.

Flores, M.M., & Hinton, V.M. (2022). The effects of a CRA-I intervention on students' number sense and understanding of addition. *Remedial and Special Education*, 43(3), 183–194.

Flynn, N., Powell, D., Stainthorp, R., & Stuart, M. (2021). Training teachers for phonics and early reading: Developing research-informed practice. *Journal of Research in Reading*, 44(2), 301–318.

Foley, E.A., Dozier, C.L., & Lessor, A.L. (2019). Comparison of components of the Good Behavior Game in a preschool classroom. *Journal of Applied Behavior Analysis*, 52(1), 84–104.

Forber-Pratt, A.J., Hanebutt, R., Minotti, B., Cobb, N.A., & Peagram, K. (2024). Social-emotional learning and motivational interviews with middle school youth with disabilities or at-risk for disability identification. *Education and Urban Society*, 56(1), 33–65.

Frankel, F.D., & Myatt, R.J. (2002). *Children's friendship training*. New York: Routledge Taylor & Francis.

Friedman, C., Rizzolo, M.C., & Spassiani, N.A. (2019). Self-management of health by people with intellectual and developmental disabilities. *Journal of Applied Research in Intellectual Disabilities*, 32(3), 600–609.

Fu, D.M., Liu, Y., & Zhang, D. (2023). The relationship between teacher autonomy support and student mathematics achievement: A 3-Year longitudinal study. *Educational Psychology*, 43(2), 187–206.

Gabova, K., Furstova, J., & Tavel, P. (2024). Wireless microphones for students who are deaf and hard of hearing: Czech teachers' perspective. *Journal of Research in Special Educational Needs*, 24(1), 68–79.

Gage, N., & Giaconia, R. (1981). Teaching practices and student achievement; Causal connections. *New York University Education Quarterly*, 12, 2–9.

Gaintza, Z., Ozerinjauregi, N., & Arostegui, I. (2018). Educational inclusion of students with rare diseases: Schooling students with spina bifida. *British Journal of Learning Disabilities*, 46(4), 250–257.

Gardner, P., & Kuzich, S. (2022). Ready to write? Investigating the writing experiences of pre-service teachers and their readiness to teach writing. *Issues in Educational Research*, 32(2), 513–532.

Gargiulo, R.M. & Metcalf, D. (2022). *Teaching in today's inclusive classrooms: A Universal Design for Learning approach* (4th ed.). Belmont, CA: Wadsworth.

Garvik, M., Idsoe, T., & Bru, E. (2014). Effectiveness study of a CBT-based adolescent coping with depression course. *Emotional and Behavioural Difficulties*, 19(2), 195–209.

Gassid, J. (2023). *A systematic review of multisensory instruction targeted toward improving literacy rates in elementary students*. ProQuest LLC: Ed.D. Dissertation, Trevecca Nazarene University. ERIC document ED635276.

Gengler, K. (2023). *Root cause analysis: Investigating factors contributing to a high rate of students at risk for reading difficulties*. ProQuest LLC, Ed.D. Dissertation, University of Massachusetts Lowell. ERIC Document ED635230.

Ghanouni, P., Jarus, T., Zwicker, J.G., Lucyshyn, J., Mow, K., & Ledingham, A. (2019). Social Stories for children with autism spectrum disorder: Validating the content of a virtual reality program. *Journal of Autism and Developmental Disorders*, 49(2), 660–668.

Gill, K., & Thompson-Hodgetts, S. (2018). Self-regulation in fetal alcohol spectrum disorder: A concept analysis. *Journal of Occupational Therapy, Schools & Early Intervention*, 11(3), 329–345.

Gill, K., Thompson-Hodgetts, S., & Rasmussen, C. (2018). A critical review of research on the Alert Program®. *Journal of Occupational Therapy, Schools & Early Intervention*, 11(2), 212–228.

Gillingham, A., & Stillman, B.W. (1956). *Remedial training for students with specific disability in reading, spelling, and penmanship*. Cambridge, MA: Educators Publishing Service.

Gillon, G., McNeill, B., Denston, A., Scott, A., & Macfarlane, A. (2020). Evidence-based class literacy instruction for children with speech and language difficulties. *Topics in Language Disorders*, 40(4), 357–374.

Gilson, C.M., & Lee, L.E. (2023). Cultivating a learning environment to support diverse gifted students. *Gifted Child Today*, 46(4), 235–249.

Givler, A. (2022). *First year teachers' perspectives of their self-efficacy to teach writing in elementary*. ProQuest LLC, Ph.D. Dissertation, Walden University. ERIC document: ED641765.

Gluck, S. (2024). *Mild, moderate, severe intellectual disability differences*. HealthyPlace: https://www.healthyplace.com/neurodevelopmental-disorders/intellectual-disability/mild-moderate-severe-intellectual-disability-differences

Golubovic, S., Božic, D., & Ilic, S. (2022). Support needs of children with cerebral palsy. *International Journal of Disability, Development and Education*, 69(3), 739–750.

Good, T.L. (2024). Reflecting on decades of teacher expectations and teacher effectiveness research: Considerations for current and future research. *Educational Psychologist*, 59(2), 111–141.

Goodman-Scott, E., Carlisle, R., Clark, M., & Burgess, M. (2017). A powerful tool: A phenomenological study of school counselors' experiences with social stories. *Professional School Counseling*, 20(1), 25–35.

Gorard, S., Siddiqui, N., & See, B.H. (2016). An evaluation of Fresh Start as a catch-up intervention: A trial conducted by teachers. *Educational Studies*, 42(1), 98–113.

Gorbunova, A., van Merrienboer, J.G., & Costley, J. (2023). Are inductive teaching methods compatible with cognitive load theory? *Educational Psychology Review*, 35(4), 111.

Gov.UK. (2020). *The Engagement Model*. Standards and testing Agency. https://assets.publishing.service.gov.uk/media/5f19be233a6f40727dc2e452/Engagement_Model_Guidance_2020.pdf

Gov.UK. (2022). *Disability Rights: Education*. https://www.gov.uk/rights-disabled-person/education-rights

Gov.UK. (2023a). *Obesity profile*. Office for Health Improvement and Disparities. https://fingertips.phe.org.uk/profile/national-child-measurement-programme

Gov.UK. (2023b). *Special educational needs in England*. https://explore-education-statistics.service.gov.uk/find-statistics/special-educational-needs-in-england

Graham, L., Bellert, A., Thomas, J., & Pegg, J. (2007). 'QuickSmart': A basic academic skills intervention for middle school students with learning difficulties. *Journal of Learning Disabilities*, 40(5), 410–419.

Graham, S., & Taylor, A.Z. (2022). The power of asking "why?": Attribution retraining programs for the classroom teacher. *Theory Into Practice*, 61(1), 5–22.

Grant-Skiba, D. (2023). Tier 2 interventions in secondary schools: Challenges and strategies. *Learning Difficulties Australia Bulletin*, 55(1), 21–23.

Grattan, G., & Demchak, M.A. (2014). Stimulus Preference Assessments. *Nevada Dual Sensory Impairment Project Newsletter*, 23(1), 1–4.

Graves, D. (1983). *Writing: Teachers and children at work*. Exeter, NH: Heinemann.

Gravråkmo, S., Olsen, A., Lydersen, S., Ingul, J.M., Henry, L., & Øie, M.G. (2023). Associations between executive functions, intelligence and adaptive behaviour in children and adolescents with mild intellectual disability. *Journal of Intellectual Disabilities*, 27(3), 715–727.

Gray, C., (2020). *The new social story book*. Illustrated edition. Arlington, TX: Future Horizons.

Greer, C.W., & Erickson, K.A. (2019). Teaching students with significant cognitive disabilities to count: Routine for achieving early counting. *Teaching Exceptional Children*, 51(5), 382–389.

Griffin, M.M., Copeland, S.R., & Maez, R. (2023). Effects of a function-based contingency and self-management intervention on the academic engagement of a student with FASD. *Education and Training in Autism and Developmental Disabilities*, 58(4), 470–479.

Grigorakis, I., & Manolitsis, G. (2021). Longitudinal effects of different aspects of morphological awareness skills on early spelling development. *Reading and Writing: An Interdisciplinary Journal*, 34(4), 945–979.

Gripton, C., & Rawluch, D. (2021). *Counting collections in the early years*. https://nrich.maths.org/14890

Grossman, P., Dean, C.G., Kavanagh, S.S., & Herrmann, Z. (2019). Preparing teachers for project-based teaching. *Phi Delta Kappan*, 100(7), 43–48.

Großmann, N., & Wilde, M. (2019). Experimentation in biology lessons: Guided discovery through incremental scaffolds. *International Journal of Science Education*, 41(6), 759–781.

Gulboy, E. (2023). Evaluating the evidence bases of the response cards strategy: A meta-analysis of single-case experimental design studies. *Education and Training in Autism and Developmental Disabilities*, 58(2), 181–197.

Güler Bülbül, Ö., & Özmen, E.R. (2021). Effectiveness of teaching story-writing strategy to students with intellectual disabilities and their non-disabled peers. *Journal of Intellectual & Developmental Disability*, 46(3), 204–216.

Haidari, S.M., Koçoglu, A., & Kanadli, S. (2023). Contribution of locus of control, self-efficacy, and motivation to student achievement: A meta-analytic structural equation modelling. *Journal on Efficiency and Responsibility in Education and Science*, 16(3), 245–261.

Hallahan, D.P., Kauffman, J.M., & Pullen, P.C. (2023). *Exceptional Learners: An Introduction to Special Education* (15th ed.). Upper Saddle River, NJ: Pearson.

Hampshire, P.K., & Hourcade, J.J. (2014). Teaching play skills to children with autism using visually structured tasks. *Teaching Exceptional Children*, 46(3), 26–32.

Hand, E.D., Lonigan, C.J., & Puranik, C.S. (2024). Prediction of kindergarten and first-grade reading skills: Unique contributions of preschool writing and early-literacy skills. *Reading and Writing: An Interdisciplinary Journal*, 37(1), 25–48.

Harris, K.R., & McKeown, D. (2022). Overcoming barriers and paradigm wars: Powerful evidence-based writing instruction. *Theory Into Practice*, 61(4), 429–442.

HASA (Hearing and Speech Agency). (2019). *Language-based learning disabilities.* https://hasa.org/topics/language-based-learning-disabilities/

Hassan, N.M., Landorf, K.B., Shields, N., & Munteanu, S.E. (2019). Effectiveness of interventions to increase physical activity in individuals with intellectual disabilities: A systematic review of randomised controlled trials. *Journal of Intellectual Disability Research*, 63(2), 168–191.

Hathcock, S.J. (2018). Interdisciplinary science through the Parallel Curriculum Model: Lessons from the sea. *Gifted Child Today*, 41(1), 28–40.

Hattie, J., & Yates, G.C.R. (2014). *Visible learning and the science of how we learn.* London: Routledge.

Hayes, H.M.R., Burns, K., & Egan, S. (2024). Becoming 'good men': Teaching consent and masculinity in a single-sex boys' school. *Sex Education: Sexuality, Society and Learning*, 24(1), 31–44.

Hays, L., Jurkowski, O., & Sims, S.K. (2024). ChatGPT in K-12 education. *TechTrends: Linking Research and Practice to Improve Learning*, 68(2), 281–294.

Helsel, L., Kelly, K., & Wong, K. (2022). Responsive teaching in the Writer's Workshop. *Reading Teacher*, 75(5), 583–592.

Henbest, V.S., & Apel, K. (2021). The relation between a systematic analysis of spelling and orthographic and phonological awareness skills in first-grade children. *Language, Speech, and Hearing Services in Schools*, 52(3), 827–839.

Hennenfent, L., Johnson, L.J., Novelli, C., & Sharkey, E. (2022). *Intensive intervention practice guide: Explicit morphology instruction to improve overall literacy skills in secondary students.* Washington, DC: Office of Special Education Programs, US Department of Education.

Hepburn, L., Beamish, W., & Alston-Knox, C.L. (2021). Classroom management practices commonly used by secondary school teachers: Results from a Queensland survey. *Australian Educational Researcher*, 48(3), 485–505.

Hiebert, E.H. (2023). Thinking through research and the science of reading. *Phi Delta Kappan*, 105(2), 37–41.

Hindin, A., & Steiner, L. (2024). Creating opportunities to read and build fluency at home. *Journal of Early Childhood Literacy*, 24(1), 217–240.

Hinduja, S., & Patchin, J.W. (2019). Connecting adolescent suicide to the severity of bullying and cyberbullying. *Journal of School Violence*, 18(3), 333–346.

Hingstman, M., Doolaard, S., Warrens, M.J., & Bosker, R.J. (2021). Supporting young struggling readers at Success for All schools in the United States and the Netherlands: Comparative case studies. *Research in Comparative and International Education*, 16(1), 22–42.

Hingstman, M., Neitzel, A.J., &Slavin, R.E. (2023). Preventing special education assignment for students with learning or behavioral difficulties: A review of programs. *Journal of Education for Students Placed at Risk*, 28(4), 380–411.

Hodgson, J. (2013). Classroom activities. *English Teaching Forum*, 51(3), 46–52.

Hoff, K.E., & Ervin, R.A. (2013). Extending self-management strategies: The use of a classwide approach. *Psychology in the Schools*, 50(2), 151–164.

Holman, K. (2023). Interventions for students with developmental dyscalculia: A systematic literature review. *Insights into Learning Disabilities*, 20(2), 135–151.

Holmdahl, A., Schad, E., Nilsson, G., & Kaldo, V. (2023). More than just a game: Teachers' experiences of the PAX Good Behavior Game. *European Journal of Psychology and Educational Research*, 6(1), 55–68.

Holmes, S.C. (2024). Inclusion, autism spectrum, students' experiences. *International Journal of Developmental Disabilities*, 70(1), 59–73.

Hopkins, S.W., Marks, A.K., & Fireman, G.D. (2023). A person-centered exploration of peer aggression and prosocial behavior in early adolescence. *Contemporary School Psychology*, 27(4), 683–695.

Horbach, J., Mayer, A., Scharke, W., Heim, S., & Günther, T. (2020). Development of behavior problems in children with and without specific learning disorders in reading and spelling from Kindergarten to Fifth Grade. *Scientific Studies of Reading*, 24(1), 57–71.

Horn, A.L., Gable, R.A., & Bobzien, J.L. (2020). Constant time delay to teach students with intellectual disability. *Preventing School Failure*, 64(1), 89–97.

Horn, A.L., Roitsch, J., Murphy, K.A. (2023). Constant time delay to teach reading to students with intellectual disability and autism: A review. *International Journal of Developmental Disabilities*, 69(2), 123–133.

Hornbeck, D., & Duncheon, J.C. (2024). "From an ethic of care to queer resistance": Texas administrator and teacher perspectives on supporting LGBTQ students in secondary schools. *International Journal of Qualitative Studies in Education (QSE)*, 37(3), 874–890.

Hornby, G., & Kauffman, J.M. (2023). Special education's zombies and their consequences. *Support for Learning*, 38(3), 135–145.

Howard, A.J., Morrison, J.Q., & Collins, T. (2020). Evaluating self-management interventions: Analysis of component combinations. *School Psychology Review*, 49(2), 130–143.

Hugh, M.L., Conner, C., & Stewart, J. (2018). *Intensive Intervention Practice Guide: Using visual activity schedules to intensify academic interventions for young children with autism spectrum disorder.* Washington, DC: Office of Special Education Programs, US Department of Education.

Hughes, E.M., Witzel, B.S., Myers, J., & Lin, T.H. (2023). Unpacking and understanding specific learning disabilities in mathematics. *TEACHING Exceptional Children*, 56(1), 26–32.

Hüseyin, F., & Nüket, A. (2023). Perfectionism and life satisfaction in gifted students. *International Journal of Psychology and Educational Studies*, 10(4), 1012–1023.

Hwang, J. (2019). Relationships among locus of control, learned helpless, and mathematical literacy in PISA 2012: Focus on Korea and Finland. *Large-scale Assessments in Education*, 7(1), 4.

Hymel, S., & Katz, J. (2019). Designing classrooms for diversity: Fostering social inclusion. *Educational Psychologist*, 54(4), 331–339.

Idawati, D., Masitoh, S., & Bachri, B.S. (2020). Application of learning mobility orientation on social skill of blind children. *Journal of Education and Learning*, 9(1), 196–204.

Inder, A., Marslen, T., & Carr, D. (2023). Introduction to multi-tiered system of supports. *Learning Difficulties Australia Bulletin*, 55(2), 26–29.

Institute of Education Sciences. (2014). Students with learning disabilities: Spelling Mastery. What Works Clearinghouse™. https://files.eric.ed.gov/fulltext/ED544745.pdf

Institute of Education Sciences. (2023). *Reading Recovery®*. https://whatworks.ed.gov

Irving, J.A., Oppong, E., & Shore, B.M. (2016). Alignment of a high-ranked PISA mathematics curriculum and the "Parallel Curriculum" for gifted students: Is a high PISA mathematics ranking indicative of curricular suitability for gifted learners? *Gifted and Talented International*, 31(2), 114–131.

Isaak, R.C., Kleinert, S.I., & Wilde, M. (2022). Learning strategies of students with and without emotional and behavioural disorders in primary school. *European Journal of Special Needs Education*, 37(5), 790–803.

Izuno-Garcia, A.K., McNeel, M.M., & Fein, R.H. (2023). Neurodiversity in promoting the well-being of children on the autism spectrum. *Child Care in Practice*, 29(1), 54–67.

Jackson. R.L., & Jung, J.Y. (2022). The Identification of Gifted Underachievement: Validity evidence for the commonly used methods. *British Journal of Educational Psychology*, 92(3), 1133–1159.

Jaeger, E.L. (2024). The potential for Common Core and Response to Intervention as intersecting initiatives: Supporting readers who struggle with high-level standards. *Reading & Writing Quarterly*, 40(2), 87–102.

James, K., & Beringer, V. (2019). Brain research shows why handwriting should be taught in the computer age. *Learning Difficulties Australia Bulletin*, 51(1), 25–30.

Johnson, H.N., Wakeman, S.Y., & Clausen, A.M. (2023). Inclusive supports and strategies to increase opportunities to respond for all learners. *TEACHING Exceptional Children*, 56(2), 72–80.

Kaczorowski, T.L., Hashey, A.I., & Di Cesare, D.M. (2019). An exploration of multimedia supports for diverse learners during core math instruction. *Journal of Special Education Technology*, 34(1), 41–54.

Kadioglu Ates, H., & Gurdag, K. (2021). Compilation study on gifted students and e-learning during the pandemic: Limitations, strengths and weaknesses. *Journal of Social Sciences* 8(54), 136–148.

Kalenjuk, E., Laletas, S. Subban, P., & Wilson, S. (2022). A scoping review to map research on children with dysgraphia, their carers, and educators. *Australian Journal of Learning Difficulties*, 27(1), 19–63.

Kalogeropoulos, P., Russo, J.A., Sullivan, P., Klooger, M., & Gunningham, S. (2020). Re-enfranchising mathematically-alienated students: Teacher and tutor perceptions of the Getting Ready in Numeracy (G.R.I.N.) Program. *International Electronic Journal of Mathematics Education*, 15(1), em0545.

Kaplan, S.N. (2024). Clusters…An additional approach to differentiation. *Gifted Child Today*, 47(1), 79–81.

Karal, M.A., & Wolfe, P.S. (2018). Social Story effectiveness on social interaction for students with autism: A review of the literature. *Education and Training in Autism and Developmental Disabilities*, 53(1), 44–58.

Karbowski, C.F. (2020). See3D: 3D printing for people who are blind. *Journal of Science Education for Students with Disabilities*, 23(1). https://doi.org/10.14448/jsesd.12.0006

Kearns, D.M., & Borkenhagen, M.J. (2024). Following the rules in an unruly writing system: the cognitive science of learning to read English. *Reading Teacher*, 77(5), 712–726.

Keen, J. (2022). Teaching writing: Process, practice and policy. *Changing English: Studies in Culture and Education*, 29(1), 24–39.

Kelly, C., Cornwell, P., Hewetson, R., & Copley, A. (2023). The pervasive and unyielding impacts of cognitive-communication changes following traumatic brain injury. *International Journal of Language & Communication Disorders*, 58(6), 2131–2143.

Kendall, L. (2023). *Challenging assumptions about highly able children*. https://mensa.org.uk/challenging-assumptions-about-highly-able-children/

Kerr, N.A. (2024). Teaching in a lonely world: Educating students about the nature of loneliness and promoting social connection in the classroom. *Teaching of Psychology*, 51(1), 93–103.

Khalid, E. (2021). *Sensory impairments: Types, effects and treatment*. https://nuprisma.com/sensory-disabilities-types-effects-and-treatment/

Khosravi, R., Dastgoshadeh, A., & Jalilzadeh, K. (2023). Writing metacognitive strategy-based instruction through flipped classroom: An investigation of writing performance, anxiety, and self-efficacy. *Smart Learning Environments*, 10(1), 48.

Kidwai, I., & Smith, P.K. (2024). A content analysis of school anti-bullying policies in England: Signs of progress. *Educational Psychology in Practice*, 40(1), 1–16.

Kim, N.J., Belland, B.R., & Axelrod, D. (2019). Scaffolding for optimal challenge in K-12 problem-based learning. *Interdisciplinary Journal of Problem-based Learning*, 13(1), 3.

Kim, Y.S.G. (2022). Co-occurrence of reading and writing difficulties: The application of the Interactive Dynamic Literacy Model. *Journal of Learning Disabilities*, 55(6), 447–464.

Kinberg, M. (2020). Real-Life nature-based experiences as keys to the Writing Workshop. *Networks: An Online Journal for Teacher Research*, 22(1), 3.

Kizilaslan, A. (2019). Linking theory to practice: Science for students with visual impairment. *Science Education International*, 30(1), 56–64.

Knoche, L.L., Boise, C.E., Sheridan, S.M., & Cheng, K.C. (2023). Promoting expressive language skills for preschool children with developmental concerns: Effects of a parent-educator partnership intervention. *Elementary School Journal*, 123(4), 513–537.

Koczela, A., & Carver, K. (2023). Understanding Circle Time practices in Montessori early childhood settings. *Journal of Montessori Research*, 9(2), 1–27.

Koegel, R.L. & Koegel, L.K. (2006). *Pivotal response treatments for autism: Communication, social and academic development*. Baltimore, MD: Brookes.

Kohout-Diaz, M. (2023). Inclusive education for all: Principles of a shared inclusive ethos *European Journal of Education*, 58(2), 185–196.

Kokkinos, T. (2020). Aspects of differentiation in teacher education: Exploring student teachers' experiences. *African Educational Research Journal*, 8(4), 814–821.

Kostewicz, D., & Kubina, R.M. (2020). A comparison of two reading fluency methods: Repeated reading to a fluency criterion and interval sprinting. *Reading Improvement*, 57(2), 86–103.

Kožuchová, M., Barnová, S., Stebila, J., & Krásna, S. (2023). Inquiry-based approach to education. *Acta Educationis Generalis*, 13(2), 50–62.

Kurth, J.A., Zagona, A.L., Walker, V.L., & Sheldon, L.,& Loman, S.L. (2024). Teachers' perspectives and knowledge of students with complex support needs and practices associated with SWPBIS. *Journal of Special Education*, 57(4), 205–218.

Kyriakos, D. (2023). Strengths and weaknesses of using educational technology in inclusive settings with limited available resources: Reflections on a classroom-based computer-mediated collaborative learning approach. *International Journal of Learning Technology*, 18(3), 279–303.

Lange, A.A., Brenneman, K., & Sareh, N. (2021). Using number games to support mathematical learning in preschool and home environments. *Early Education and Development*, 32(3), 459–479.

Lantolf, J.P. (2024). On the value of explicit instruction: The view from sociocultural theory. *Language Teaching Research Quarterly*, 39, 281–304.

Lawson, C.A., McGuire, S., Hodges, R., Gray, R., McGuire, S.Y., Killingbeck, M., & Segovia, J. (2021). Recipe for success: Teaching students metacognitive and self-regulatory learning strategies. *Learning Assistance Review*, 26(2), 149–178.

Lee, J.S., & Yeung, C.Y. (2022). Assisted discovery-based learning for literature studies. *Innovations in Education and Teaching International*, 59(5), 543–554.

Lee, K., Cascella, M., & Marwaha, R. (2024a). *Intellectual disability*. National Center for Biotechnology Information. https://www.ncbi.nlm.nih.gov/books/NBK547654/

Lee, S.M., & Oh, Y. (2017). The mediator role of perceived stress in the relationship between academic stress and depressive symptoms among E-Learning students with visual impairments. *Journal of Visual Impairment & Blindness*, 111(2), 123–134.

Lee, Y.F., Chen, P.Y., & Cheng, S.C. (2024b). Improve learning retention, self-efficacy, learning attitude and problem-solving skills through e-books based on sequential multi-level prompting strategies. *Education and Information Technologies*, 29(3), 3663–3680.

Leijen, A., Arcidiacono, F., & Baucal, A. (2021). The dilemma of inclusive education: Inclusion for some or inclusion for all. *Frontiers in Psychology*, 12, 633066.

Lequia, J.L., Vincent, L.B., Lyons, G.L., Asmus, J.M., & Carter, E.W. (2023). Individualized education programs of high school students with significant disabilities. *Education and Training in Autism and Developmental Disabilities*, 58(1), 22–35.

Levesque, K.C., Breadmore, H.L., & Deacon, S.H. (2021). How morphology impacts reading and spelling: Advancing the role of morphology in models of literacy development. *Journal of Research in Reading*, 44(1), 10–26.

Lillehaug, H.A., Klevberg, G.L., & Stadskleiv, K. (2023). Provision of augmentative and alternative communication interventions to Norwegian preschool children with cerebral palsy: Are the Right Children Receiving Interventions? *Augmentative and Alternative Communication*, 39(4), 219–229.

Lim, Z., & Lee, S.H. (2019). Effects of an interview article writing intervention using class-wide social network site on writing abilities and self-esteem of students with intellectual disabilities and peers' attitudes. *Journal of Special Education Technology*, 34(1), 27–40.

Lindner, K.T., Schwab, S., Emara, M., & Avramidis, E. (2023). Do teachers favor the inclusion of all students? A systematic review of primary schoolteachers' attitudes towards inclusive education. *European Journal of Special Needs Education*, 38(6), 766–787.

Lindo, E.J., Weiser, B., Cheatham, J.P., & Allor, J.H. (2018). Benefits of structured after-school literacy tutoring by university students for struggling elementary readers. *Reading & Writing Quarterly*, 34(2), 117–131.

Lipscomb, A.H., Anderson, M., & Gadke, D.L. (2018). Comparing the effects of Classdojo with and without tootling intervention in a postsecondary special education classroom setting. *Psychology in the Schools*, 55(10), 1287–1301.

Liu, H., Zhang, Y., & Jia, J. (2024). The design of guiding and adaptive prompts for intelligent tutoring systems and its effect on students' mathematics learning. *IEEE Transactions on Learning Technologies*, 17, 1379–1389.

Loft, P., Long, R., & Danechi, S. (2020). *Support for more able and talented children in schools (UK)*. Briefing Paper 9065. House of Commons Library.

Loh, S.Y., Ee, S.I., & Marret, M.J. (2023). Sensory processing and its relationship to participation among childhood occupations in children with autism spectrum disorder: Exploring the processing profile of differences. *International Journal of Developmental Disabilities*, 69(2), 226–237.

Lohmann, M.J., Hovey, K.A., & Gauvreau, A.N. (2023). Universal Design for Learning (UDL) in inclusive preschool science classrooms. *Journal of Science Education for Students with Disabilities*, 26(1), 4.

Long, L.C., & Erwin, A. (2020). IGNITE: Empowering high ability underachieving students to become focused learners in mainstream classes. *Gifted Education International*, 36(3), 237–249.

Lovaas, O.I., & Smith, T. (2003). Early and intensive behavioral interventions in autism. In A.E. Kazdin & J. R. Weisz (Eds.) *Evidence-based psychotherapies for children and adolescents* (pp. 325–340). New York: Guilford Press.

Love, D.J. (2022). *ClassDojo new age classroom management.* ProQuest LLC, Ed.D. Dissertation: Chicago School of Professional Psychology. ERIC Document. ED621253.

Loveless, B. (2024). *Pros and cons of gifted learning programs in schools.* https://www.educationcorner.com/gifted-education-pros-cons/

Lu, J. (2022). Cracking the formula: How should Australia be teaching maths under the national curriculum, *The Guardian* [newspaper], 12 February 2022.

Lum, J.D.K., Radley, K.C., Tingstrom, D.H., Dufrene, B.A., Olmi, D.J., & Wright, S.J. (2019). Tootling with a randomized independent group contingency to improve high school class-wide behavior. *Journal of Positive Behavior Interventions,* 21(2), 93–105.

Lundberg, A., Petersen-Brown, S., Houlihan, D.D., Panahon, C., & Wagner, D. (2023). Applying peer tutoring to spelling with elementary-aged students. *Journal of Applied School Psychology,* 39(2), 107–129.

Lyndon, H. (1989). 'I did it my way': An introduction to Old Way–New Way. *Australasian Journal of Special Education,* 13, 32–37.

Lyons, M.E. (2024). Within-classroom play: Cultivating autonomy, competence, and relatedness during the transition to kindergarten. *Early Childhood Education Journal,* 52(1), 155–165.

Ma, X., & Xin, Y.P. (2024). Teaching mathematics word problem solving to students with autism spectrum disorder. *Journal of Special Education,* 58(1), 47–58.

Macquarie University. (2023). *Teaching children with intellectual disability.* https://www.mq.edu.au/faculty-of-arts/departments-and-schools/macquarie-school-of-education/news-and-events/news/news/teaching-children-with-intellectual-disabilities

Magableh, I.S., & Abdullah, A. (2022). Differentiated instruction effectiveness on the secondary stage students' reading comprehension proficiency level in Jordan. *International Journal of Evaluation and Research in Education,* 11(1), 459–466.

Magnusson, C., Roe, A., & Blikstad-Balas, M. (2019). To what extent and how are reading comprehension strategies part of language arts instruction? A study of lower secondary classrooms. *Reading Research Quarterly,* 54(2), 187–212.

Maker, C.J., & Pease, R. (2021). Building on and extending the characteristics of gifted learners: Implementing the Real Engagement in Active Problem Solving (REAPS) teaching model. *Australasian Journal of Gifted Education,* 30(2), 5–25.

Maker, C.J., Pease, R., & Bahir, A.K. (2024). Profiles of exceptionally talented students in science, technology, engineering, and mathematics (STEM): An exploration using Q factor analysis. *Roeper Review,* 46(1), 7–26.

Malik, S., Abd Manaf, U.K., Ahmad, N.A., & Ismail, M. (2018). Orientation and mobility training in special education curriculum for social adjustment problems of visually impaired children in Pakistan. *International Journal of Instruction,* 11(2), 185–202.

Mammadov, S., & Tozoglu, D. (2023). Autonomy support, personality, and mindset in predicting academic performance among early adolescents: The mediating role of self-determined motivation. *Psychology in the Schools,* 60(10), 3754–3769.

Manolev, J., Sullivan, A., & Slee, R. (2019). The datafication of discipline: ClassDojo, surveillance and a performative classroom culture. *Learning, Media and Technology,* 44(1), 36–51.

Marsh, J. (2023). *How to use dictation in spelling instruction.* https://howtospell.co.uk/how-to-use-dictation-in-spelling-instruction

Marsili, F., Dell'Anna, S., & Pellegrini, M. (2023). Giftedness in inclusive education: A systematic review of research. *International Journal of Inclusive Education*. https://doi.org/10.1080/13603116.2023.2190330

Martin, B.L., Sargent, K., Van Camp, A., & Wright, J. (2018). *Intensive intervention practice guide: Increasing opportunities to respond as an intensive intervention.* Washington, DC: US Department of Education, Office of Special Education Programs.

Mason, L., & Otero, M. (2021). Just how effective is Direct Instruction? *Perspectives on Behavior Science*, 44(2–3), 225–244.

Maycock, K.W. (2019). Chalk and talk versus flipped learning: A case study. *Journal of Computer Assisted Learning*, 35(1), 121–126.

Mays, D. (2020). Making plans for Michael: Providing for a student with moderate learning difficulties in a secondary academy. *Support for Learning*, 35(1), 83–100.

Mazurek, M.O. (2014). Loneliness, friendship and well-being in adults with autism spectrum disorders. *Autism*, 18(3), 223–232.

Mazurek, M.O., Curran, A., Burnette, C., & Sohl, K. (2019). ECHO Autism STAT: Accelerating early access to autism diagnosis. *Journal of Autism and Developmental Disorders*, 49(1), 127–137.

McCoach, D. B., Siegle, D., & Rubenstein, L.D. (2020). Pay attention to inattention: Exploring ADHD symptoms in a sample of underachieving gifted students. *Gifted Child Quarterly*, 64(2), 100–116.

McCollow, M.M., & Hoffman, H.H. (2019). Supporting social development in young children with disabilities: Building a practitioner's toolkit. *Early Childhood Education Journal*, 47(3), 309–320.

McConkey, R., Sadowsky, M., & Shellard, A. (2019). An international survey of obesity and underweight in youth and adults with intellectual disabilities. *Journal of Intellectual & Developmental Disability*, 44(3), 374–382.

McCracken, T., Chapman, S., & Piggott, B. (2023). Inclusion illusion: A mixed-methods study of preservice teachers and their preparedness for inclusive schooling in health and physical education. *International Journal of Inclusive Education*, 27(4), 507–525.

McDaniel, S.C., Coogler, C., & Guyotte, K. (2024). 'It's a process': Preliminary educator perceptions of Tier 2 implementation barriers, facilitators, and attitudes. *Journal of Applied School Psychology*, 40(1), 1–24.

McGrath, P. (2019). Education in Northern Ireland: Does it meet the needs of gifted students? *Gifted Education International*, 35(1), 37–55.

McKay, J., & Sridharan, B. (2024). Student perceptions of collaborative group work (CGW) in higher education. *Studies in Higher Education*, 49(2), 221–234.

McKnight, L. (2023). Teaching writing by formula: Empowerment or exclusion? *International Journal of Inclusive Education*, 27(5), 571–585.

McKoy, S., & Merry, K.E. (2023). Engaging advanced learners with differentiated online learning. *Gifted Child Today*, 46(1), 48–56.

McMahan, A., & Maricle, D.E. (2020). Epilepsy: What school psychologists should know. *Communique*, 49(2). 10–13.

McMurray, S. (2020). Learning to spell for children 5–8 years of age: The importance of an integrated approach to ensure development of phonic, orthographic and morphemic knowledge at compatible levels. *Dyslexia*, 26(4), 442–458.

McNeill, B.C., Gillon, G., & Gath, M. (2023). The relationship between early spelling and decoding. *Language, Speech, and Hearing Services in Schools*, 54(3), 981–995.

Meeks, L., & Stephenson, J. (2020). Australian preservice teachers and early reading instruction. *Australian Journal of Learning Difficulties*, 25(1), 65–82.

Mendini, M., & Peter, P.C. (2019). Research note: The role of smart versus traditional classrooms on students' engagement. *Marketing Education Review*, 29(1), 17–23.

Meral, B.F., Wehmeyer, M.L., Palmer, S.B., Ruh, A.B., & Yilmaz, E. (2023). Parenting styles and practices in enhancing self-determination of children with intellectual and developmental disabilities. *American Journal on Intellectual and Developmental Disabilities*, 128(4), 282–301.

Meredith-Murphy, J., Hawkins, R.O., & Nabors, L. (2020). Combining social skills instruction and the Good Behavior Game to support students with emotional and behavioral disorders. *Contemporary School Psychology*, 24(2), 228–238.

Mesibov, G.B., Shea, V., & Schopler, E (2005). *The TEACCH approach to Autism spectrum disorders*. New York: Kluwer Academic-Plenum.

Michael, R., Attias, J., & Raveh, E. (2019). Cochlear implantation and social-emotional functioning of children with hearing loss. *Journal of Deaf Studies and Deaf Education*, 24(1), 25–31.

Michaud, G., & Ammar, A. (2023). Explicit Instruction within a task: Before, during, or after? *Studies in Second Language Acquisition*, 45(2), 442–460.

Mieres, D., Losilla, J.M., Pérez, E., & Cambra, C. (2024). linguistic intervention strategies speech-language pathologists use with children using cochlear implants. *Journal of Deaf Studies and Deaf Education*, 29(1), 60–71.

Miesner, H.R., Blair, E.E., Packard, C.C., Macgregor, L., & Grodsky, E. (2023). Instructional coordination for Response to Intervention: How organizational contexts shape Tier 2 interventions in practice. *American Journal of Education*, 129(4), 565–592.

Miller, R.E. (2024). Pandora's can of worms: A year of generative AI in higher education. *Libraries and the Academy*, 24(1), 21–34.

Miravete, S. (2023). Should talented students skip a grade? A literature review on grade skipping. *European Journal of Psychology of Education*, 38(2), 903–923.

Miskimon, K., Jenkins, L.N., & Kaminski, S. (2023). Direct and indirect effects of bullying victimization on academic performance and mental health among secondary school students. *School Mental Health*, 15(1), 220–230.

Mølster, T., & Nes, K. (2018). To what extent does information and communication technology support inclusion in education of students with learning difficulties? *Universal Journal of Educational Research*, 6(4), 598–612.

Montacute, R. (2018). *Potential for success: Fulfilling the promise of highly able students in secondary schools*. London: Sutton Trust.

Mood, D., Sheldon, R., Tabangin, M., Wiley, S., & Meinzen-Derr, J. (2022). Technology assisted language intervention (TALI) for children who are deaf/hard of hearing: Promising impact on pragmatic skills. *Deafness & Education International*, 24(4), 334–355.

Moriña, A., Carballo, R., & Castellano-Beltran, A. (2024). A systematic review of the benefits and challenges of technologies for the learning of university students with disabilities. *Journal of Special Education Technology*, 39(1), 41–50.

Morris, D. (2023). The case for tutoring struggling readers in the primary grades. *Reading & Writing Quarterly*, 39(2), 104–119.

Morrison, J.Q., Hawkins, R.O., & Collins, T.A. (2020). Evaluating the cost-effectiveness of the Dyslexia Pilot Project: A multitiered system of supports for early literacy. *Psychology in the Schools*, 57(4), 522–539.

Morse, T.E. (2023). Designing appropriate small group intensive instruction within an MTSS for students with low incidence disabilities. *Journal of the American Academy of Special Education Professionals*, 89(Spring-Summer Issue), 101.

Mousavi, E., Akbarfahimi, N., Moein, S., & Vahedi, M. (2023). A study of the relationship between executive function and school function in children with cerebral palsy. *Journal of Occupational Therapy, Schools & Early Intervention*, 16(2), 160–172.

Mukamal, R. (2021). *Technology tools for children with low vision*. American Academy of Ophthalmology. https://www.aao.org/eye-health/tips-prevention/technology-apps-devices-children-blind-low-vision

Mund, M., & Neyer, F.J. (2019). Loneliness effects on personality. *International Journal of Behavioral Development*, 43(2), 136–146.

Murawski, W.W., & Scott, K.L. (Eds.). (2019). *What really works with Universal Design for Learning*. Thousand Oaks, CA: Corwin.

Murnan, R., & Cornell, H. (2023). Digital tools to support self-regulation in the writing process for exceptional learners. *Journal of Special Education Technology*, 38(4), 547–554.

Murray, A.L., Booth, T., Eisner, M., Auyeung, B., Murray, G., & Ribeaud, D. (2019). Sex differences in ADHD trajectories across childhood and adolescence. *Developmental Science*, 22(1), e12721.

Mutflu, Y., & Akgün, L. (2019). Using computer for developing arithmetical skills of students with mathematics learning difficulties. *International Journal of Research in Education and Science*, 5(1), 237–251.

NAGC-CEC (National Association for Gifted Children-Council for Exceptional Children). (2013). *Teacher preparation standards in gifted and talented education*. Washington, DC: National Association for Gifted Children.

Nagl, S. (2020). The power of Workshop. *Networks: An Online Journal for Teacher Research*, 22(2), 5.

Nalls, A.J., & Wickerd, G. (2023). The Jigsaw Method: Reviving a powerful positive intervention. *Journal of Applied School Psychology*, 39(3), 201–217.

National Autistic Society [UK]. (2018). *Causes of autism*. https://www.autism.org.uk/about/what-is/asd.aspx

National Council on Teacher Quality. (2023). *Reading foundations: Technical Report*. New York: NCTQ.

NCES (National Centre for Education Statistics). (2023). *Students with disabilities*. Washington, DC: Institute of Education Sciences.

Neese, B. (2023). *15 Assistive technology tools & resources for students with disabilities*. https://www.teachthought.com/technology/assistive-technology/

Neilson, R. (2019). Spelling: Enabler or disabler? *Learning Difficulties Australia Bulletin*, 51(1), 22–24.

Nelson, G., & Powell, S.R. (2018). A systematic review of longitudinal studies of mathematics difficulty. *Journal of Learning Disabilities*, 51(6), 523–539.

Nelson, K.A., & Eckert, T.L. (2024). Examining student adherence within a cover-copy-compare intervention. *Psychology in the Schools*, 61(5), 2019–2035.

Nelson, P.M., Parker, D.C., & Van Norman, E.R. (2018). Subskill mastery among elementary and middle school students at risk in mathematics. *Psychology in the Schools*, 55(6), 722–736.

Nese, R.N., Kittelman, A., Strickland-Cohen, M.K., & McIntosh, K. (2023). Examining teaming and Tier 2 and 3 practices within a PBIS framework. *Journal of Positive Behavior Interventions*, 25(1), 16–22.

Neumeister, K.L.S. (2024). Maximizing the potential of twice-exceptional learners: Creating a framework of stakeholder supports. *Gifted Child Quarterly*, 68(1), 19–33.

Nielsen, T.C., Nassar, N., Boulton, K.A., Guastella, A.J., & Lain, S.J. (2024). Estimating the prevalence of autism spectrum disorder in New South Wales, Australia: A data linkage study of three routinely collected datasets. *Journal of Autism and Developmental Disorders*, 54(4), 1558–1566.

Nipe, T.A., Dowdy, A., Quigley, J., Gill, A., & Weiss, M.J. (2018). Increasing the wearing of multiple prescription prosthetic devices. *Education and Treatment of Children*, 41(3), 331–344.

Noltemeyer, A., Palmer, K., James, A.G., & Petrasek, M. (2019). Disciplinary and achievement outcomes associated with School-Wide Positive Behavioral Interventions and Supports implementation level. *School Psychology Review*, 48(1), 81–87.

O'Neill, A. (2024). Was Humpty Dumpty right? Towards a functional definition of e-learning. *Education and Information Technologies*, 29(2), 2093–2115.

OECD. (2007). *Students with disabilities, learning difficulties and disadvantages: Policies, statistics, and indicators.* Paris: OECD.

OECD. (2019a), *The heavy burden of obesity: The economics of prevention.* Paris: OECD Publishing: https://doi.org/10.1787/f563de08-en

OECD (2019b). *PISA 2018 results. V.3. What school life means for students.* Paris: OECD Publishing.

OECD (2022). *How to support gifted students to reach their full potential.* https://oecdedutoday.com/gifted-education/

Office of English Language Acquisition. (2021). *English learners in gifted and talented programs.* Washington, DC: Office of English Language Acquisition.

Ofsted (2021). *Supporting SEND: How children and young people's special educational needs (SEN) are met in mainstream schools.* London: Ofsted.

Ögülmüş, K. (2021). The effect of the POW + C-SPACE strategy on writing skills of students with specific learning difficulties attending classes in the resource room. *International Journal of Psychology and Educational Studies*, 8(3), 242–253.

Ohtani, K., & Hisasaka, T. (2018). Beyond intelligence: A meta-analytic review of the relationship among metacognition, intelligence, and academic performance. *Metacognition and Learning*, 13(2), 179–212.

Okcu, B., & Sozbilir, M. (2019). Designing a bulb to teach electric circuits to visually impaired students. *Physics Teacher*, 57(2), 99–101.

Olivieri, C. (2020). Childhood obesity, health & nutrition and its effects on learning. *Journal for Leadership and Instruction*, 19(1), 31–37.

Oppong, E., Shore, B.M., & Muis, K.R. (2019). Clarifying the connections among giftedness, metacognition, self-regulation, and self-regulated learning: Implications for theory and practice. *Gifted Child Quarterly*, 63(2), 102–119.

Orton, S.T. (1937). *Reading, writing and speech problems in children.* New York: Norton.

OT Toolbox. (2023). *Alert Self-Regulation Program.* https://www.theottoolbox.com/alert-program-self-regulation-program

Otero, T.M., & Naglieri, J.A. (2023). PASS neurocognitive assessment of children with autism spectrum disorder. *Psychology in the Schools*, 60(2), 452–459.

Pacheco, O., & Huertas, A. (2022). Effects of a writing strategy on improving text production skills among primary school students. *Knowledge Management & E-Learning*, 14(1), 1–14.

Page, S.V., Zimmerman, D.M., & Pinkelman, S.E. (2023). A systematic review of dependent group contingencies (197z–2019). *Journal of Positive Behavior Interventions*, 25(3), 198–209.

Papanthymou, A., & Darra, M. (2022). Perceptions of primary school teachers regarding the implementation of differentiated instruction to students with learning difficulties. *World Journal of Education*, 12(5), 19–39.

Park, I., & Kim, Y.R. (2018). Effects of TEACCH structured teaching on independent work skills among individuals with severe disabilities. *Education and Training in Autism and Developmental Disabilities*, 53(4), 343–352.

Park, J., Bryant, D.P., & Shin, M. (2022). Effects of interventions using virtual manipulatives for students with learning disabilities: A synthesis of single-case research. *Journal of Learning Disabilities*, 55(4), 325–337.

Park, M.N., Moulton, E.E., & Laugeson, E.A. (2023). Parent-assisted social skills training for children with autism spectrum disorder: PEERS for preschoolers. *Focus on Autism and Other Developmental Disabilities*, 38(2), 80–89.

Partington, P., Major, G., & Tudor, K. (2024). Deaf students' perception of wellbeing and social and emotional skill development within school: A critical examination of the literature. *International Journal of Disability, Development and Education*, 71(1), 55–68.

Pas, E.T., Ryoo, J.H., Musci, R., & Bradshaw, C.P. (2019). A state-wide quasi-experimental effectiveness study of the scale-up of school-wide positive behavioral interventions and supports. *Journal of School Psychology*, 73, 41–55.

Paseka, A., & Schwab, S. (2020). Parents' attitudes towards inclusive education and their perceptions of inclusive teaching practices and resources. *European Journal of Special Needs Education*, 35(2), 254–272.

Passolunghi, M.C., Cargnelutti, E., & Pellizzoni, S. (2019). The relation between cognitive and emotional factors and arithmetic problem-solving. *Educational Studies in Mathematics*, 100(3), 271–290.

Pawelski, C.E. (2007). Conductive Education. In A.M. Bursztyn (Ed.) *The Praeger handbook of special education* (pp. 84–88). Westport, CT: Praeger.

Payne, S.B., & Swanson, E. (2023). Supporting families to motivate their middle school student during homework time. *TEACHING Exceptional Children*, 55(6), 422–430.

Paz-Baruch, N., Leikin, M., & Leikin, R. (2022). Not any gifted is an expert in mathematics and not any expert in mathematics is gifted. *Gifted and Talented International*, 37(1), 25–41.

Pearson Publishing. (2024). *Rapid phonics: An early intervention program.* https://www.pearson.com/en-au/schools/primary/literacy/rapid-phonics/

Perkins, M., Roe, J., Postma, D., McGaughran, J., & Hickerson, D. (2024). Detection of GPT-4 generated text in higher education: Combining academic judgement and software to identify generative AI tool misuse. *Journal of Academic Ethics*, 22(1), 89–113.

Peterson, J.M., Borders, C.M., & Ely, M.S. (2023). Prevalence of educationally significant disabilities among deaf and hard of hearing students. *American Annals of the Deaf*, 167(5), 583–596.

Piaget, J. (1963). *Origins of intelligence in children.* New York: Norton.

Picken, A. (2023). *Scottish education performance falling, says study.* BBC Scotland News. https://www.bbc.com/news/uk-scotland-67580173

Piekema, L., Ten Brug, A., Waninge, A., & van der Putten, A. (2024). From assistive to inclusive? A systematic review of the uses and effects of technology to support people with pervasive support needs. *Journal of Applied Research in Intellectual Disabilities*, 37(2), e13181.

Pierce, E. (2022). *Gifted and talented programs: What parents need to know.* https://www.usnews.com/education/k12/articles/gifted-and-talented-programs-what-parents-should-know

Pierce, S., & Maher, A.J. (2020). Physical activity among children and young people with intellectual disabilities in special schools: Teacher and Learning Support Assistant perceptions. *British Journal of Learning Disabilities*, 48(1), 37–44.

Pilgrim, J. (2022). The science of reading: An analysis of Texas Literacy Standards for Teacher Certification. In *TALE Turns Ten: A Decade of Literacy, Service, and Advocacy*, Texas Association for Literacy Education Yearbook 9, pp. 63–74.

Pistav Akmese, P., Kyhan, N., & Isikogan Ugurlu, N. (2023). Written language characteristics of deaf and hard of hearing students in terms of the components of the language. *Journal of Psycholinguistic Research*, 52(6), 2093–2117.

Pitts, L., Gent, S., & Hoerger, M.L. (2019). Reducing pupils' barriers to learning in a special needs school: Integrating Applied Behaviour Analysis into Key Stages 1–3. *British Journal of Special Education*, 46(1), 94–112.

Pletcher, B.C., Nicol, M., Harper, T., Hollenbaugh, M., Johnson, R., & Staples, M. 2023a). "A first look at teaching": The impact of a tutorial program on first-grade children and their tutors. *Reading Psychology*, 44(8), 936–964.

Pletcher, B.C., Robertson, P., & Watson, K. (2023b). Engaging preservice teachers in interdisciplinary collaboration and intervention in a reading clinic setting. *Preventing School Failure*, 67(4), 282–296.

Plucker, J., Glynn, J., Healey, G., & Dettmer, A. (2018). *Equal talents, unequal opportunities: A report card on state support for academically talented low-income students* (2nd ed.). Landsdowne, VA: Jack Kent Cooke Foundation.

Poast, M., Skidmore, S.T., & Zientek, L.R. (2021). Multiplication facts in the continuum of skills. *Journal of College Reading and Learning*, 51(1), 58–77.

Pokorski, E.A. (2019). Group contingencies to improve class-wide behavior of young children. *Teaching Exceptional Children*, 51(5), 340–349.

Poling, D.V., & Smith, S.W. (2023). Perceptions about verbal aggression: Survey of secondary students with emotional and behavioral disorders. *Journal of Emotional and Behavioral Disorders*, 31(1), 14–26.

Pontecorvo, E., Higgins, M., Mora, J., Lieberman, A.M., Pyers, J., & Caselli, N.K. (2023). Learning a sign language does not hinder acquisition of a spoken language. *Journal of Speech, Language, and Hearing Research*, 66(4),1291–1308.

Porta, T., & Todd, N. (2024). The impact of labelling students with learning difficulties on teacher self-efficacy in differentiated instruction. *Journal of Research in Special Educational Needs*, 24(1), 108–122.

Poulter, B. (2023). '*We are concerned*': *California professors frustrated over university system's revised math standards.* https://dailycaller.com/2023/07/07/california-professors-frustrated-over-university-systems-revised-math-standards/

Powell, S.R., Akther, S.S., Yoon, N.Y., Berry, K.A., Nemcek, C. Fall, A.M., & Roberts, G. (2023). The effect of addition and subtraction practice within a word-problem intervention on addition and subtraction outcomes. *Learning Disabilities Research & Practice*, 38(3), 182–198.

Pratiwi, D.I., & Waluyo, B. (2023). Autonomous learning and the use of digital technologies in online English classrooms in higher education. *Contemporary Educational Technology*, 15(2), ep423.

Prizant, B., Wetherby, A.M., Laurent, A.C., & Rydell, P.J. (2006). *The SCERTS® Model: A comprehensive educational approach for children with autism spectrum disorders*. Baltimore, MD: Brookes.

Pytash, K.E., Morgan, D.N., & Testa, E. (2023), Learning in practice: What preservice teachers report learning about writing in a middle school role-based field experience. *Literacy Research and Instruction*, 62(4), 305–326.

Quinn, M., & Bliss, M. (2021). Moving beyond tracing: The nature, availability and quality of digital apps to support children's writing. *Journal of Early Childhood Literacy*, 21(2), 230–258.

Rabideau, L.K., Stanton-Chapman, T.L., & Brown, T.S. (2018). Discrete Trial Training to teach alternative communication: A step-by-step guide. *Young Exceptional Children*, 21(1), 34–47.

Ralli, M., Papadopoulou, S., Pantinaki, S., & Apostolakis, M. (2023). The strategic planners of writing: A Tier 2 intervention writing program. *Insights into Learning Disabilities*, 20(1),1–25.

Ramberg, J., & Watkins, A. (2020). Exploring inclusive education across Europe: Some insights from the European Agency statistics on inclusive education. *FIRE: Forum for International Research in Education*, 6(1), 85–101.

Ramirez, G., Fries, L., Gunderson, E., Schaeffer, M.W., Maloney, E.A., Beilock, S.L., & Levine, S.C. (2019). Reading anxiety: An early affective impediment to children's success in reading. *Journal of Cognition and Development*, 20(1), 15–34.

Ramos, S., & de Andrade, A.M. (2016). ICT in Portuguese reference schools for the education of blind and partially sighted students. *Education and Information Technologies*, 21(3), 625–641.

Ramos-Carbo, S., Vulchanov, V., & Vulchanov, M. (2021). Different ways of making a point: a study of gestural communication in typical and atypical early development. *Autism Research*, 14, 984–996.

Redford, K. (2019). Assistive technology: Promises fulfilled. *Educational Leadership*, 76(5), 70–74.

Regan, K., Evmenova, A.S., Sacco, D., Schwartzer, J., Chirinos, D.S., & Hughes, M.D. (2019). Teacher perceptions of integrating technology in writing. *Technology, Pedagogy and Education*, 28(1), 1–19.

Reimers, C. (2020). *Longitudinal analysis of behavior screening data in a school district implementing School-Wide Positive Behavior Interventions and Supports*. ProQuest LLC, Ed.S. Dissertation, University of Nebraska at Omaha. ERIC document number: ED597652.

Reis, S.M., & Peters, P.M. (2021). Research on the Schoolwide Enrichment Model: Four decades of insights, innovation, and evolution. *Gifted Education International*, 37(2), 109–141.

Renzulli, J.S. & Reis, S.M. (2014) *The Schoolwide Enrichment Model: A how-to guide for talent development* (3rd ed.). Waco, TX: Prufrock Press.

Reynolds, M., Buckingham, J., Madelaine, A., Arakelian, S., Bell, N., Pogorzelski, S., Wheldall, R., & Wheldall, K. (2021). What we have learned: Implementing MiniLit as an intervention with young struggling readers. *Australian Journal of Learning Difficulties*, 26(2), 113–125.

Ribeiro, F.S., Tonoli, M.C., Ribeiro, D.P., & Santos, F.H.D. (2017). Numeracy deficits scrutinized: Evidences of primary developmental dyscalculia. *Psychology & Neuroscience*, 10(2), 189–200.

Rice, M., Erbeli, F., & Wijekumar, K. (2024). Phonemic awareness: Evidence-based instruction for students in need of intervention. *Intervention in School and Clinic*, 59(4), 269–273.

Ridgely, N.C., Pallathra, A.A., Raffaele, C.T., Rothwell, C., & Rich, B.A. (2023). Adaptation of the PEERS for young adults' social skills curriculum for college students with autism spectrum disorder. *Focus on Autism and Other Developmental Disabilities*, 38(4), 234–244.

Rippel, M. (2024). *How to do spelling dictation.* https://blog.allaboutlearningpress.com/spelling-dictation/

Ritchotte, J.A., Matthews, M.S., & Flowers, C.P. (2014). The validity of the Achievement-Orientation Model for gifted middle school students: An exploratory study. *Gifted Child Quarterly*, 58(3), 183–198.

Rochford, D. (2016). *Review of assessment for pupils working below the standard of national curriculum tests (The Rochford Review): Final report*. London: Standards and Testing Agency.

Rodgers, D.B., & Loveall, S.J. (2023). Writing interventions for students with intellectual and developmental disabilities: A meta-analysis. *Remedial and Special Education*, 44(3), 239–252.

Rodriguez, S., Allen, K., Harron, J., & Qadri, S.A. (2019). Making and the 5E Learning Cycle. *Science Teacher*, 86(5), 48–55.

Roiha, A., & Polso, J. (2021). The 5-Dimensional Model: A tangible framework for differentiation. *Practical Assessment, Research & Evaluation*, 26(1), 20.

Rojo, M., King, S., Gersib, J., & Bryant, D.P. (2023). Rational number interventions for students with mathematics difficulties: A meta-analysis. *Remedial and Special Education*, 44(3), 225–238.

Rojo, M., & Wakim, N. (2023). Teaching whole number addition and subtraction to students with learning disabilities. *Intervention in School and Clinic*, 58(3), 190–197.

Ronimus, M., Eklund, K., Pesu, L., & Lyytinen, H. (2019). Supporting struggling readers with digital game-based learning. *Educational Technology Research and Development*, 67(3), 639–663.

Rosenblum, L.P., Cheng, L., & Beal, C.R. (2018). Teachers of students with visual impairments share experiences and advice for supporting students in understanding graphics. *Journal of Visual Impairment & Blindness*, 112(5), 475–487.

Rouse, H., Goudie, A., Rettiganti, M., Leath, K., Riser, Q., & Thompson, J. (2019). Prevalence, patterns, and predictors: A statewide longitudinal study of childhood obesity. *Journal of School Health*, 89(4), 237–245.

Ruderman, M. (2016). *Children's vision and eye health: A snapshot of current national issues*. Chicago, IL: National Center for Children's Vision and Eye Health at Prevent Blindness.

Rudy, L.J. (2023). *The Rapid Prompting Method for treating autism*. https://www.verywellhealth.com/what-is-the-rapid-prompting-method-for-treating-autism-259937

Russell, D. (2024). *What is explicit instruction?* https://www.teachermagazine.com/au_en/articles/teaching-resource-what-is-explicit-instruction?utm_source=CM&utm_medium=Bulletin&utm_campaign=16April

Rutter, S., & Atkinson, C. (2024). How educational psychologists use cognitive behavioural therapy interventions: A systematic literature review. *Educational Psychology in Practice*, 40(1), 96–120.

Saavedra, A.R., & Rapaport, A. (2024). Key lessons from research about project-based teaching and learning. *Phi Delta Kappan*, 105(5), 19–25.

Sabatier, E., Leybaert, J., & Chetail, F. (2024). Orthographic learning in French-speaking deaf and hard of hearing children. *Journal of Speech, Language, and Hearing Research*, 67(3), 870–885.

Samuelsson, J., Holmer, E., Johnels, J.A., Palmqvist, L., Heimann, M., Reichenberg, M., & Thunberg, G. (2024). My point of view: Students with intellectual and communicative disabilities express their views on speech and reading using Talking Mats. *British Journal of Learning Disabilities*, 52(1), 23–35.

Sanal, S.Ö., & Elmali, F. (2024). Effectiveness of realistic math education on mathematical problem-solving skills of students with learning disability. *European Journal of Special Needs Education*, 39(1), 109–126.

Sanders, S., & Garwood, J.D. (2022). Assessment of effective strategy instruction and reading comprehension. *Preventing School Failure*, 66(4), 320–326.

Sandjojo, J., Zedlitz, A.E.E., Gebhardt, W.A., Hoekman, J., den Haan, J., & Evers, A.W.M. (2019). Effects of a self-management training for people with intellectual disabilities. *Journal of Applied Research in Intellectual Disabilities*, 32(2), 390–400.

Satherley, D., & Norwich, B. (2022). Parents' experiences of choosing a special school for their children. *European Journal of Special Needs Education*, 37(6), 950–964.

Satsangi, R., Miller, B., & Savage, M.N. (2019). Helping teachers make informed decisions when selecting assistive technology for secondary students with disabilities. *Preventing School Failure*, 63(2), 97–104.

Savage, M. (2023). Quarter of a million children enter secondary school without basic maths and English. *The Guardian* [newspaper], 12 February 2023.

Schardt, A.A., Miller, F.G., & Bedesem, P.L. (2019). The effects of CellF-Monitoring on students' academic engagement: A technology-based self-monitoring intervention. *Journal of Positive Behavior Interventions*, 21(1), 42–49.

Scharer, P.L. & Zutell, J. (2003). The development of spelling. In N. Hall, J. Larson & J. Marsh (Eds) *Handbook of early childhood literacy*. London: Sage.

Scholes, L. (2024). Reading for digital futures: A lens to consider social justice issues in student literacy experiences in the digital age. *Cambridge Journal of Education*, 54(1), 71–88.

Schrieber, S.R., Ware, M.E., & Dart, E.H. (2023). Student interview-informed behavior contracts for high school students identified as at risk. *Behavioral Disorders*, 49(1), 31–45.

Schulze, M.A. (2016). Self-management strategies to support students with ASD. *Teaching Exceptional Children*, 48(5), 225–231.

Schwab, S. (2019). Friendship stability among students with and without special educational needs. *Educational Studies*, 45(3), 390–401.

Scott, T.M. (2023). Not a roll of the dice: Increasing the probability of student success. *TEACHING Exceptional Children*, 55(4), 286–287.

Seage, S.J., & Türegün, M. (2020). The effects of blended learning on STEM achievement of elementary school students. *International Journal of Research in Education and Science*, 6(1), 133–140.

Seidl, A.H., Indarjit, M., & Borovsky, A. (2024). Touch to learn: Multisensory input supports word learning and processing. *Developmental Science*, 27(1), e13419.

Serhan, D., & Almeqdadi, F. (2020). Students' perceptions of using MyMathLab and WebAssign in mathematics classroom. *International Journal of Technology in Education and Science*, 4(1), 12–17.

Serki, N., & Bolkan, S. (2024). The effect of clarity on learning: Impacting motivation through cognitive load. *Communication Education*, 73(1), 29–45.

Serry, T., Rose, M. & Liamputtong, P. (2014). Reading Recovery teachers discuss Reading Recovery: A qualitative investigation. *Australian Journal of Learning Difficulties*, 19(1), 61–73.

Setty, E. (2021). Sex and consent in contemporary youth sexual culture: The 'ideals' and the 'realities.' *Sex Education: Sexuality, Society and Learning*, 21(3), 331–346.

Shafiullah, S., & Akay, C. (2023). Challenges of visually impaired university students in education: A meta-synthesis study. *Journal on Educational Psychology*, 16(3), 46–60.

Shalit, E., & Dotan, D. (2024). Exploring the linguistic complexity of third-grade numerical literacy. *Cognitive Research: Principles and Implications*, 9, Article 48.

Shaw, A. (2017). Inclusion: The role of special and mainstream schools. *British Journal of Special Education*, 44(3), 292–312.

Shaw, N. (2023). Insights into cognitive processes operating during classroom learning. *Journal of Pedagogical Research*, 7(3), 125–139.

Shepherd, C. (2021). More able learners: Key terminology and definitions. National Association for Able Children in Education. https://www.nace.co.uk/blogpost/1764156/367215/More-able-learners-key-terminology-and-definitions

Sherawat, J., & Punia, P. (2022). Impact of adoption of information and communication technologies (ICTs) in teaching mathematics to intellectually disabled children. *Mathematics Teaching Research Journal*, 14(1), 41–66.

Sherry, M.B. (2019). Emergence and development of a dialogic whole-class discussion genre. *Dialogic Pedagogy*, 7, 27–57.

Siegle, D., McCoach, D.B., & Roberts, A. (2017). Why I believe I achieve determines whether I achieve. *High Ability Studies*, 28(1), 59–72.

Sigstad, H.M.H., & Garrels, V. (2023). Which success factors do young adults with mild intellectual disability highlight in their school-work transition? *European Journal of Special Needs Education*, 38(4), 573–587.

Silva, P.N., & Maricle, D.E. (2021). Spina bifida: What school psychologists should know. *Communique*, 50(2), 10–12.

Simmons, C.R., Miller, R.D., Uphold, N.M., & Horn, S.E. (2023). Teaching students with a mild intellectual disability to respond to strangers using computer-based video instruction. *Journal of Special Education Technology*, 38(4), 527–538.

Slater, Z. & Chambers, G. (2024). Primary teachers' perceptions of whole-class teaching and learning in English primary schools: An exploratory study of perceived benefits, challenges and effective practice. *Education 3–13*, 52(4), 536–550.

Slavin, R., Madden, N.A., Chambers, B., & Haxby, B. (2009). *Two Million Children: Success for All* (2nd ed.). Thousand Oaks, CA: Corwin Press.

Slavin, R.E., & Madden, N.A. (2013). Success for All at 27: New developments in whole-school reform. *Journal of Education for Students Placed at Risk*, 18(3–4), 169–176.

Smith, B., Spooner, F., & Wood, C.L. (2013). Using embedded computer-assisted explicit instruction to teach science to students with autism spectrum disorder. *Research in Autism Spectrum Disorders*, 7(3), 433–443.

Smith, T., Mruzek, D.W., & Mozingo, D. (2015). Sensory integration therapy. In Foxx, R.M., & Mulick, J.A. (Eds.). *Controversial therapies for autism and intellectual disabilities: Fad, fashion, and science in professional practice.* New York: Routledge.

Snowling, M.J., Lervåg, A., Nash, H.M., & Hulme, C. (2019). Longitudinal relationships between speech perception, phonological skills and reading in children at high-risk of dyslexia. *Developmental Science*, 22(1), e12723.

Soares, D.A., Harrison, J.R., Melloy, K., Baran, A., & Mohlmann, M. (2022). Practice-to-research: Responding to the complexities of inclusion for students with emotional and behavioral disorders with recommendations for schools. *NASSP Bulletin*, 106(2), 77–108.

Song, S., Li, T., Quintero, M., & Wang, Z. (2023). The link between math anxiety and math achievement: The role of afterschool learning. *Journal of Numerical Cognition*, 9(3), 418–432.

Sonnemann, J., Hunter, J., & Stobart, A. (2023). How to embed small group tuition in schools: A guide for school leaders. *Learning Difficulties Australia Bulletin*, 55(1), 17–20.

Spiker, A. (2023). Opportunities for equity in writing instruction: A framework for teacher preparation. *Teacher Educators' Journal*, 16(2), 21–40.

Spooner, F., Root, J.R., Saunders, A.F., & Browder, D.M. (2019). An updated evidence-based practice review on teaching mathematics to students with moderate and severe developmental disabilities. *Remedial and Special Education*, 40(3), 150–165.

Stanczak, A., Jury, M., Aelenei, C., Pironom, J., Toczek-Capelle, M., & Rohmer, O. (2024). Special education and meritocratic inclusion. *Educational Policy*, 38(1), 85–103.

Steenbergen-Hu, S., Makel, M.C., & Olszewski-Kubilius, P. (2016). What one hundred years of research says about the effects of ability grouping and acceleration on K-12 students' academic achievement: Findings of two second-order meta-analyses. *Review of Educational Research*, 86(4), 849–899.

Steenbergen-Hu, S., Olszewski-Kubilius, P., & Calvert, E. (2020). The effectiveness of current interventions to reverse the underachievement of gifted students: Findings of a meta-analysis and systematic review. *Gifted Child Quarterly*, 64(2), 132–165.

Sternberg, R.J. (2024). Individual, collective, and contextual aspects in the identification of giftedness. *Gifted Education International*, 40(1), 3–24.

Sternberg, R.J., & Rodriguez-Fernández, M.I. (2024). Humanitarian giftedness. *Gifted Education International*, 40(1), 92–115.

Stockall, N. & Dennis, L.R. (2014). Using pivotal response training and technology to engage preschoolers with autism in conversations. *Intervention in School and Clinic*, 49(4), 195–202.

Stornaiuolo, A., Higgs, J., Jawale, O., & Martin, R.M. (2024). Digital writing with AI platforms: The role of fun with/in generative AI. *English Teaching: Practice and critique.* 23(1), 83–103.

Stratton, J. (2023). Implicit and explicit instruction in the second language classroom: A study of learner preferences in higher education. *Unterrichtspraxis/Teaching German*, 56(2), 103–117.

Stultz, S.L. (2017). Computer-assisted mathematics instruction for students with specific learning disability: A review of the literature. *Journal of Special Education Technology*, 32(4), 210–219.

Summers, C. (2000). *Collaborative action research summary. How to help children learn to read.* https://eric.ed.gov/?q=decodable+books&id=ED439395

Sumner, E., Nightingale, R., Gurney, K., Prunty, M., & Barnett, A.L. (2024). Doing the "write" thing: Handwriting and typing support in secondary schools in England. *Literacy*, 58(1), 25–36.

Sutherland, K.S., Conroy, M.A., McLeod, B.D., Kunemund, R., & McKnight, K. (2019). Common practice elements for improving social, emotional, and behavioral outcomes of young elementary school students. *Journal of Emotional and Behavioral Disorders*, 27(2), 76–85.

Sutherland, M., Furjanic, D., Harmida, J., & Clarke, B. (2024). Using the number line to develop understanding of whole number magnitude and operations. *Intervention in School and Clinic*, 59(3), 158–164.

Sweller, J. (1988). Cognitive load during problem solving: Effects on learning, *Cognitive Science*, 12, 257–285.

Sweller, J. (2023). The development of cognitive load theory: Replication crises and incorporation of other theories can lead to theory expansion. *Educational Psychology Review*, 35(4), 95.

Tan, C. (2018). Whither teacher-directed learning? Freirean and Confucian Insights. *Educational Forum*, 82(4), 461–474.

Taylor, J., & Sailor, W. (2024). A case for systems change in special education. *Remedial and Special Education*, 45, 125–135.

Tee, A., & Reed, P. (2017). Controlled study of the impact on child behaviour problems of Intensive Interaction for children with ASD. *Journal of Research in Special Educational Needs*, 17(3), 179–186.

Templeton, S. (2020). Stages, phases, repertoires, and waves: Learning to spell and read words. *Reading Teacher*, 74(3), 315–323.

Thomas, G., Dobson, G., & Loxley, A. (2023). The increasing use of private special schools: A policy gap for inclusive education. *British Educational Research Journal*, 49(6), 1357–1371.

Thompson, J.L., Wood, C.L., Preston, A., Stevenson, B. (2019). Teaching unison responding during small-group Direct Instruction to students with autism spectrum disorder who exhibit interfering behaviors. *Education and Treatment of Children*, 42(1), 1–23.

Tiernan, B. (2022). Inclusion versus full inclusion: Implications for progressing inclusive education. *European Journal of Special Needs Education*, 37(5), 882–890.

Tomlinson, C. & Imbeau, M.B. (2014). *A differentiated approach to the Common Core: How do I help a broad range of learners succeed with challenging curriculum?* Alexandria, VA: Association for Supervision and Curriculum Development.

Tomlinson, C.A., & Imbeau, M.B. (2023). *Leading and managing a differentiated classroom* (2nd ed.). Alexandria, VA: ASCD.

Tomlinson, C.A., Kaplan, S.N., Purcell, J.H., Leppien, J.H., Burns, D.E., Renzulli, J.S., Imbeau, M.B. & Strickland, C.A. (2008). *The Parallel Curriculum* (2nd ed.), Thousand Oaks, CA: Corwin Press.

Tripathi, I., Moody, C.T., & Laugeson, E.A. (2024). Parent perspectives on treatment: A mixed methods analysis of PEERS® for preschoolers. *Autism: The International Journal of Research and Practice*, 28(2), 390–402.

Troia, G. (2014). *Evidence-based practices for writing instruction* (Document No. IC-5). University of Florida. https://ceedar.education.ufl.edu/tools/innovation-configuration/

UNESCO. (1994). *The Salamanca Statement and Framework for action on special needs education*: Adopted by the World Conference on Special Needs Education; Access and Quality. Salamanca, Spain, 7–10 June 1994.

UNESCO (2020). *Towards inclusion in education: status, trends and challenges: The UNESCO Salamanca Statement 25 years on*. https://www.unesco.org/en/articles/new-publication-paving-way-toward-inclusion-education

UNESCO (2023). *Inclusive education*. https://www.ibe.unesco.org/en/glossary-curriculum-terminology/i/inclusive-education

Unicef. (2024). *Behind the numbers: Ending school violence and bullying*. Geneva: Unicef.

Unwin, K.L., Powell, G., & Jones, C.R.G. (2021). The use of multi-sensory environments with autistic children: Exploring the effect of having control of sensory changes. *Autism: The International Journal of Research and Practice*, 26(6), 1379–1394.

Urquhart, N., Lee, J., & Wood, E. (2024). Get that App! Examining parents' evaluations of numeracy apps. *Journal of Research in Childhood Education*, 38(3), 337–351.

US Department of Education. (2004). *Individuals with Disabilities Education Improvement Act, Public Law 108-446:108th Congress*. https://idea.ed.gov/download/statute.html

Vadasy, P.F., & Sanders, E.A. (2021). Introducing phonics to learners who struggle: Content and embedded cognitive elements. *Reading and Writing: An Interdisciplinary Journal*, 34(8), 2059–2080.

van Vijfeijken, M., van Schilt-Mol, T., van den Bergh, L., Scholte, R.H.J., & Denessen, E. (2023). How teachers handle differentiation dilemmas in the context of a school's vision: A case study. *Cogent Education*, 10(1), 2165006.

VanTassel-Baska, J. (2015). Common Core State Standards for students with gifts and talents. *Teaching Exceptional Children*, 47(4), 191–198.

VanTassel-Baska, J. (2019). Are we differentiating effectively for the gifted or not? A commentary on differentiated curriculum use in schools. *Gifted Child Today*, 42(3), 165–167.

Vatterott, C. (2018). *Rethinking homework: Best practices that support diverse needs* (2nd ed.). Alexandria, VA: Association for Supervision and Curriculum Development.

Verdonck, M., Wright, H., Hamilton, A., & Taylor, J. (2024). The educator's experience of using flipped classrooms in a higher education setting. *Active Learning in Higher Education*, 25(1), 25–40.

Veytsman, E., Baker, E., Martin, A.M., Choy, T., Blacher, J., & Stavropoulos, K. (2023). Perceived and observed treatment gains following PEERS: A preliminary study with Latinx adolescents with ASD. *Journal of Autism and Developmental Disorders*, 53(3), 1175–1188.

Vicker, B. (2002). *What is the Picture Exchange System or PECS?* https://www.iidc.indiana.edu/irca/articles/what-is-the-picture-exchange-communication-system-or-pecs.html

Virues-Ortega, J., Julio, F.M., & Pastor-Barriuso, R. (2013). The TEACCH program for children and adults with autism: A meta-analysis of intervention studies. *Clinical Psychology Review*, 33(8), 940–953.

Vogl, K. & Preckel, F. (2014). Full-time ability grouping of gifted students: Impacts on social self-concept and school-related attitudes. *Gifted Child Quarterly*, 58(1), 51–68.

Waghorn, E. (2024). *New report says Australian children are among the most bullied in the world*. https://www.rmit.edu.au/news/media-releases-and-expert-comments/2024/may/school-bullying

Wai, J., & Worrell, F.C. (2021). How talented low-income kids are left behind. *Phi Delta Kappan*, 102(4), 26–29.

Walker, V.L., Conradi, L.A., Strickland-Cohen, M. K., & Johnson, H.N. (2023). School-wide positive behavioral interventions and supports and students with extensive support needs: A scoping review. *International Journal of Developmental Disabilities*, 69(1), 13–28.

Walsh-Aziz, M.L., Schick, B., & Lederberg, A. (2024). Fingerspelling used in classrooms by teachers of the deaf and hard-of-hearing. *Journal of Deaf Studies and Deaf Education*, 29(1), 30–39.

Waltz, S.B. (2019). Tutor training for service learning: Impact on self-efficacy beliefs. *Mentoring & Tutoring: Partnership in Learning*, 27(1), 26–43.

Wang, J., & Jou, M. (2023). The influence of mobile-learning flipped classrooms on the emotional learning and cognitive flexibility of students of different levels of learning achievement. *Interactive Learning Environments*, 31(3), 1309–1321.

Wang, L., & Li, J. (2019). Development of an innovative dual-coded multimedia application to improve reading comprehension of students with imagery deficit. *Journal of Educational Computing Research*, 57(1), 170–200.

Wang, W.L., & Kuo, C.Y. (2019). Relationships among teachers' positive discipline, students' well-being and teachers' effective teaching: A study of special education teachers and adolescent students with learning disabilities in Taiwan. *International Journal of Disability, Development and Education*, 66(1), 82–98.

Wass, M., Ching, T.Y.C., Cupples, L., Wang, H.C., Lyxell, B., Martin, L., Button, L., Gunnourie, M., Boisvert, I., McMahon, C., & Castles, A. (2019). Orthographic learning in children who are deaf or hard of hearing. *Language, Speech, and Hearing Services in Schools*, 50(1), 99–112.

Waters, C.L. (2020). Covering the bases: Pairing sign with spoken word in early childhood settings. *Young Exceptional Children*, 23(3), 130–142.

Watkins, L., O'Reilly, M., Kuhn, M., & Ledbetter-Cho, K. (2019). An interest-based intervention package to increase peer social interaction in young children with autism spectrum disorder. *Journal of Applied Behavior Analysis*, 52(1), 132–149.

Weale, S. (2020). Schools converting toilet blocks into isolation booths. *The Guardian* [online]. 18 January 2020. https://uk.news.yahoo.com/schools-converting-toilet-blocks isolation-170100289.html

Webber, C., Patel, H., Cunningham, A., Fox, A., Vousden, J., Castles, A., & Shapiro, L. (2024). An experimental comparison of additional training in phoneme awareness, letter-sound knowledge and decoding for struggling beginner readers. *British Journal of Educational Psychology*, 94(1), 282–305.

Werfel, K.L., & Hendricks, A.E. (2023). The contribution of phonological processing to reading and spelling in students with cochlear implants. *Language, Speech, and Hearing Services in Schools*, 54(3), 967–980.

Westwood, P. (2021). Integration to inclusion in Hong Kong: Not an easy progression. *Australasian Journal of Special and Inclusive Education*, 45(2), 268–280.

Westwood, P. (2023). Counting really counts. *Learning Difficulties Australia Bulletin*, 55(2), 14–15.

Westwood, P. (2024). *Inclusive and adaptive teaching: Meeting the challenge of diversity in the classroom* (3rd ed.). London: Routledge.

Wheldall, K., Wheldall, R., Madelaine, A., Reynolds, M., & Arakelian, S. (2017). Further evidence for the efficacy of an evidence-based, small group, literacy intervention program for young struggling readers. *Australian Journal of Learning Difficulties*, 22(1), 3–13.

Whitney, T., & Ackerman, K.B. (2023). Effects of a digital fluency-based reading program for students with significant reading difficulties. *Journal of Special Education Technology*, 38(3), 262–273.

WHO (World Health Organization). (2023). *Blindness and vision impairment.* https://www.who.int/news-room/fact-sheets/detail/blindness-and-visual-impairment

WHO (World Health Organization). (2024). *Deafness and hearing loss.* https://www.who.int/news-room/fact-sheets/detail/deafness-and-hearing-loss

Wienen, A.W., Reijnders, I., van Aggelen, M.H., Bos, E.H., Batstra, L., & de Jonge, P. (2019). The relative impact of school-wide positive behavior support on teachers' perceptions of student behavior across schools, teachers, and students. *Psychology in the Schools*, 56(2), 232–241.

Williams, G.J., & Larkin, R.F. (2023). Translation and transcription processes in the writing skills of children with developmental language disorder: A systematic review. *Topics in Language Disorders*, 43(4), 283–301.

Williams, K.R. (2006). The Son-Rise Program intervention for autism: Prerequisites for evaluation. *Autism: The International Journal of Research & Practice*, 10(1), 86–102.

Williams, V.C. (2021). Using social stories to decrease negative behaviors in students with autism and other disabilities. *Journal of the American Academy of Special Education Professionals*, Fall 2021, 116–121.

Witter, M., & Hattie, J. (2024). Can teacher quality be profiled? A cluster analysis of teachers' beliefs, practices and students' perceptions of effectiveness. *British Educational Research Journal*, 50(2), 653–675.

Witzel, B., & Myers, J.A. (2023). Solving algebraic word problems using general heuristics instruction. *Teaching Exceptional Children*, 56(1), 52–60.

Wolter, J.A. & Dilworth, V. (2014). The effects of a multi-linguistic morphological awareness approach for improving language and literacy. *Journal of Learning Disabilities*, 47(1), 76–85.

World Council for Gifted and Talented Children. (2021). *Global principles for professional learning in gifted education*. https://world-gifted.org/professional-learning-global-principles.pdf

Wright, R. (2003). Mathematics Recovery: A program of intervention in early number learning, *Australian Journal of Learning Disabilities*, 8(4), 6–11.

Yi, J., Kim, W., & Lee, J. (2022). Effectiveness of the SCERTS model-based interventions for autistic children: A systematic review. *Journal of Speech, Language, and Hearing Research*, 65, 2662–2676.

Yildirim, H.H., & Roveshenov, A. (2022). Designing of volunteer reader mobile application for visually impaired individuals. *Paper presented at the Annual Meeting of the International EJER Congress 2022*. ERIC Document ED624178.

Young, J., & Donovan, W. (2022). *Online and on course: Digital learning creates a path for at-risk students*. White Paper No. 242. Boston, MA: Pioneer Institute for Public Policy Research.

Yu, L., & Zhu, X. (2018). Effectiveness of a SCERTS model-based intervention for children with autism spectrum disorder in Hong Kong: A pilot study. *Journal of Autism and Developmental Disorders*, 48(11), 3794–3807.

Zauderer, S. (2023). *What is discrete trial training?* https://www.crossrivertherapy.com/aba-therapists/discrete-trial-training

Zhang, J., Martella, R.C., Kang, S.W., Yenioglu, B.Y. (2023). Response to intervention (RTI)/multi-tiered systems of support (MTSS): A nationwide analysis *Journal of Educational Leadership and Policy Studies*, 7(1), 1–25.

Zoder-Martell, K.A., Floress, M.T., Skriba, H.A., & Taber, T.A. (2023). Classroom management systems to address student disruptive behavior. *Intervention in School and Clinic*, 58(5), 361–370.

Zurbriggen, C.L.A., Hofmann, V., Lehofer, M. & Schwab, S. (2023). Social classroom climate and personalised instruction as predictors of students' social participation. *International Journal of Inclusive Education*, 27(11), 1223–1238.

Index

For Product Safety Concerns and Information please contact our EU
representative GPSR@taylorandfrancis.com
Taylor & Francis Verlag GmbH, Kaufingerstraße 24, 80331 München, Germany

www.ingramcontent.com/pod-product-compliance
Ingram Content Group UK Ltd.
Pitfield, Milton Keynes, MK11 3LW, UK
UKHW022238080725
460580UK00005B/280

9 781032 984384